Hybrid Conflicts
— and —
Information Warfare

Hybrid Conflicts
— and —
Information Warfare

New Labels, Old Politics

edited by
Ofer Fridman
Vitaly Kabernik
James C. Pearce

LYNNE
RIENNER
PUBLISHERS

BOULDER
LONDON

Published in the United States of America in 2019 by
Lynne Rienner Publishers, Inc.
1800 30th Street, Boulder, Colorado 80301
www.rienner.com

and in the United Kingdom by
Lynne Rienner Publishers, Inc.
Gray's Inn House, 127 Clerkenwell Road, London EC1 5DB

Library of Congress Cataloging-in-Publication Data
Names: Fridman, Ofer, 1979– editor. | Kabernik, Vitaly, 1975– editor. |
  Pearce, James C., 1991– editor.
Title: Hybrid conflicts and information warfare : new labels, old politics /
  edited by Ofer Fridman, Vitaly Kabernik, James C. Pearce.
Description: Boulder, Colorado : Lynne Rienner Publishers, Inc., [2018] |
  Includes bibliographical references and index.
Identifiers: LCCN 2018025762 | ISBN 9781626377516 (hardcover : alk. paper)
Subjects: LCSH: Hybrid warfare. | Information warfare. | IS (Organization) |
  Propaganda—Middle East—History—21st century.
Classification: LCC U167.5.I8 H928 2018 | DDC 355.4—dc23
LC record available at https://lccn.loc.gov/2018025762

British Cataloguing in Publication Data
A Cataloguing in Publication record for this book
is available from the British Library.

Printed and bound in the United States of America

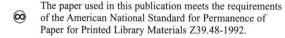

5 4 3 2 1

Contents

Foreword

Free exchange of ideas has always resided at the heart of the community of scholars. This book was born of the ambition to create an open space for dialogue and research at a time when a fresh chill was entering international relations between Russia and Western states. In January 2017 academics from Europe, the United States, and Russia met in London to offer diverse perspectives on the information warfare of hybrid conflicts. For two days, experts in strategic communications, strategic theory, and international relations reflected on how dramatic changes in information technologies had affected the way we see global politics, including fueling talk of a new Cold War.

Whether the latter thoughts might prove to be unfounded, a group of scholars nevertheless sought to mine a richer understanding of transformations in the political use of misinformation and disinformation. Significantly, they went on to explore broader fields of analysis, embracing complexities surrounding the concept of hybridity when applied to the changing nature of interstate conflict. They questioned what it means to speak of information warfare, particularly in the context of East-West relations, and how such thinking could be extended to the challenge of the Islamic State, an insurgent movement that at the time held sway over stretches of sovereign territory in Syria and Iraq. The recurring backdrop to these discussions was the dynamic character of a global media landscape that had come about in little more than a generation. Those years had seen two-thirds of the world's population acquire the means to communicate their ideas and opinions as and when they choose through the use of personal mobile phones and the World Wide Web. Few if any states have remained immured to their reach:

few have failed to recognize their potential in projecting foreign policy or stirring up trouble in rival states.

The King's Centre for Strategic Communications (KCSC) at King's College London was created to innovate and develop such engaging approaches. KCSC has rapidly established itself as a focal point for the study of strategic communications. It now acts as a global hub where networks of scholars and practitioners can freely exchange research and experience. And it is from this same center that a hundred postgraduate students graduate each year, specializing in strategic communications before going on to enrich the worlds of government, diplomacy, military, aid and development, and journalism.

So it was with great pleasure that, for this international conference, KCSC was able to draw on generous funding from the Gerda Henkel Foundation in Germany, research and funding support from the International Centre for Counter-Terrorism in The Hague, and the participation of six scholars from Moscow and Saint Petersburg facilitated through the Centre for Military-Political Research at Moscow State Institute of International Relations. KCSC is also grateful for the observations of those audiences who participated across the two days. Their expert knowledge greatly benefited the final chapters in this collection, which we trust will stimulate further thought.

If strategic communications is in part about seeking desired change in audience behavior, then this book offers a modest contribution to building creative and diplomatic bridges in the spirit of better mutual understanding.

—*Neville Bolt*
Director, King's Centre for Strategic Communications

1

Hybrid Conflicts and Information Warfare

Ofer Fridman, Vitaly Kabernik,
and James C. Pearce

Two significant events marked the year 2014 as a turning point in the history of international security: the Russian involvement in the Ukrainian crisis and the rise of the Islamic State in Syria and Iraq. The most focal characteristic, which these two independently evolved confrontations share, is not necessarily the relative success of political actors (either Russia or the Islamic State) in achieving their territorial gains, but rather their successful use of informational space by an effective employment of novel communication capabilities. The Information Revolution that had been occurring for the past two decades has finally manifested itself in the way that political players conduct, interpret, and perceive conflicts. The concept of *hybrid warfare* was one of the first attempts of the expert community to address this rapidly changing character of conflicts, where a smart employment of newly available technologies to influence the hearts and minds of targeted audiences offers significantly better results than any real actions.

It is important to note that there was little novelty in the idea itself, as disinformation campaigns, propaganda, and other attempts to use informational space for political goals have been around for thousands of years. However, while the manipulation of information successfully executed by an adversary is a virus, as old as politics itself, today's information technologies allow this virus to be disseminated much further and much faster than ever before. It does not necessarily mean that the virus is stronger or the victims are weaker. It simply means that more people are exposed—and this alone offers a huge advantage to anybody who attempts to influence hearts and minds in the post–Information Revolution era of the early twenty-first century.

1

The technological and informational revolutions of the past two decades have amplified the danger posed by nonmilitary means and methods of political struggle, in general, and in the information dimension in particular. While the Western world is preoccupied by the Kremlin's alleged interference in the US presidential elections in 2016 or Russia's other alleged attempts to subvert and destabilize the Western democracies by successful information operations, Russian decisionmakers are notably anxious about Western attempts to manipulate Russian information against the current government. Moreover, the rapid success of the Islamic State in recruiting thousands of young people across the world surprised both Russia and the West, demonstrating the new dangers of the manipulated flow of information multiplied by modern communication technologies.

In light of these developments, three main issues have been occupying the academic and professional discourse in regard to contemporary conflicts. The first one has been the idea of increasing hybridity between different military and nonmilitary means and methods employed by political players to achieve their goals without escalating to an outright open armed confrontation. The second one has been the increasing role of the informational dimension as a virtual space, used to promote certain political goals, either domestically or internationally, or both. The third major topic has been the rise of the Islamic State with a whole set of problems and threats that it brought to international security and stability. While it seems that the core territorial base of the Islamic State has been destroyed, it is difficult to conclude the same about its ideology and its influence spread through the modern communication technologies. Moreover, as several chapters of this book point out, there are much bigger geopolitical problems that allow to the ideology of the Islamic State to flourish, and the main lessons that the rest of the world should learn rest not in the tactics of counterinsurgency but in the field of strategic communications.

In analyzing the parallel discourses that have developed in the West and Russia on these three topics, it is possible to point to two main narratives. While discussing the role of hybridity and the information dimension in international relations, both Russian and Western scholars and experts swiftly fall into the field of mutual accusations. Their conceptual understandings of the hybrid environment, as well as the importance of influence and control of information for achieving political goals, are starkly similar. Moreover, when it comes to analyzing the hybrid activity of the Islamic State, or the way it exploits the information dimensions, it seems that Russian and Western opinions share even more similarities than differences.

This book brings, for the first time, both Russian and Western scholars to discuss the most sensitive and timely topics such as the role and nature of hybridity, information warfare, and strategic communications in contemporary world politics. The unique academic collaboration presented in this book takes place at a challenging time in international relations, as a confluence of conflict-related insecurities has given rise to a sense of deep crisis. Closely associated with this are concerns relating to the increasing use of propaganda, espionage, subversion, and cyberattacks by state and nonstate actors. Such concerns have recently taken a prominent role in the contemporary international public discourse. The current political climate presents challenges to the free academic exchange of views and opinions, yet also renders it of critical importance. This book offers a dialogue on pressing issues relating to international order, peace and security, and building bridges between societies by fostering and supporting the development of a more inclusive international public discourse.

The book consists of three main conceptually interconnected parts. Each section includes two chapters written by Russian scholars and two written by Western scholars. One of the most important rationales of the book is that these chapters are not structured as one versus the other, but to represent a dialogue of opinions. In other words, the purpose is not to contrast the Russian and the Western views on hybridity, strategic communications, or the Islamic State's propaganda, but rather to offer one integrated discourse that benefits from both Eastern and Western perspectives on conflicts in the twenty-first century.

After this brief introduction, Part 1 of the book focuses on the idea of hybridity in contemporary conflicts. In the opening chapter, David Betz discusses the development of the idea of hybridity in Western military thought, its advantages and weaknesses, as well as the main contribution of the concept of the so-called hybrid war to the Western political-military debate and decisionmaking processes. While the concept has been widely discussed in the existent literature,[1] Chapter 2 offers a fresh perspective by analyzing the Russo-Japanese War and arguing that the concept of *hybrid war* is simply an answer to contemporary erroneous expectations for wars to be easy, cheap, and decisive.

This insight into the Western understanding of hybridity is followed by Chapters 3 and 4 by Georgy Filimonov and Vitaly Kabernik, respectively. While the first sheds light on the Russian interpretation of "color revolution" in the context of hybrid war and points to the conceptual differences between the Western and the Russian approaches to hybridity, the second offers an in-depth historical-conceptual analysis of the

Russian approach through the prism of Russian traditional military thinking. These two chapters come to bridge an important gap in the currently available literature in English on the Russian understanding of hybridity. Since 2014, many Western scholars have tried to analyze Russian actions through the Western prism of hybrid war; however, the amount of research conducted to analyze the Russian perspective has been limited.[2] Chapters 3 and 4 fill this important lacuna.

The final contribution in Part 1, Chapter 5 by Ofer Fridman, compares the Russian and the Western perspectives on hybridity, making an attempt to answer one of the most important questions regarding this debate: Is hybrid war something new, in either the Western or the Russian interpretations, or is it just a new title used for the politicization of very old elements of political confrontation?

Part 2 of this book focuses on the role of strategic communications and information warfare. It opens with Chapter 6 by Mervyn Frost and Nicholas Michelsen, who discuss the ethical dimensions of informational confrontations. The world has become envisioned as beset by irreconcilable clashes of interpretations. In the turbulent information space of the twenty-first century, people have become less deferential, more questioning, and—thanks to social media—have access to too many opinions, some of which might intentionally distort the truth. One notable concern is that the criteria for identification of one's international political and military opponents widen to include anyone who threatens an actor's command of the informational space. Amid rising geopolitical tensions and public anxiety associated with campaigns by hostile state and nonstate actors seeking to shape public opinion and attitudes in pursuit of their own strategic objectives, the chapter seeks to shed light on the unavoidable ethical dimensions that arise in this information war. It aims to elucidate the ethical dimensions of acts of strategic communication, within which are included those acts referred to as *information war* by reference to the global practices within which they take place.

This general introduction to the topic is followed by a dialogue between Matthew Armstrong and Radomir Bolgov, who discuss the relations between politics and information warfare, the former presenting the case of the United States in Chapter 7 and the latter the case of Russia in Chapter 8. In his chapter, Armstrong traces the political history of the United States Information Agency (USIA)—the agency established during the Cold War to centralize and coordinate the battlefield of the minds and wills of the public on both sides of the iron curtain. Analyzing the internal politics that surrounded the establishment and the activity of the USIA, Armstrong argues that the United States never properly armed itself for the reality of the information warfare it was embroiled in, neither during the Cold War nor after it (when the agency was abolished in 1999). Therefore, Armstrong's argument goes, in the turbulent information environment of the twenty-first century with many players who attempt to subvert US stability and interests through informational space, the United States lacks a historical precedent to draw on.

In the chapter that follows Armstrong's, Bolgov underlines the complexity of discourse and the nexus of different ideas in Russian professional and scholarly publications on information warfare. While some Western scholars claim to crack the so-called Russian information warfare,[3] Bolgov argues that in Russia itself the understanding of what this type of confrontation should (or should not) be is full of contradictions fed by different political and ideological factors. He provides an overview of the approaches to information warfare in the Russian political and expert community, including an analysis of the legal and doctrinal framework of information warfare policy in Russia. For the first time, Bolgov combines political, ideological, and theoretical factors involved in the Russian conceptualization of information warfare as well as the practical activity of actors in charge of related policies in Russia.

In Chapter 9, which closes Part 2, Oxana Timofeyeva takes Bolgov's arguments further, elaborating on the conceptual understanding of the information dimension in contemporary conflicts and on the Russian interpretation of this phenomenon. The biggest problem surrounding the discourse about information warfare in Russia, according to Timofeyeva, is a variety of different actors (military, politics, media, etc.) that attempt to manipulate the concept to suit their own agendas. After examining several recent cases of information-psychological operations conducted in the Russian media space, Timofeyeva discusses and criticizes a controversial tool created in the political environment of information warfare by the Russian Institute for Strategic Studies for monitoring the level of anti-Russian narratives in the media publications of different countries.

Based on the conceptual foundations created in the first two parts of this book, Part 3 analyzes the case of the Islamic State and its success to utilize the informational domain for a variety of goals. While Charlie Winter's in-depth analysis in Chapter 10 of the propaganda campaign launched by the Islamic State during the battle for Mosul mainly focuses on its domestic aspects, in Chapter 11 Vladimir Sotnikov discusses the implications of the successful strategic communications of the Islamic State for global security and stability. Since Winter examines in detail the information operations conducted by the Islamic State on a tactical and operational level, and Sotnikov presents the strategic framework of the organization's actions, these two chapters uniquely complement each other by presenting for the first time the full picture of its information warfare.

In Chapter 12, Akhmet Yarlykapov examines the effectiveness of the Islamic State's propaganda in the North Caucasus. Basing his analysis on sociological and anthropological research and surveys, he points to different propaganda methods used by the Islamic State to recruit new fighters and their astonishing level of success.

In the closing chapter of Part 3 (Chapter 13), Craig Whiteside draws a conceptual line between all previously discussed topics. He argues that regardless of the title—whether it is hybrid, information, or political warfare—the contemporary conflict has become a multimodal affair with a great emphasis on the information domain, and the case of the Islamic State is a good illustration of this phenomenon.

In the concluding chapter of the book, Chapter 14, James C. Pearce makes an attempt to connect between conceptual debates and practical examples presented in the book. He ultimately comes to a conclusion that although the labels used to describe events change, there is little novelty in the politics that shape and direct them.

Notes

1. For example, Timothy McCulloh and Richard Johnson, *Hybrid Warfare* (Tampa: MacDill Air Force Base, Joint Special Operations University Press, 2013); Frank Hoffman, *Conflict in the Twenty-First Century: The Rise of Hybrid Warfare* (Arlington, VA: Potomac Institute for Policy Studies, 2007); Williamson Murray and Peter Mansoor, eds., *Hybrid Warfare: Fighting Complex Opponents from the Ancient World to the Present* (Cambridge: Cambridge University Press, 2012).

2. For example, Andrew Korybko, *Hybrid Wars: The Indirect Adaptive Approach to Regime Change* (Moscow: RUDN University, 2015); Ofer Fridman, *Russian "Hybrid Warfare": Resurgence and Politicisation* (London: Hurst, 2018).

3. For example, Keir Giles, *Handbook of Russian Information Warfare* (Rome: NATO Defense College, 2016); Rod Thornton, "The Changing Nature of Modern Warfare; Responding to Russian Information Warfare," *RUSI Journal* 160, no. 4 (2015): 40–48; Jolanta Darczewska, "The Anatomy of Russian Information Warfare: The Crimean Operation, A Case Study," Point of View No. 42 (Warsaw: Centre for Eastern Studies, 2014); Keir Giles, "The Next Phase of Russian Information Warfare" (Riga, Latvia: NATO Strategic Communications Centre of Excellence, 2016); Mark Galeotti, *Hybrid War or Gibridnaya Voina? Getting Russia's Non-Linear Military Challenge Right* (Prague: Mayak Intelligence, 2016).

PART 1

The Concept of Hybridity in Conflicts

2

The Idea of Hybridity

David Betz

In the sixteen years since the 2002 advent of the war on terror, howsoever named, *hybrid war* has undoubtedly emerged as the most popular term of use in defense and strategy for describing the apparently topsy-turvy character of contemporary conflicts. Despite its ubiquity in the discourse, the term is deployed variously by different characters and institutions. It would be a mistake, therefore, to assume a single, consistently agreed-to, meaning that is speaking only of the West, for that matter; in other countries, as other chapters in this book discuss, the term sometimes has a quite different connotation.

My understanding of the concept as I use it in this chapter is essentially drawn from the work of Frank Hoffman, who more than any other academic author can lay claim to be its godfather. As he explains it, hybrid wars are characterized by the simultaneous incorporation of different modes of warfare—conventional, irregular, and terroristic (not incidentally, themselves discrete categorizations that many experts dispute). These multimodal forms of warfare can be conducted by both state and nonstate actors and, crucially distinctively, are said to occur at the same time in the same place—or "battlespace" in the jargon of doctrine, which in turn must be understood as being nonlinear, comprising multiple domains beyond the physical including electronic, cyber, or even more abstractly cognitive or virtual.

The first chief characteristic of hybridity is the "convergence" of warfare types on a mutant form that defies easy categorization in accordance with habitual frames of reference: while some nonstate actors are acquiring state-like capabilities and organization, some state actors deliberately don the proverbial "dwarf's clothing" of the guerrilla. In either case. there are multiple impetuses. Perhaps most interestingly in the case of the latter is the desire of many states to intentionally blur the distinction of war/not war for reasons of avoiding the legal restrictions that formally declared states of war impose as well as out of a fear of the escalatory consequences of openly warring, especially with nuclear-armed states. The second chief characteristic of hybridity is the combination of tactics and nontypical means such as criminality, which is employed to sustain the hybrid force, to facilitate the disruption of the target nation and protract the conflict. These combinations are not merely coincidental; rather, they are "fused" in a deliberate strategy designed to produce synergistic effects.[1]

Extant British strategic thinking draws explicitly on these influential ideas, extending them even further in an alliterative description of the future character of conflict: congested, cluttered, contested, connected, and constrained. A wag would be tempted to add the word *confused* to the list of Cs, but the joke is diminished by the frank recognition by its victims of the reality of their situation. Moreover, it hardly is only practitioners who are at sea because the academy is just as mystified on the seemingly simple question, What is war?[2]

In this chapter, I argue that our ancestors would frown on this confusion and regard our need for hyphenated and portmanteau concepts of war to be immature. I illustrate the retrograde character of hybridity with reference mainly to British (and, passingly, to Russian) military history of the nineteenth century to demonstrate that statesmen and commanders of the not-so-distant past would have found the concept obvious and therefore superfluous.

Strategic Context

The nineteenth century is often referred to as the "long peace." After the defeat of Napoleon at Waterloo in 1815, no wars occurred among the five major European powers for almost forty years. The dominant conception of war through this period up to, and to an extent beyond, World War I was based largely on the ideas of the Swiss-born general Antoine-Henri Jomini who served under the French flag through most of the Napoleonic Wars until opportunistically defecting to Russia in 1813. The gist of Jominian military thought may be said to comprise two elements: first, that victory is achieved through the defeat of the enemy's army on the battlefield; and, second, that the key to said defeat is the calculated application of a small number of "fundamental principles" to war, among which the most important is the concentration of the maximum power of one's own military force against the weakest, most decisive, point of the military force of one's enemy. "Strategy," he defined succinctly as the "art of making war upon the map" while the leitmotif of operations, to judge from his many epigrammatic advisements to commanders, was above all to be "brisk, bold, impetuous, perhaps even sometimes audacious."[3]

The resemblance of these ideas to the late twentieth and early twenty-first century's fascination with such things as "shock and awe," "rapid decisive operations," and "full spectrum dominance" are readily apparent. Sticking with the nineteenth century, though, for the time being, a very interesting thing is how far the actual practice of warfare departed from the theory even then. Close to home, the major preoccupation of Europe's major armies was the suppression of the multitude of internal revolts associated with the effects of the Industrial Revolution, the rise of liberal ideals, and later the emergence of class-based proto Marxist-Leninist "people's wars," including in the case of the anarchist movement a violent and highly effective transnational ideological terror network. Further abroad, largely at the same time, these armies were mainly engaged in wars of imperial expansion and pacification of subject populations, which we might describe in the jargon of today as "asymmetric." In such wars, more often as not there was no enemy army to defeat, certainly not one organized along the same lines, similarly equipped, and trained to operate conventionally in the manner of European forces. Decisive engagements were few and far between in them—indeed, this was a rather "harassing form of warfare . . . most difficult to bring to a satisfactory conclusion . . . protracted, thankless, and invertebrate," in the words of the preeminent theorist of "small wars" of the day, the British soldier C. E. Callwell.[4] Leaving aside the relatively few major wars of the century such as the American Civil War, the wars of German reunification, and Franco-Prussian War, the wars of the nineteenth century were decidedly hybrid. A few examples are illustrative.

Hybrid War Nineteenth-Century Style

In late June of 1806, just over half a year and half a world away from Vice Admiral Horatio Nelson's victory over the French and Spanish fleet at Trafalgar, British forces under the command of Admiral Sir Home Popham landed at the Rio de la Plata, Argentina aiming to capture

Buenos Aires and ultimately to seize one of the greatest and richest Spanish colonies in South America. Initially, the results were extremely congenial. A superior Spanish military force was quickly routed at the cost of a handful of British casualties and Buenos Aires was occupied on the march. Popham had acted independently on his own judgment as a commander, which was not wholly unusual given the technology of communications of the day in the context of a global conflict, having convinced himself that the people of the region were "groaning under the tyranny" of Spain and eager for liberation. He also considered that here was an opportunity to counter allied setbacks in the European theater—notably Napoleon's huge victory at the Battle of Austerlitz in December 1805—with a splendid little war in the South Atlantic.[5]

The fury that the maverick Popham caused government ministers back in London, who considered that he had contemptuously exceeded his authority, was to an extent assuaged by reassurances of the importance of the colony and the immense profits that the bold action would cause to accrue to English traders. *The Times* triumphantly editorialized on the news:

> The circumstances which attended this success are in the highest degree honourable to the British name, and to the character of our brave army. . . . By our success in La Plata, where a small British detachment has taken one of the greatest and richest of the Spanish colonies, Buonaparte must be convinced that nothing but a speedy peace can prevent the whole of Spanish America from being wrested from his influence, and placed forever under the protection of the British Empire.[6]

In other words, one might say, "Mission Accomplished." The then vast sum of over a million dollars was sent back to Britain by frigate along with six wagonloads of other booty—primarily Jesuit's bark (a valuable antimalarial) and mercury. A large quantity of arms and ammunition was also seized from abandoned and surrendered Spanish armories. Financial markets in the City of London soared on anticipation that the good times would roll. Unfortunately, the mood of buoyancy was not to last. Indeed, by the time that these treasures landed in Britain, and reinforcements had been dispatched, events had already turned decidedly for the worse.

While the British certainly did plunder the assets of the deposed Spanish regime, they took care to otherwise not "exasperate" the local population (as Callwell nearly a century later would enjoin practitioners of small wars to do). Thus, private property was untouched; the population (regarded as liberated rather than conquered) was protected; local government, courts, and tax authorities were permitted to continue as normal; and the place of the Catholic Church in society was unmolested. It was to little avail, however, as the remnants of the regular Spanish forces under the skillful command of Santiago de Liniers y Bremond, a Knight of the Order of Malta in the service of Spain, organized a powerful popular insurgency out of a ragbag of soldiers ("bitter enders," let's call them), civilians, and gauchos. The result was a bitter humiliation of British arms, which resulted in the court martial of the officer in charge of operations—ironically, not Popham, who escaped ignominy, but General John Whitelocke who had arrived in May 1807 with a small army under orders to recover the worsening situation. The fighting in the town and suburbs of Buenos Aires proved insurmountably difficult for the British, who discovered that the thick walls and flat roofs of the Spanish colonial urban landscape cut through by narrow alleys turned the place into a practically endless series of discontinuous ambushes. From the roofs, they were assailed by a great proportion of the population with hand grenades, musket fire, stones, and boiling water while seemingly at the turning of every street corner they were blasted by Spanish cannons loaded with grapeshot stationed behind deep ditches. The mood of the aftermath was recorded by a British officer, Lieutenant Colonel Lancelot Holland:

> We were ordered to march out without arms. It was a bitter task, everyone felt it, the men were all in tears. We were marched through the town to the Fort. Nothing could be more mortifying than our passage through the streets amidst the rabble who had conquered us. They were dark-skinned people, short and ill-made, covered with rags, armed with long muskets and some a sword. There was neither order nor uniformity among them.[7]

The war is generally unremembered now by Britons, though not by Argentinians for whom it was a precursor to revolution and independent nation building. It was indubitably hybrid, according to an objective understanding of the concept's main underpinnings. Certainly, there was a mix of regular and irregular modes of warfare, and it also included the exploitation of clan, tribal, and illicit networks for the sustainment of the insurgent fighting forces. The final battles on the streets of Buenos Aires featured a mix of the most primitive arms deployed alongside what were then cutting-edge ones—cunning savagery, continuous improvisation, rampant organizational adaptation—de Liniers achieved the operational and tactical fusion of these things in the same battle-space, though it would not have been described as such then. This says nothing of the political complexity of the conflict, which had tendrils linking events of a nature local to the theater, such as the three-way tension between Spanish colonial rulers, indigenous peoples, and their British liberators cum conquerors, into governments in Paris, Madrid, and London, as mentioned already, and on multiple levels—not least being the interaction of the conflict with financial markets. There was, too, a media dimension: first, in the enthusiastic boosting of Popham—who was acutely conscious of his celebrity—and, as the war progressed, second, with the public pillorying of Whitelocke.

In 1996 United States Marine Corps commandant, General Charles Krulak, declared in a speech to the Royal United Services Institute in London that "the future of war is not the son of Desert Storm, but the stepchild of Chechnya and Somalia."[8] The line has become a staple in the literature on future war and a touchstone of the hybrid war thesis. He might as well have talked of the stepchild of La Plata. One wonders how many would catch the reference, though the truth is that a passing familiarity with practically any of Victoria's wars should suffice to trigger recognition—the Sikh Wars, the Burma Campaigns, both forays into Afghanistan, the Opium War, the Second China War, all would fit this pattern. Moreover, neither is it the case that this period was technologically more static; quite the opposite, in fact, as the armies of the day grappled with adaptation to, inter alia, the advent of steamships and railroads, telegraphic communications, rapid-fire rifles, and breach-loading artillery, any one of which might be argued revolutionary in import. And neither, as it is generally supposed, did the industrial powers always have technical or tactical superiority over their foes.

War's Virtual Dimension

It could be said that the key difference today, however, is information technology specifically, and the density of global interconnectedness of people, ideas, and things that has burgeoned in the past half-century particularly with the advent of the Internet. There is a vast literature on this subject in relation to every aspect of society—politics, economics, culture, friendships, and society—typically encapsulated under the rubric of globalization. It is self-evident that our lives are increasingly intertwined with those of distant others, producing a condition that

Zygmunt Bauman has called "liquid modernity." There is no longer an intellectual "outside," it is said, and nothing can now occur to people completely "over there" without bearing on "how people in all other places live, hope, or expect to live."[9]

It is hard to gainsay these ideas precisely, yet they deserve and benefit from some cautious exposure to historical comparison. For instance, in the hybrid wars literature, the Lebanese Shiite militia cum political party Hezbollah is described as a sort of prototype of the concept on account of its effective blend of regular and irregular tactics, its quasi-state-like deployment of some high-tech weapons, and in general its ability to go toe to toe with the powerful organized military forces of Israel in 2006. All of these, though, as witnessed, were apparent in some cases as far back as 1806. A more ambiguous point is Hezbollah's apparent mastery of "perception dominance," by which is meant not just dominating one's foe physically but undermining them morally and psychologically, tunneling out their base of support domestically as well as their reputation internationally.

Indeed, for a long time, it has been ventured in the literature on counterinsurgency that the reason that big states lose small wars is that they are exhausted morally rather than physically. This is in large part the central reasoning to accounts of the US defeat in Vietnam and equally may well be applied to the failed expeditionary campaigns of the war on terror, especially the NATO mission in Afghanistan. Hezbollah's effort in this perceptual domain of war is said to have been particularly exemplary, however:

> Not until this war have networks actually projected in real time the grim reality of the battlefield pictures of advancing or retreating troops in southern Lebanon, homes and villages being destroyed during bombing runs, old people wandering aimlessly through the debris, some tailed by children hugging tattered dolls, Israeli airplanes attacking Beirut airport, Hezbollah rockets striking northern Israel and Haifa—all conveyed live as though the world had a front row seat on the blood and gore of modern warfare.[10]

It is true that soldiers and statesmen today are increasingly preoccupied with the apparent breakdown of what journalist Andrew Marr describes as the "wall of willed incomprehension, between civilians at home and those killing" caused, he says, specifically by the arrival of real-time, or near to real-time, digital imagery of conflict spreading virally on the network flows of globalization.[11] The effects of this are considered to be manifold and interrelated, though two are worth high-lighting particularly. First, it brings the beliefs and ideals of a multitude of spatially distant actors into the strategic mix; and, second, crucially, though rarely addressed directly in the proliferating literature on strategic communications, it brings the mood of the home population of expeditionary forces potentially decisively into play. Britain's General Sir David Richards, commander of the International Security Assistance Force (ISAF) in Afghanistan in 2006 at the point historians are quite likely to determine the war's outcome became apparent, puts it this way: "Conflict today, especially because so much of it is effectively fought through the medium of the Communications Revolution, is principally about and for the people—hearts and minds on a mass scale."[12]

Be that as it may, how much is really different? The case is easily overstated. Consider, for example, the Second Anglo-Boer War of 1899–1902 in which, again in scenes resonant with the post–April 2003 Iraq War, the then preeminent world power was badly mauled by a highly motivated, tactically skillful, and well-armed local force of religious fanatics, though ultimately it muscled its way to victory through a combination of superior manpower and a massive complex of networked blockhouses that shut down the mobility of Boer commandos. This was in addition to population control measures that nowadays would almost certainly be deemed to constitute war crimes. Boer political leaders worked with a good deal of success in foreign capitals from where they hoped to draw support to bring attention to harsh British measures against Boer noncombatants. Effectively, they sought to weaponize the media channels of the day, seeking to mobilize moral opprobrium against the British. In the French press, for instance, Field Marshal Horatio Kitchener was pictured as a monster feasting on Boer corpses, Britain was accused of genocide, and the British Empire as a whole was characterized as a dim and overweight bully. In another biting French newspaper illustration, a British soldier was pictured kicking a pregnant Boer woman in the belly while she attempted to shield a group of toddlers cowering in terror in her shadow—other British soldiers in the background are seen smiling and egging him on. Such representations were commonplace.[13]

The effects were not limited to foreign populations. The British government was certainly concerned about the fragility of domestic opinions about the war. The "hysterical, euphoric relief" that followed the breaking of the siege of the British garrison at Mafeking and subsequent lionization of the commander Colonel Robert Baden-Powell is a testament to the public's fear of national humiliation at the hands of yet another ragbag force of irregulars. Contemporary accounts of the war illustrate the palpable mood of apprehension, fear of isolation, and dismay at the likely prospect of defeat:

> Nowhere had Britain a friend. France, Russia, and Germany were equally outspoken in bitter and contemptuous criticism. . . . And the most grievous feature of our defeats was that they were inflicted by a people numerically weak, without an army in the true sense—by a number of peasants and farmers upon the very flower of the British Army. The strongest, the best appointed, and, it was hoped, the best led force that had ever left our shores, equipped with all the contrivances of modern war, with field telegraphs, war balloons, howitzers, naval guns and lyddite shells, had failed . . . the British people had been brought face to face with the tragic realities of war. The scales fell from all eyes; it was clear to every man that this was a struggle for life or death, a struggle in which defeat must mean the loss of South Africa and the shaking of the British Empire to its very foundations, and in which victory at the best could never regain for us what we had forfeited—our reputation before the world.[14]

It was, moreover, not simply Britain's place in the eyes of the world—its pride in itself was equally challenged. Ministers were in particular concerned with domestic upset over harsh tactics against Boer civilians employed by the army, as it attempted desperately to separate Boer commandos from their base of support among the civilian population. Such tactics included the widespread burning of farms; collective punishment of local communities for attacks on railways, sniping, and ambushes of British patrols; and, most controversially, the erection of concentration camps into which noncombatants were interned en masse. There was an obvious point to such tactics, but at the same time the justificatory accounts of them were freighted with an equally obvious awareness that a moral line had been crossed—and it was not clear that Britain was on the right side of it:

> The determination of the Boers to wage a guerrilla war had compelled the British Generals, notwithstanding their reluctance to employ severe measures, to take steps to deal with the outwardly non-combatant Boer population. The enemy's custom of wearing no uniform, except that of the British troops—in itself a grave infraction of the laws of war—and their habit of resuming their peaceful avocations and returning to their farms when they required rest from their labour of derailing trains and sniping British sentries, coupled with their invariable practice of using

the farms as arsenals and bases of operations, and with their proved determination to respect no oaths of neutrality, no solemn promise to refrain from hostile action, had driven our Generals, in spite of themselves, to this course. It was not entered upon until the provocation given had been almost past endurance, and such as would have been tolerated by no other army in the world.[15]

On the whole, the British population accepted the rationalizations given and its support for the war did not collapse—as, for example, the Russian population accepted the pulverization of Grozny in Chechnya through the 1990s; the Israeli population has accepted the periodic pounding of south Lebanon, the West Bank, and Gaza over decades; the US population accepted the flattening, inter alia, of Fallujah, Iraq; and the world generally accepts the ongoing operations against the Islamic State in the course of which Mosul is being turned into a plain of rubble. It was a near-run thing, however, that could well have gone otherwise.

Reader, forgive another long quote from an account of the war at the time, it is necessary because to paraphrase it diminishes the sense of parallel with the modern era. It concerns the opinions (and putative personality) of Emily Hobhouse, an English peace activist and social liberal, who in early 1901 was permitted by British authorities to visit the concentration camps, in which it should be noted many thousands actually did perish of hunger and disease, on the proviso that she should not make political use of her findings.

> No sooner had [Hobhouse] returned to England than she produced a report in which she drew what pro-Boers called a "terrible picture" of the camps. She made no allowance whatever for the special difficulties of war, and forgot the fact that to keep a large population of hostile noncombatants supplied, while their husbands and brothers and sons were daily cutting the railways, was a stupendous task. She knew nothing of the normal conditions of Boer life, or of the state of dirt and squalor in which a large proportion of the camp inmates usually lived. She did not test or analyse what these people told her but, so long as they were to the discredit of her country, eagerly accepted their stories, though men who had lived for years in the Transvaal could have shown her how little Boer assertions, when uncorroborated, were to be trusted. . . . A report may be judged by its recommendations, and Miss Hobhouse's, with the elegant impracticability of the sentimentalist, could only suggest that the Boer women should be turned loose once more. . . . Not content with her report, however, she delivered a series of partisan addresses throughout England, and per-

mitted herself to be made the unconscious instrument of the Boer plot-
ters in Europe, who caught up her words, reprinted them, translated
them, heightening the colour at times, and scattered them broadcast
throughout the world, the result being to increase the animosity felt
abroad towards Britain, which was already only too bitter.[16]

It takes little imagination to hear such lines, with the change of
"Boer" to "Chechen," "Palestinian," or "Afghan," and "impracticable
sentimentalist" to "Amnesty International" or "Human Rights Watch,"
as though they were emerging from the mouth of a current government
spokesperson struggling to explain one of today's seemingly intractable
morally compromised hybrid conflicts. The effects of real-time imagery
on the basic problem of how governments manage the domestic perception of conflicts in which their forces are engaged abroad are easily
overstated. If there is a difference, it is one of fine degree.

Having dwelled somewhat lengthily on nineteenth-century British
military history, it is perhaps predictable to conclude this section with
a few lines from the foremost cultural chronicler of these hybrid wars of
yore, Rudyard Kipling. They are, however, apposite and serve to mark
quite important observations. Take, for instance, this verse from "The
Young British Soldier," written in 1895 as a description of the Second
Anglo-Afghan War:

> *When you're wounded and left on Afghanistan's plains,*
> *And the women come out to cut up what remains,*
> *Jest roll to your rifle and blow out your brains*
> *An' go to your Gawd like a soldier.*

Were the Victorians really so innocent and unknowing of the "blood and
gore" of warfare? It is hard to square the existence of such naïveté with
a society in which such poetically graphic imagery was a popular best-
seller, taught in schools, reprinted in popular newspapers, read in concert halls and pubs. Consider too the opening lines of "The Lesson"
written as a sort of epigraph of the Boer War, which I have just discussed, but which really ought to be taken as rather timelessly relevant:

> *Let us admit it fairly, as a business people should,*
> *We have had no end of a lesson: it will do us no end of good.*
> *Not on a single issue, or in one direction or twain,*
> *But conclusively, comprehensively, and several times and*
> *Again.*

Lessons of the Russo-Japanese War

A more recent development of the hybrid wars thesis is its application by many governments of the NATO alliance, and the alliance when speaking in its own right, to describe Russia's activities vis-à-vis the Baltic states, Georgia, and especially Ukraine. The conjectured elements of Russian hybrid warfare include the combination of regular and irregular formations, the manipulation of political divisions in the target state, economic pressure, diplomatic obfuscation, and a concerted and well-organized information campaign. Its distinction from other examples of hybridity rests, apparently largely, on the degree of state involvement. Whereas in other conflicts the belligerents on at least one side are objectively nonstate actors, or, as with Hezbollah, are arguably *quasi*-nonstate actors, in the case of Russia's "little green men" it requires a willing suspension of disbelief not to recognize them as uniformed, regularly equipped, organized, trained, and disciplined Russian troops with their unit markings removed. It is an effective strategic gambit, to judge from the degree of consternation it has provoked in NATO defense circles as well as the popular press, and military fiction. Russia pretends that it is not actively directly engaged in objectively warlike behavior on its periphery and, so far, most other states accept the pretense because they fear the escalatory consequences of doing otherwise.

The adroitness with which Russia exercises these tactics perhaps comes down to the fact that it is well practiced with them. History shows this well. If there is something hybrid to this particular way of war, which in terms of the obvious combination of means military and nonmilitary, intertwined with a coherent deception campaign stretching from the political through the strategic to the tactical levels of war, there would seem to be, it is not new; its existence now is not due to any particular technological development either. There is no major or minor aspect of hybrid war that is not perfectly evident, for an example, among several possible others, in the 1904–1905 Russo-Japanese War. Rather like Britain's Argentine adventure a century earlier, the Russo-Japanese War was a highly politically complex across a range of vectors—regionally between the belligerents and the countries they were fighting over and globally multilaterally via various commercial interests as well as entangling alliances, notably that between Japan and Britain. Russia was a politically troubled empire—though its economy was growing at the time—while Japan was an energetic and ambitious one. Japan was relatively weak militarily, having abandoned its antique mode of warfare, based on the samurai cult of the sword, only about two generations before. But it was learning fast and was capable of bold action. Both countries were vying for political mastery over a third country (Korea), which Japan would subsequently repress savagely until its own defeat and occupation by the United States in World War II. But the conflict was also nested within a larger contest for dominance of yet another, even larger, country (China) where, to muddy the waters even further, essentially every major player of the day felt it had a commercial or political stake (and, to a greater or lesser extent, the military presence to back it up).

In the interests of brevity, a précis: the war came down to competing imperial ambitions in Korea and Manchuria between Russia and Japan; its major battles were fought in southern Manchuria on land and in the seas around Korea. Japanese military forces inflicted a series of striking defeats on Russia, on land and at sea. For Japan, it was a gigantic success which, despite the war being overshadowed by World War I, was seen as highly significant at the time on account of it being the first instance in modern history in which an Asiatic power defeated a European one decisively. For Russia, it was a disaster militarily, but the political effects were even worse—the widespread revolts of 1905, which were put down, presaged the revolution of 1917.

Russian tactics in the war, however, perhaps because they failed, have not received as much attention as they merit. For one thing, as noted, they are interesting because of the extent to which they mirror what are described as the precepts of twenty-first-century hybrid warfare, starting with the use of regular troops in a quasi-irregular, ambiguously uniformed manner well in advance of the commencement of openly hostile operations. In the spring of 1903 (by which point, many years of diplomatic and cutthroat economic maneuvering had already passed), Tokyo observed that Russian forces had crossed the river Yalu into Korea and established there a seemingly permanent presence. As Japan saw it, Russia had extracted from a weak Korean government—in modern parlance, nearly a "failed state," a consequence in no small part of the meddling of its neighbors—a concession to cut timber in its northern territory. Russia claimed, at first, that its forces were simply unarmed woodcutters and, second, after being challenged on the veracity of the point, that if they were armed it was only for self-protection from Korean bandits, a condition necessitated by the malgovernance of the country. Essentially, the Japanese believed that Russia, under a cloud of promises and reassurances to the contrary, was invading and occupying Korea—in which view they were probably correct. Instead of little green men, Russia was advancing by battalions of woodcutters. At the same time, Russia was said, again according to contemporaneous accounts (in this case from the British, who were sympathetic to Japan) to be fomenting disorder in Korea:

> Now the Korean Emperor would protest his attachment to Russia, and now again, stricken with panic, he would insist on his devotion to Japan, and produce by the ream ordinances of reform to which no one paid the slightest attention. In all directions disorder appeared. The Tonghaks, who had risen in 1894, and so brought on the war between Japan and China, once more broke into rebellion. The crowds in the capital menaced all foreigners, and guards were hurriedly obtained for the various foreign Legations. The wildest stories were in circulation and were credited. Now it was said that Japan was pouring disguised soldiers into Korea; now that the Russian "woodcutters" in the north were moving south.[17]

On top of that, there was a befuddling and exasperating diplomatic campaign of obfuscation and delay by the Russians to protract negotiations that, in the Japanese view, were designed simply to forestall the outbreak of hostilities while Russia covertly prepositioned supplies and gathered its army and naval forces. Furthermore, it was argued by Japan and Britain that the French and German press corps were riddled with Russian agents from which points of editorial privilege they were blasting international political opinion with absurd stories. The object of this alleged collusion and procrastination was said to be to delay the onset of war until conditions were more favorable to Russia.

> Day followed day, week followed week, and there was no Russian reply [to a Japanese proposal]. The Japanese minister at St. Petersburg, M. Kurino, pressed not once but repeatedly for an answer. He was put off with evasive words. Now Count Lamsdorff was just about to resume control of the negotiations—and he was supposed to be in favour of peace—now this point or that had to be referred to Admiral Alexeieff at the other end of Asia. It might almost have been supposed that the Russians were ignorant of the art of telegraphy.[18]

The tactics and techniques employed by Russia in the early twentieth century, its efforts to prepare the battlespace as we would now put it, prior to the formal outbreak of conflict through a combination of means—overt and covert, diplomatic and military, and economic, all blended toward a common goal—are in themselves interesting. Their parallel with observed tactics of the moment is unmistakable. The point of observing them, however, is not simply to remark that there is nothing new under the sun because that itself is a banal point, well understood since Old Testament times. It rather is that when we presume the opposite, that things are unprecedented and uniquely complex because of technological change, say (as is the current habit), it has the effect of severing current decisionmakers from hard-learned lessons of the past, both good and bad, that pertained to situations every bit as confounding of those of the present.

Conclusion

War is the extension of politics by other means. It is intrinsically human and war is about, for, and by people. People are hugely ingenious, never more so than when their situation is kill or be killed by some other human who wants to compel them to do their will. There is no reason to expect that it should stay within the boundaries of the labels that we might attach to it—regular, irregular, conventional, unconventional—because history shows that it does not. None of the wars that I discussed in this chapter behaved so agreeably as to have begun when they were supposed to have begun (or ended when they were supposed to have ended), were fought solely (or even primarily) by military means, or stayed confined to one theater of conflict, and the military means employed in them comprised a range of types, uniformed and nonuniformed, sometimes literally rag wearing. Sometimes the weak win because they are strong in the things that really matter, and are wise and creative enough to recognize and act on them.

Some years ago, at a dinner with Hoffman, I remarked that if we had a mature understanding of war then we would have no need of the concept of hybrid war. However, as we did not have such an understanding, it had some important utility. The most self-defeating mental habit in Western strategy for many decades now has been the tendency to place technology in the center of the frame of analysis, as though all problems stem from a foe's better grasp of how to employ this or that new development in weapon systems, and as though all solutions lie in our achievement of the same.

Our ancestors understood war better; they seem less frequently to have expected wars to be easy, cheap, and decisive and were better prepared, therefore, to deal with the world as it was, not as they wished it to be. I think they would have found appending the word *hybrid* to war to be superfluous, maybe even indulgent. That said, if interrogating hybridity brings us back to a more mature understanding of war, more realistic if not realist, then perhaps it could be an intermediate step forward.

Notes

1. Frank Hoffman, *Conflict in the Twenty-First Century: The Rise of Hybrid Wars* (Arlington, VA: Potomac Institute for Policy Studies, 2007).

2. Hew Strachan, "The Changing Character of War," Europaeum Lecture delivered at the Graduate Institute of International Relations, Geneva, 9 November 2006, p. 2.

3. Antoine-Henri Jomini, "The Art of War," trans. Colonel John N. Greely and Major Robert C. Cotton, in *The Roots of Strategy,* Book 2 (Mechanicsburg, PA: Stackpole Books, 1987), p. 393.

4. C. E. Callwell, *Small Wars: Their Principles and Practice,* 3rd ed. (Abingdon: Purnell Book Services, 1976), p. 27.

5. The section of this chapter dealing with the British in Argentina in 1806–1807 is based on Ian Hernon, *The Savage Empire: Forgotten Wars of the Nineteenth Century* (Stroud, Gloucestershire: Sutton, 2000).

6. *The Times,* quoted in ibid., p. 9.

7. Lieutenant Colonel Lancelot Holland, quoted in ibid., p. 1.

8. Charles Krulak, "The United States Marine Corps in 21st Century," *RUSI Journal* 141, no. 4 (1996): 25.

9. Zygmunt Bauman, quoted in David Betz, *Carnage and Connectivity: Landmarks in the Decline of Conventional Military Power* (London: Hurst, 2014), p. 4.

10. Hoffman, *Conflict in the Twenty-First Century,* p. 38.

11. Andrew Marr, journalist, quoted in Betz, *Carnage and Connectivity,* p. 130.

12. Sir David Richards, commander of the International Security Assistance Force (ISAF) in Afghanistan, quoted in Betz, *Carnage and Connectivity,* p. 128.

13. Thomas Pakenham, *The Boer War,* illustrated ed. (London: Weidenfeld and Nicolson, 1979) is the classic work on this subject. It includes many of the illustrations noted in this section on the Boer War.

14. H. W. Wilson, *With the Flag to Pretoria: A History of the Boer War of 1899–1900,* vol. 1 (London: Harmsworth Brothers, 1900), p. 205.

15. H. W. Wilson, *After Pretoria: The Guerrilla War,* vol. 1 (London: Amalgamated Press, 1909), p. 496.

16. Ibid., pp. 500–502.

17. H. W. Wilson, *Japan's Fight for Freedom: The Story of the War Between Russia and Japan,* vol. 1 (London: Amalgamated Press, 1905), p. 80.

18. Ibid., pp. 73–74.

3

The Color Revolutions in the Context of Hybrid Wars

Georgy Filimonov

Revolutions in military affairs usually occur as a result of fundamental changes created by scientific and technological advancements, which serve as a driving force behind the development in the means of armed struggle, in the ways to build up and train armed forces, and in the methods of warfighting and conducting combat operations.[1] In the case of hybrid warfare, however, there is no need to develop new weapon systems and sophisticated ways to employ them since the core of this type of confrontation is generally based on already existing components of interstate struggle. In other words hybrid war, a combination of adversary's nonlinear actions, is not a product of a revolutionary impulse in military affairs, but merely a special organizational model that offers enhanced methods and better structure required to achieve concrete military and political objectives.[2] This is especially the case when an external controlling power (international actor) needs to minimize the risks of conventional (open) confrontation and employs various destructive forces, providing them with different types of situational support such as camouflaging the presence and involvement of military contingents or providing a superficial (informational) cover-up for covert subversive operations.[3]

The concept of hybrid warfare describes a situation where an external controlling power brings the protest-potential masses (which are usually unaware of being exploited) and different types of destructive opposition forces (e.g., terrorist, extremist, and criminal groups) to the forefront of the fight against adversary political regimes.[4] Hence, by conducting hybrid war, an external controlling power gains great operational capabilities to achieve its military and political goals without escalating into full-scale conventional fighting. In this chapter, I discuss the Russian conceptualization of hybrid warfare, as it is presented in the ongoing military, academic, and professional discourses in Russia, focusing on the role and place of the color revolutions as a core element of this type of contemporary interstate confrontations.

Hybrid Warfare: The Western Origins

The *Quadrennial Defense Review (QDR) 2010*—an official strategic policy document—uses the term *hybrid war* to capture the increasing "complexity of war, the multiplicity of actors involved, and the blurring between traditional categories of conflict."[5] According to the document, this approach to warfare is not entirely novel. It calls for the United States to prepare itself for such challenges because, in the near future, hybrid techniques will be employed against the country by both state and nonstate actors. Therefore, it is not surprising that there is an ongoing political-academic-military debate in many Western countries regarding the need to counter different threats posed by this hybrid war. For example, this message was reflected in a joint declaration following the 2014 NATO Wales summit, which defined such wars as "threats where a wide range of overt and covert military, paramilitary, and civilian measures is employed in a highly integrated design."[6]

According to Nathan Freier of the Center for Strategic and International Studies, in the future the United States will face a combination of four types of threats—traditional, irregular, catastrophic, and disruptive. Freier suggests that such a combined hybrid threat may be posed by any actor that employs at least two of these modes of conflict, thus ultimately conducting a hybrid type of warfare that would involve different nonmilitary and nonviolent measures of influence such as informational, political, and economic.[7] Vice Admiral Arthur K. Cebrowski and analyst John J. Garstka, who were called to rethink the traditional approaches to warfighting and substitute them with a concept of network-centric warfare (NCW), elaborated the main idea of this theory. According to Cebrowski and Garstka, this concept better explains the needs of the US Army by applying modern information technologies to ensure its qualitative advantage on the battlefield.[8] Therefore, it seems right to argue that, in the Western perspective, war is turning into a network phenomenon, thereby transforming hostilities into a type of network process. Regular armies, intelligence activities, innovation and cutting-edge technologies, journalism and diplomacy, economic processes and social transformations, civilian populations and military professionals, active units and separate loosely knit groups—all are integrated into a single network through which information is circulated and a war is conducted. According to John Arquilla, NCW is characterized by exploitation of communication and information technologies, the most important of which is known as "swarming" and involves unarmed protesters and largely decentralized combatant units.[9]

In 2015, the Pentagon published *The National Military Strategy of the United States of America 2015*—a concept paper that replaced the previous document from 2011. This document not only referred to hybrid conflicts as a blend of conventional and irregular forces with a variety of methods and means of combat, but it also blamed Russia for using such tactics. Specifically, it stated that "such 'hybrid' conflicts may consist of military forces assuming a non-state identity, as Russia did in the Crimea. . . . Hybrid conflicts also may be comprised of state and non-state actors working together toward shared objectives, employing a wide range of weapons such as we have witnessed in eastern Ukraine."[10] This is a clear demonstration of the US bias toward the term *hybrid war* since when it comes to hybrid methods that the United States itself employs against Russia, Washington is reluctant to recognize them as such.[11]

Hybrid war is a multidimensional phenomenon that integrates several aspects of fighting—military, informational, economic, political, and sociocultural—into a single domain. What makes it particularly distinctive is a combination of military and nonmilitary influences, which are extended simultaneously across multiple battlefields and therefore require well-organized multivector counteraction. Due to the technological expertise of the Western world in the twenty-first century, the latest advances in military affairs, availability of highly sophisticated communication systems, vast experience in the field of information technologies and control of mass media have all created a better opportunity for the West to conduct hybrid operations against its adversaries without economic and material costs of traditional (conventional) warfare.[12]

Hybrid War in the Russian Conceptual Debate

In Russia, there is an understanding that the US-led West has mastered hybrid warfare as part of its "intelligent" approach to warfighting that allows it to avoid an undesired escalation into an open large-scale confrontation of regular armies. These multilayered operations blend military measures (irregular rebel tactics, use of special operations forces, fighting in information and cyber spaces, economic and political pressures) with civilian aspects of struggle (popular protests).[13] The civilian component, accompanied by a range of destructive techniques for dismantling political regimes (color revolutions), plays one of the most important roles in these hybrid confrontations. While the civilian component is mainly based on the political protests of the population, if necessary, it can be complemented with covert military measures. Military theorist Evgeny Messner, who developed his concept of "subversion war" during the Cold War, was among the first to argue that, in the future, battle lines of conflicts would be dissolved across the territories of the conflicting countries, thus turning political, social, and economic aspects into the most dominant dimensions of war. At the same time, a greater role would be given to destructive influences on the civilian population:

> Each fighting side would create and nurture partisan movement inside the territory of its adversaries, promoting different oppositionist and defeatist parties and offering them ideological, material, financial and propaganda support. It would employ all available means and methods to fuel civilian disobedience, sabotage, subversion and terror. . . . [Simultaneously] the government and the armed forces of this fighting side would engage their own population and the population in occupied territories in the fight against enemy agents, who attempt to do the same [inside its own territory].[14]

Moreover, Messner identified seven main methods of subversion war— propaganda, obstruction, sabotage, subversion, terror, guerrilla, and rebellion—specifically emphasizing propaganda as the most important element in subversion war.[15]

Regardless of this early conceptualization, the Russian expert community lacks a common understanding of the concept of hybrid warfare. According to Pavel Tsygankov, one of the defining features of hybrid warfare is that it takes advantage of the broad possibilities provided by modern information technologies, which have become instrumental in the intentional distortion of facts and deliberate dissemination of false information and fake stories. According to Tsygankov, hybrid warfare also includes an application of the different techniques of social manipulation and falsification of history because hybrid war antagonizes the whole population and includes all areas of social life such as politics, the economy, social development, and culture.[16] Developing his ideas further, Tsygankov states:

> In reality, "hybrid wars" have become one of the most frequently employed by the U.S. and the rest of the West methods of foreign policy. The U.S. employs these methods, drawing on its vast (though not always successful) experience of toppling inconvenient regimes in various countries through a combination of military and non-military means. Moreover, it does not hesitate to lie or manipulate facts, disregard human casualties and ignore international and political implications of is actions.[17]

Thus, Tsygankov explains a hybrid nature of many contemporary armed conflicts by suggesting that the US political elite implements these techniques in its attempt to preserve its supremacy on the global arena. Moreover, he argues that Russia's expert community gives insufficient attention to this phenomenon because, while the Russian literature provides a basis for further study of that subject, "the West is not only outpacing us in quantity of information-propagandistic publications on this topic, but it also has a serious approach within its expert and academic communities intended to study this phenomenon (though that approach cannot be considered absolutely free from an ideological bias against Russia)."[18]

On the one hand, some Russian scholars examine the concept of hybrid war through the lens of different associated theories, such as network-centric war, managed chaos, and the destructive political techniques of color revolutions, considering them all as the structural components of the hybrid type of warfare.[19] On the other hand, there are those who distinguish between these concepts, advocating the relevance of one particular concept.[20] The most important fact, however, is that all of these researchers agree that hybrid war is a serious threat to Russia's national security. Therefore, it is not surprising that the studies devoted to the hybridization of warfare have stirred up interest not only among military professionals, but also in the civilian expert community. Sergei Glazyev, associate member of the Russian Academy of Sciences and adviser to the president, suggests an examination of hybrid war from the perspective of geopolitics and current US approaches to ensure its unilateral global dominance. According to Glazyev,

> The contemporary form of waging warfare between countries, which has become known among experts as "hybrid war," is completely

different from different wars that we had witnessed until today. Because today, military force is used as a last-resort argument, when the adversary has already been defeated and should be punished [for his previous resistance]. The ultimate defeat of the adversary is achieved by a creation of chaos.[21]

In his opinion, contemporary wars are conducted by weapons based on new age technologies, which first of all include information and communication technologies and high-precision weapons. Such wars, according to Glazyev, enable the US military to maintain its systemic supremacy on the battlefield and to minimize its losses. Moreover, he states that "[these technologies] are reinforced by cognitive techniques that turn the mass media into a highly effective psychotropic weapon of mass destruction used against people's consciousness, and diplomacy into a psycho-paralysing weapon used against the political will of the adversary's leadership."[22]

Mikhail Delyagin, director of the Institute for Problems of Globalization, also emphasizes the geopolitical scale of hybrid warfare which, he believes, is a euphemism for global competition. He states that "[hybrid war] is a struggle that seeks to destroy the adversary, to completely eliminate the independence of his governing system and bring him under your full control. Hybrid war aims to reduce the adversary country [from its status as an independent state] to a territory under your own authority."[23] Delyagin highlights the multifaceted nature of this phenomenon, emphasizing the effectiveness of such means as propaganda, bribery, political scheming, espionage, political assassination, and staging of civil unrest.

Vladimir Karyakin, a leading research fellow at the Russian Institute for Strategic Studies, highlights the importance of the phenomena of color revolutions and hybrid wars in current international confrontations. He also qualifies destructive political techniques as an essential element of hybrid war. According to Karyakin, in hybrid wars both military and nonmilitary methods are used for achieving domestic and international political aims, by utilizing protest movements to ensure a nonviolent struggle for power. If it does not lead to the anticipated result, fueling of the political tensions allows protest movements to transform into a color revolution and, if required, into a civil war that turns into hybrid war as in the Middle East and in Ukraine.[24] On the one hand, it can be concluded that Russian experts on hybrid wars hold somewhat similar views on this phenomenon. But on the other, it becomes obvious that, despite this shared understanding, there is no common conceptual definition of *hybrid war* in Russia, nor of its structural features and technological aspects of its implementation.

The Dangers of Hybrid Wars

In analyzing joint efforts of civilian and military scholars, its seems possible to establish a common understanding of the concept of hybrid threats, thus enabling experts, military officials, and civilians to comprehend the true nature of this type of conflict rather than examine different interrelated actions of the adversary as separate actions. For example, some experts tend to interpret illegitimate international sanctions and overwhelming external pressure as a routine element of tense international relations, and an orchestrated civilian unrest that involves the public as a "democratic" form of political expression.[25] Various political groups of extremists, sometimes including terror organizations, are often regarded as groups of frenzied radicals and not as a tool carefully concocted by intelligence services to play a part in much larger international confrontations.[26] An examination of all these factors together, however, offers a greater picture and highlights the importance of the coordinating activities by an external power, an international actor who facilitates different (seemingly unrelated) actions. Examples include the application of sanctions and external pressure, and the staging of civil unrest, followed by international provocations and attempts to topple the regime by covert connivance with extremist movements and terrorist groups.

Frank G. Hoffman, US military theoretician who coined the term *hybrid war,* believes that the twenty-first century will be marked by hybrid warfare because "we see the convergence of military force and the interagency community, of states and non-state actors, and of the capabilities they are armed with. Of greatest relevance are the converging modes of war. What once might have been distinct operational types or categorizations among terrorism and conventional, criminal, and irregular warfare have less utility today."[27] According to Hoffman, hybrid wars would involve a whole range of different types of warfare, including conventional capabilities, irregular tactics and formations, as well as terrorist attacks, indiscriminate violence, and criminal disorders, that will be waged by both states and various nonstate actors. Therefore, it seems right to argue that, due to its use of different disruptive methods, hybrid warfare has the potential to grow into a special type of conflict that takes place without a formal declaration of war or, in other words, confrontations that erase the familiar line between the state of peace and the state of war. In such confrontations, adversaries pursue the strategy of destruction and attrition which, nowadays, could be implemented in both global and regional conflicts.

An employment of destructive political techniques (color revolutions) in an attempt to achieve certain political goals involves different nonmilitary methods, which often prove to be more effective than military ones. A color revolution is the initial step in destabilizing the situation in a targeted country, where the general goal is to overthrow the adversary political regime. This color revolution scenario is predominantly based on the employment of information warfare methods, when an important role is played by intelligence agencies, special forces, and other military formations that are capable of turning the tide of events.[28] To implement its subversive color revolution strategy, an external controlling power preliminarily trains destructionists and quasi-military combat formations, and creates sustainable channels of economic, military, political, and other types of support, secretly transferring necessary weapons and equipment. In an addition, these destructionists and their supervisors increasingly try to covertly exploit the population's protest potential, planning to involve private military companies or special operations forces in different stages of this process. If the attempted coup fails, the confrontation emphasis shifts toward the use of force, and implementation of military measures. Thus, color revolutions become the initial (transitional) stage of a much bigger hybrid war.[29]

An implementation of such a hybrid scenario, where a successful coup d'état is followed by the establishment of an aggressive regime that promotes instability and violence, has great potential for escalation into a large-scale confrontation, or even a full-scale conventional war. Therefore, it is not surprising that one of the biggest external military threats to Russia, as stated in its Military Doctrine is the "establishment in the states bordering Russia, including as a result of overthrowing legitimate governments, of regimes that pursue a policy threatening Russia's interests."[30] In other words, hybrid warfare is an extremely dangerous type of confrontation because it blurs the line between war and peace by intentionally destabilizing not only individual states, but also entire regions, without a clear declaration of war. This is best demonstrated by the series of color revolutions, which have become commonly known as the Arab Spring, that toppled political regimes across the Middle East, notably Libya, Tunisia, and Egypt. The entire region was plunged into chaos by several external (Western) powers that waged hybrid war against local political regimes by implementing different political techniques intended to stage color revolutions against them.

Color Revolutions in the Context of Hybrid Wars

In an attempt to construct a comprehensive understanding of all factors that create a color revolution, it is important to elaborate this concept further. *Color revolution* is a term that refers to specific techniques intended to stage a coup d'état and establish external control over the political situation in a targeted country. This usually is achieved by artificially manufactured political instability, where political blackmail is employed to pressure the government and youth protest movements serve as the most powerful destabilizing factor. Despite considerable dissimilarities between countries in which color revolutions have occurred (geopolitically, socially, economically, and internationally), it is difficult not to recognize the same organizational scheme, which has included instigating patterned youth protest movements, building a politically active crowd, and turning the combined political force of both against the incumbent government as a means of political blackmail.[31] Moreover, it seems reasonable to argue that color revolutions have little to do with the fulfillment of reasonable hopes and aspirations of the popular majority. It is important to understand that modern-day political upheavals do not work toward the same goals as previous classic revolutions, which sought to change the polity and forms of ownership or to recast the entire social system. Since the ultimate objective of any color revolution is to instigate a coup d'état, thus forcibly seizing and retaining power, it seems right to argue that a color revolution is a tool in the global struggle for power that targets the political legitimacy and coherence of adversaries.[32]

There are two main conditions required for a successful color revolution. The first one underlines the necessity of political instability in a targeted country, coupled with the crisis of the incumbent government (if the political situation in the country is stable, it should be artificially disrupted to achieve this necessary condition). The second condition signifies the necessity of specially organized protest movements (based on a particular network of different organizations).[33] These two types of preconditions also shape the main characteristics of a color revolution: (1) the instability allows it to influence the local authorities through political blackmail; (2) the external control of protest movements is used as the main tool for influencing (blackmailing) the authorities because that allows them to maintain the instability.[34] Therefore, it seems right to argue that color revolutions resemble real revolutionary movements only superficially because, unlike actual revolutions that are driven by the natural flow of history, color revolutions are specific political techniques cunningly disguised as spontaneous processes. It can also be noted that these processes are staged with almost theatrical dramaturgy, when certain (mainly Western) political scientists try to frame them as a self-induced and spontaneous expression of the will of people, who suddenly have decided to reclaim their right to govern their own country.[35]

There are two major viewpoints among experts regarding the causes of color revolutions: while some claim that color revolutions occur as an outcome of natural evolutionary political-social-economic processes,[36] others suggest that they are carefully staged processes designed to establish political control over an adversary.[37] Those who believe that color revolutions are outcomes of natural societal developments argue that the causes of these revolutions rest in the objective social antagonism that develops into different forms of civilian revolts and mass protests of an oppressed population. In these cases, possible causes include poverty, frustration with the ruling regimes, aspiration for democratic changes, and the demographic situation.[38] On the contrary, a closer analysis of the sociopolitical situation in nearly any country where a color revolution took place shows that the existing antagonisms and social divisions did act as a catalyst for the revolutionary events, but that they were not the primary or only cause. For example, in Egypt, before the color revolution broke out, the government had provided subsidies on flatbread, making this basic food product obtainable for the poorest groups of the country's population. In Libya, people had received a natural resource rent (and many other subsidies), which was so high that the population had stopped working altogether, necessitating the importation of an immigrant workforce from different African countries, including Egypt. In Tunisia, the most democratic of all African autocracies, the standard of living had nearly equaled that of southern France (Provence and Languedoc) and even exceeded that of southern Italy. In Syria, one of the reasons for the upsurge in protest movements was that Bashar al-Assad (by his own initiative) decided to ease his authoritarian rule and initiated liberal transformations, which were immediately exploited by radical Islamists and their sponsors in the United States.[39] Therefore, it is not surprising that there are those who tend to see color revolutions as carefully staged political interventions, pointing to recurrences of the same scenario in various countries around the world, which in fact are very different in terms of their social, economic, and political problems. The main argument of these scholars and experts is that all color revolutions evolve in the same pattern and, since the likelihood of the same event following the same pattern under different conditions is next to none, there should be a "guiding hand" that shapes and directs each one of these events.[40]

Drawing on these conclusions, the proponents of the staging interpretation of color revolutions point to a number of attributes that reject a color revolution as a spontaneous popular uprising. According to these scholars, every color revolution has certain characteristics that point to its nature as a carefully employed set of techniques. First, the employed methods are natural attributes of the Western (Anglo-Saxon) foreign policy and its typical work style. Second is the conformity of every revolution's plan to a similar template (or scenario)—all color revolutions unfold by following the same scenario based on the same patterned scheme. Third, the ways in which all protest movements are organized and employed, regardless of the place of the color revolution, are reminiscent of the reflexive control techniques (also invented by the United States). Fourth, there are certain recurring peculiarities in selecting and putting forward revolutionary leaders. Finally, some color revolutions lacked any revolutionary ideology as such, proving that these revolutions had been forged.[41] It is possible to argue that color revolutions are often called techniques or tools of "soft power," as it was defined by Joseph Nye.[42] Based on the law of assimilation, it is possible to assume that color revolutions are in fact nonviolent techniques employed for regime change. Such an approach, however, is inadequate and often leads to confusion, suggesting that color revolutions should be considered as a softer, and hence more progressive and less dangerous, way of influencing authoritarian regimes. Therefore, it is not surprising that certain voices promote color revolutions as an alternative, and more peaceful, form of armed coup.[43] However, it seems difficult to unambiguously determine the greater danger to global security: color revolutions or local armed conflicts. In fact, the outcomes of the color revolutions in the Middle East, which plunged the whole region into a state of managed chaos, is a clear testimony that the former is as dangerous as the latter, if not more. In other words, since the color revolution is one of the foundation stones of hybrid warfare, it is essentially a tool of a global struggle for power and, therefore, by its very nature, can be as bloody as any other type of war.

Stages of the Color Revolution

While every stage is prepared and executed independently, the success of each subsequent stage depends on the successful preparation and implementation of the previous one. The first stage is the inception (preparation).[44] It implies identifying and aligning forces, classifying different political actors as "friends" and "foes" (i.e., as possible allies and prominent adversaries). In an addition to this division, during this stage the external controlling power carefully identifies certain social groups that could be easily manipulated against the existing political regime. The main criterion for choosing this targeted audience is their attitudes toward the goals, values, underlying concepts, and demands of the external controlling (destructive) power. Before implementing any activities in practice, every detail and action will be carefully modeled and analyzed. This modeling phase can take between a few months to several years (depending on the set goals; the involvement of the masses; the intensity of domestic, regional, and global political developments, etc.). This preparatory analysis takes into account not only the targeted audience and the political, social, and economic state of affairs in the country and the region, but also the personality and political status of each leader or head (of state agencies, political parties and movements, large businesses, mass media, etc.) individually. This also includes a particular focus on the preliminary alignment of political forces, military leadership, and other governmental institutions, in an attempt to examine the possibility of influencing them through various means and methods, including discrediting techniques and manipulation. It is important to note that a carefully selected incompetent political figure, with neither decisionmaking experience nor adequate skills, may serve as a targeted key link in the governance system at a moment of crisis. Thus, the main purpose of the preparation stage is to probe and monitor possible ways to influence high-level political-military-economic decisionmaking. The process of this monitoring may include launching various activities such as political activist campaigns and dissemination of false stories, with subsequent assessment of the targeted audience's response.

The second stage is the alignment of forces. It aims to divide all political actors between those who will eventually find themselves in power (and form necessary forces around them) and those who will be sacrificed for the sake of the revolution and, thus, removed from the political scene. This period is usually marked by the appearance of new figures and movements on the domestic political stage and the emergence of new leaders. During this process, a particular significance is given to personal qualities of the existing and emerging political and military leaders, their habits, inclinations, and even health conditions. The aim of the external controlling power is to identify the frontline players to clearly divide them between friends (whose activity should be supported) and foes (whose actions should be undermined). The duration of this stage may vary between several months and two to three years.

The third stage is the actual destabilization of the political situation in the targeted country, which is characterized by an avalanche of different political, economic, social, and sometimes military developments. Any color revolution begins with a carefully organized protest movement. Already during the previous stages, several potential protest movements have been set up as a network consisting of clandestine cells, consisting of a local leader with three or four core activists under his or her supervision. When the time comes, these networks will bring together thousands of activists, who will constitute the core of public unrest. This network form of organization of protest movements resembles, to a certain degree, the organizational mechanisms of terrorist networks. When all preparations are accomplished, these networked protest movements will take the general public to the streets of large cities at a prearranged and carefully calculated signal, which is generally described as an "incident." For example, the revolutions in Yugoslavia (2000), Ukraine (2004), and Georgia (2004) were triggered by the declaration of unfair elections, which served as a staged incident that initiated the scenario of a color revolution. It is very important that these destabilizing incidents will draw the attention of the entire society and be widely discussed and interpreted, causing public anxiety and allowing the rise of the spontaneous behavior of the masses. The destabilization process will be instigated further within one or several politically active social networks, such as students or workers, focusing on specific economic and social demands that are most relevant for the targeted audience.

The next part of the third stage is bringing the dissatisfied social groups onto the streets to protest to voice their demands, thus provoking wider political and social resonance. As soon as the incident triggers social strife, the prepared and trained-in-advance protest networks will take the public to the streets, where well-organized groups of activists will act as catalysts for spontaneous mass demonstrations attracting more and more people. As the demands of the protesters receive wide media coverage, this allows for the introduction of new political actors: these are specially trained figures who make carefully designed political demands aimed to bring the situation to a higher level of political confrontation. Since during this stage, large numbers of people get involved in the political movement within a short period of time, it is the most crucial and costly stage for those who execute the color revolution scenario. On the one hand, the main driving force behind these political protests consists of the most financially and socially dissatisfied masses, who have nothing to lose and therefore are easily manipulated by an idea of political change. On the other hand, motivation of these groups requires financial and material resources, which often include cash rewards or provision of food, alcohol, clothing, and so forth. One of the techniques employed to heat up the population, attract new supporters and unite them against political foes, is turning the situation into a show or a sort of perform-ance. At this stage, a vital role belongs to different nonstate structures, foundations, and private companies that provide financial support for the unfolding scenario. The duration of this stage depends on the extent of the leaders' involvement and their skills, and it may vary between a few hours to several weeks.

The fourth stage is the revolution itself. It is characterized by riots, actions of civil disobedience, organized protests, and violent actions aimed at the destruction of the existing political power and seizing con-trol of the country. These actions go beyond the commonly established legal boundaries, and the development of this stage depends on the suc-cessful performance during each of the previous stages. The success of this stage usually depends on the number of people brought onto the streets and the extent of the leaders' involvement. For the planning, preparation, and implementation of mass riots and demonstrations, the prepared and trained-in-advance networks control the flow of informa-tion in a way that minimizes the number of people capable to grasp the entire picture. Single individuals emotionally fuse with the crowd, and revolutionary symbols and rhetoric are used to identify friend and foe. This allows for manipulation of the crowd through different psycholog-ical techniques that influence people's subconscious, instilling new val-ues and imperatives, thus reprogramming their personal values and political desires. Each action during this stage is provided with a facade of legitimacy because all movements are presented as leaderless, having self-coordinators who were forced by the people's will to lead them in this revolution of justice. This period usually turns out to be relatively brief and will not last more than a few days.

The fifth stage indicates the breakdown of the existing political sys-tem, leading to the legitimation of the external controlling power and the proclamation of a new political regime. During this stage, the general pub-lic experiences increased psychoemotional stress due to the destruction of the existing governance system and the signs of social-political-economic crisis that follow. This is the most suitable moment for the external controlling power to model a new lifestyle according to new (democratic) standards and patterns, without any risk of possible retaliation. It is also the best moment to outlaw the opposing side (foes and their supporters).

The sixth and final stage focuses on returning the situation to a general legal framework. It implies final elimination of the opposing side by accusations of corruption, tyranny, exploitation, and so forth; thus, placing friends in a variety of state government posts via democratic processes and establishing new vertical of power that receives orders from the external power in return for economic, military, and political assistance.

Conclusion

Destructive political techniques of color revolutions have become a crucial factor in international relations and, having no less destabilizing potential than conventional armed conflicts, these techniques significantly endanger the international stability and security system. According to Russian defense minister, Sergey Shoigu, "Colour revolutions are increasingly taking the form of warfare and are developed according to the rules of the art of war."[45] The promoters and sponsors of such popular uprisings tend to use a very adaptive approach, successfully combining military force with the techniques of color revolutions; thus, inevitably promoting the dangerous emergence of hybrid warfare. This evolution of warfare into new methods of achieving military and political goals poses qualitatively new challenges to the state. Superiority in aggregate military power can no longer be a guarantee against foreign aggression because, in this hybrid warfare, domestic security becomes a target for the interested external actors (external controlling powers). Therefore, a successful engagement in this type of complex confrontation requires taking into account the shift of internal and external threats, meticulous and comprehensive analysis of the international situation and domestic political factors, and careful neutralization of every single interacting element.

International confrontation strategies shift toward unconventional hybrid forms, and the unconstitutional coup d'état in Ukraine supported by the United States and its Western allies as well as the attempts to organize something similar in Russia are yet greater evidence of this. The ultimate goals of hybrid warfare, and color revolutions as an integral part of it, are similar to that of conventional wars—complete destabilization of the sociopolitical-economic situation in the targeted country that will lead to the collapse of the existing political regime, thus allowing it to be replaced with new politically friendly and externally controlled forces.

As Shoigu concludes in his statement at the Moscow Conference on International Security: "Socio-economic and political problems of certain states are used to replace nationally oriented governments with those that are controlled from the outside . . . and ensure that their sponsors have unfettered access to the country's resources."[46]

Notes

1. Jeffrey Collins and Andrew Futter, "Razmyshleniya o revolutsii v voennom dele i yeye vliyanii na prinyatie resheiy" [Reflecting on the Revolution in Military Affairs and Its Influence on Decision-Making Processes], *Rossiya v Global'noy Politike,* 28 January 2016, www.globalaffairs.ru/valday/Razmyshleniya-o-revolyutcii -v-voennom-dele-i-ee-vliyanii-na-prinyatie-reshenii-17952.

2. For example, Alexander Bartosh, "Gibridnaya voyna: Interpretatsii i real'nost'" [Hybrid War: Interpretations and Reality], *Nezavisimoe Voennoe Obozrenie,* 16 September 2016, http://nvo.ng.ru/concepts/2016-09-16/1_war.html; Vasily Belozerov and Alexey Solov'ev, "Gibridnaya Voyna v otechestvennom politicheskom i nauchnom diskurse" [Hybrid War in Domestic Political and Academic Discourse], *Vlast',* no. 9 (2015): 5–11; Vladimir Krasnoslobodtsev, Alexander Raskin, and Igor Tarasov, "Gibridnaya voyna: Ponyatiye, sushchnost', napravleniye protivodeystviya" [Hybrid War: Definition, Nature, the Direction of Counter-Measurement], *Strategicheskaya stabil'nost'* 1, no. 74 (2016): 6–9.

3. Alexander Naumov, "Myagkaya sila i tsvetnye revolutsii" [Soft Power and Color Revolutions], *Rossiyskiy zhurnal pravovykh issledovaniy* 6, no. 1 (2016): 73–86.

4. Igor Panarin, *Gibridnaya voyna protiv Rossii, 1816–2016 gg* [Hybrid War Against Russia, 1816–2016] (Moscow: Goryachaya Liniya-Telekom, 2016).

5. US Department of Defense, *Quadrennial Defense Review (QDR) 2010* (Washington, DC: US Department of Defense, February 2010), p. 8.

6. North Atlantic Treaty Organization, *Wales Summit Declaration: Issued by the Heads of State and Government Participating in the Meeting of the North Atlantic Council in Wales from 4 to 5 September 2014* (Brussels: NATO, 5 September 2014), p. 3.

7. Nathan Freyer, "The Defense Identity Crisis: It's a Hybrid World," *Parameters* 39, no. 3 (2009): 81–94.

8. David Alberts, John Garstka, and Frederic Stein, *Network Centric Warfare: Developing and Leveraging Information Superiority* (Washington, DC: Command and Control Research Program, 1999).

9. John Arquilla and David Ronfeldt, *Swarming and the Future of Conflict* (Santa Monica: RAND, 2000).

10. US Joint Chiefs of Staff, *The National Military Strategy of the United States of America 2015* (Washington, DC: US Joint Chiefs of Staff, June 2015), p. 4.

11. Panarin, *Gibridnaya voyna protiv Rossii.*

12. Bartosh, "Gibridnaya voyna."

13. Tatyana Nevskaya, "Informatsionnaya sostavlyayushchaya gibridnykh voyn" [The Information Component of Hybrid Wars], *Vestnik Moskovskogo universiteta, Seriya 18, Sotsiologiya i politologiya* 4 (2015): 281–284.

14. Evgeny Messner, *Vsemirnaya Myatezhvoyna* [Worldwide Subversion-War] (Moscow: Zhukovskoye Pole, 2004), p. 57.

15. Ibid.

16. Pavel Tsygankov, "Gibridnyye Voyny: Ponyatiya, interpretatsii i real'nost'" [Hybrid Wars: Definitions, Interpretations and Reality], in *"Gibridnyye Voyny" v khao-*

tiziruyushchemsya mire XXI veka ["Hybrid Wars" in the Chaotizing World of the 21st Century], ed. Pavel Tsygankov (Moscow: Moscow University Press, 2015), p. 21.

17. Ibid., p. 24.

18. Ibid., p. 5.

19. For example, Andrew Korybko, *Hybrid Wars: The Indirect Adaptive Approach to Regime Change* (Moscow: RUDN University, 2015), p. 25; Andrey Demidov, "Ot myagkoy sily k upravlyaemomu khaosu" [From "Soft Power" to "Managed Chaos"], *Geopoliticheskiy zhurnal,* no. 4 (2014): 86–93; Igor Nikolaychuk, "O suchshnosti gibridnoy voyny v kontekste sovremennoy voenno-politicheskoy situatsii" [On the Essence of the Hybrid War in the Context of the Contemporary Military-Political Situation], *Problemy natsional'noy strategii* 36, no. 3 (2016): 85–104.

20. For example, Mikhail Delyagin, "Novyye tekhnologii tsvetnykh revolyutsiy: Ne gotov'tes' k pozavcherashney voyne" [New Techniques of Color Revolutions: Stop Preparing Yourself for the Yesterday's War], *DelyaginRU,* http://delyagin.ru /articles/187-pozitsija/36321-novye-tehnologii-tsvetnyh-revoljutsii-ne-gotovtes-k -pozavcherashnei-voine (accessed 12 August 2017).

21. Sergei Glazyev, "Gibridnaya voyna i kontrol' nad Rossiyey" [Hybrid War and Control over Russia], *Izborskiy Klub,* 18 May 2015, https://izborsk-club.ru/5589.

22. Sergei Glazyev, "Kak ne proigrat' v voyne" [How Not to Lose in a War], *Glazyev, Sergei—Ofitsial'nyy sayt,* 30 July 2014, www.glazev.ru/sodr_ssn/368/.

23. Delyagin, "Novyye tekhnologii tsvetnykh revolyutsiy."

24. Vladimir Karyakin, "'Gibridnyye voyny' kak faktor vozrastaniya nestabil'nosti v zonakh sopernichestva mirovykh derzhav" ["Hybrid Wars" as a Factor of Increasing Instability in the Zones of Rivalry Between the World Powers], in *"Gibridnyye Voyny" v khaotiziruyushchemsya mire XXI veka* ["Hybrid Wars" in the Chaotizing World of the 21st Century], ed. Pavel Tsygankov (Moscow: Moscow University Press, 2015), p. 223.

25. For example, Dmitry Baluev, "Evolutsiya ekonomicheskikh sanktsiy kak instrumenta vneshney politiki" [Evolution of Economic Sanctions as an Instrument of Foreign Policy], *Mezhdunarodnye Prozessy,* no. 38 (2014): 23–33; James Lindsay, "Trade Sanctions as Political Instrument: A Re-Examination," *International Studies Quarterly* 30, no. 2 (June 1986): 153–173.

26. For example, Mukhtar Yakh'ev, "DAESh: Ideyno-politicheskie istoki terroristicheskoy organizatsii" [ISIS: Ideological and Political Origins of a Terrorist Organization], *Islamovedenie,* no. 4 (2016): 16–29; Denis Brilev, "Genezis i sushchnost' radilal'nogo islamizma v kontekste globalizatsionnykh prozessov" [Genesis and Essence of Radical Islamism in the Context of the Globalization Processes], *Vestnik VolGU, Seriya 9,* no. 8 (2010): 5–9.

27. Frank Hoffman, "Hybrid Warfare and Challenges," *Joint Forces Quarterly,* no. 52 (2009): 34.

28. For example, Georgy Filimonov, Oleg Karpovich, and Andrey Manoylo, *Tekhnologii "myagkoy" sily na vooruzhenii SShA: Otvet Rossii* [The US Techniques of "Soft" Power: Russia's Response] (Moscow: RUDN University, 2015), p. 423; Alexander Bartosh, "Kompleks podryvnykh tekhnologiy 'Tsvetnaya Revolyutsiya— Gibridnaya Voyna' kak ugroza natsional'noy bezopasnosti Rossii" [The Complex of Subversive Techniques "Color Revolution—Hybrid War," as a Threat to the Russia's National Security], *Bezopasnost' Yevrazii* 1 (2015): 245–247.

29. For example, Bartosh, "Gibridnaya voyna"; Andrey Manoylo, "Tekhnologii 'tsvetnykh revolyutsiy' v sovremennykh proyavleniyakh 'gibridnykh voyn'" [The Techniques of "Color Revolutions" in Contemporary Expressions of "Hybrid Wars"], in *"Gibridnyye Voyny" v khaotiziruyushchemsya mire XXI veka* ["Hybrid Wars" in the Chaotizing World of the 21st Century], ed. Pavel Tsygankov (Moscow:

Moscow University Press, 2015); Alexander Raskin, "Setevyye Tekhnologii v gibridnoy voyne" [Network-Centric Technologies in Hybrid War], *Informatsionnyye voyny* 1, no. 37 (2016): 2–4.

30. "Voennaya doktrina Rossiyskoy Federatsii" [Military Doctrine of Russian Federation], *Rossiyskaya Gazeta,* 30 December 2014, https://rg.ru/2014/12/30/doktrina-dok.html.

31. Andrey Manoylo, "Tsvetnye revolutsii i tekhnologii demontazha politicheskikh rezhimov" [Color Revolutions and the Techniques to Dismantle Political Regimes], *Mirovaya Politika,* no. 1 (2015): 1–19.

32. Vladimir Kotlyar, "K voprosu o 'gibridnoy voyne' i o tom, kto zhe yeye vedet na Ukraine" [On the Question About "Hybrid War" and About Who, After All, Wages It in Ukraine], *Mezhdunarodnaya zhizn',* no. 8 (2015): 58–72.

33. Manoylo, "Tekhnologii 'tsvetnykh revolyutsiy.'"

34. Filimonov, Karpovich, and Manoylo, *Tekhnologii "myagkoy" sily na vooruzhenii SShA,* p. 413.

35. Anna Aryamova, "'Tsvetnye revolutsii' kak instrument vneshney politiki stran anglo-amerikanskogo politicheskogo bloka" ["Color Revolutions" as an Instrument of Foreign Policy in the Countries of the Anglo-American Political Block], *Vlast',* no. 8 (2015): 206–210; Igor Panarin, "Gladiatory gibridnoy voyny" [The Gladiators of Hybrid War], *Ekonomicheskiye Strategii* 2 (2016): 65; Andrey Budaev, "Gibridnyye voyny SShA v gosudarstvakh Latinskoy Ameriki: Podkhody i praktika primeneniya" [The Hybrid Wars of the USA in the States of Latin America: The Methods and Practice of Employment], in *"Gibridnyye Voyny" v khaotiziruyushchemsya mire XXI veka* ["Hybrid Wars" in the Chaotizing World of the 21st Century], ed. Pavel Tsygankov (Moscow: Moscow University Press, 2015).

36. Andrey Movchan, "Ekonomika 'tsvetnykh revolyutsii': Kak snizhenie syr'evykh dokhodov razrushaet diktaturi" ["Color Revolutions" Economy: How the Decline in Resource Revenues Destroys Dictatorships], Moskovskiy Tsentr Karnegi, http://carnegie.ru/2015/10/29/ru-pub-61818; Tat'yana Vorozheykina, "Ukraina: Neutrachennye ill'uzii" [Ukraine: Not Yet Lost Illusions], Moskovskiy Tsentr Karnegi, http://carnegie.ru/proetcontra/56724 (accessed 12 August 2017).

37. Aryamova, "'Tsvetnye revolutsii' kak instrument vneshney politiki"; Panarin, "Gladiatory gibridnoy voyny."

38. Movchan, "Ekonomika 'tsvetnykh revolyutsii'"; Vorozheykina, "Ukraina."

39. See Manoylo, "Tekhnologii 'tsvetnykh revolyutsiy'"; Filimonov, Karpovich, and Manoylo, *Tekhnologii "myagkoy" sily na vooruzhenii SShA,* p. 415.

40. Bartosh, "Kompleks podryvnykh tekhnologiy"; Manoylo, "Tekhnologii 'tsvetnykh revolyutsiy.'"

41. Manoylo, "Tsvetnye revolutsii i tekhnologii."

42. Joseph Nye, *Soft Power: The Means to Success in World Politics* (New York: Public Affairs, 2004).

43. Naumov, "Myagkaya sila i tsvetnye revolutsii."

44. This section is based on Georgy Filimonov, Nikita Danyk, and Maxim Yurakov, *Perevorot* [Coup D'état] (Saint Petersburg: Piter, 2016). See also Filimonov, Karpovich, and Manoylo, *Tekhnologii "myagkoy" sily na vooruzhenii SShA*; Korybko, *Hybrid Wars;* Pavel Tsygankov, ed., *"Gibridnyye Voyny" v khaotiziruyushchemsya mire XXI veka* ["Hybrid Wars" in the Chaotizing World of the 21st Century] (Moscow: Moscow University Press, 2015).

45. Sergey Shoigu, speech delivered at the Third Moscow Conference on International Security, 23 May 2014 (in Russian), http://mil.ru/et/news/more.htm?id=11929731@egNews.

46. Ibid.

4

The Russian Military Perspective

Vitaly Kabernik

In analyzing contemporary publications, it is difficult not to notice that the term *hybrid war* or *hybrid warfare* implies so many different meanings and interpretations. The term is used in different contexts and can describe almost any form of international hostilities, including sanctions, proxy wars, cyber threats, and propaganda. In numerous attempts to differentiate those activities from the state of war, some have tried to reintroduce the term *political warfare* introduced by George Kennan back in 1948.[1] Notably, Frank Hoffman, the author of hybrid warfare's definition, criticized the concept of political warfare, pointing out that these types of activities should not be called warfare at all to avoid misconceptions.[2]

In this chapter, I focus on the Russian military views of the idea of hybrid warfare, which are sometimes in line with the definition proposed by Hoffman, though not always. Yet one similarity is clear: both approaches fundamentally refuse to consider any type of political hostilities or competition as a war, unless armed violence steps in to replace the laws of peacetime. Contemporary political discourse is characterized by a broad usage of the term *hybrid war* and everyone seems to have their own respective understanding.[3] This is true for both Western and Russian studies that tend to use the term *war* to describe some extreme form of tensions between nations, nonstate actors, and so forth.

War and Warfare in Russian Military Thinking

Russian military thinking not only defines *war* as a sociopolitical phenomenon, but going further it discriminates between war and warfare, and this discrimination is important for a better understanding of Russian concepts.[4] *War* is a state of society while *warfare* is viewed by Russian military scholars as activities associated with armed conflict, a practical implementation of combat principles. Hence, according to this understanding, there just cannot be a hybrid war, or a cyberwar,[5] or any other sort of war. Instead, certain forms and modalities of warfare, including hybrid, informational, or others that can be used during a war, which in turn are viewed as a full-spectrum conflict involving armed violence as the predominant way to resolve political or other contradictions. According to the views of the Russian military, warfare is a mandatory element of any war. This in turn introduces another layer (or, more accurately, layers) for analysis.[6] While war itself is the state of the society, different forms of warfare can be used to fight a war.

The state of war in Russian military tradition is associated with the introduction of martial law, breaking of diplomatic relations while suppression of internal and external opposition is carried out using significantly different means. Army General Makhmut Gareev points out that such forms of political struggle as economic competition or propaganda efforts become different in the state of war. He provides an example that in peacetime the pressure toward a violating state is executed in the form of sanctions or information campaigns while in the state of war enemy informational outlets or objects critical for the economy will be destroyed kinetically.[7] However, this understanding of the state of war is blurred nowadays with the introduction of the hybridity concept, presenting a multitude of gradations between war and peace. Thus, we should choose a definition of *hybrid warfare* to operate further through this chapter. It is important to emphasize certain points made by Hoffman in his works. For example, he states that "at the strategic level, many wars have had regular and irregular components. However, in most conflicts, these components occurred in different theaters or in distinctly different formations. In Hybrid Wars, these forces become blurred into the same force in the same battlespace."[8] Interestingly, this last part of the explanation is often dropped during discussions of hybrid warfare. The fusion between regular and irregular forces in the same battlespace is important to differentiate between hybrid warfare and proxy wars, armed resistance, guerrilla warfare, and so forth.

In another example, Hoffman states that "in compound war (CW), there is a deliberate simultaneous use of a regular main force with dispersed irregular forces. . . . Thus, CWs are conflicts with regular and irregular components fighting simultaneously under unified direction. The complementary effects of compound warfare are generated by its ability to exploit the advantages of each kind of force and by the nature of the threat posed by each kind of force."[9] While compound warfare is genuinely different from hybrid warfare, some scholars tend to mix those together.[10] The presence of joint command of irregular and regular forces should not lead to calling the conflict hybrid. Most military conflicts in the past included the use of irregular forces, but those fought in the different battlespace are sometimes mistakenly called "hybrid." These two points are important to differentiate between hybrid and other, sometimes seemingly similar, modalities of warfare. To better understand Russian military concepts, it is also important to recall the concept of *asymmetric conflict,* widely used in Russian military circles. This concept is not genuine for the Russian military. The term was introduced by Andrew Mack in 1975 as part of a reflection on the Vietnam War, and this experience was studied deeply in Soviet military circles.[11] While there are a number of speculations regarding the understanding of asymmetric conflict, Russian military scholars tend to outline the following characterizing criteria:

- Wide involvement of irregular forces not recognized as independent actors by the international community;
- Clear ideological agenda used by the weaker irregular actor;
- Qualitative military superiority of one of the actors of a conflict;
- Nontraditional organizational models of the nonstate actors or forces involved in a conflict—including network-centric organization or a hybrid between traditional hierarchies and network-based command and control principles;
- Resorting to insurgency operations and defensive strategies aimed at the attrition of the superior actor of conflict.[12]

An important addition to those criteria is explicitly underlined in Russian military studies: at least one of the actors of asymmetric conflict is a nonstate actor.[13] When both actors of a conflict are state actors with their respective military organizations, this is viewed as *symmetric engagement,* which is in line with the definitions given by Thomas Hammes.[14]

Remarkably, some of the criteria mentioned to define asymmetric conflict in Russian military tradition reflect the "seven principles" describing a "hybrid war" by Timothy McCulloh and Richard Johnson in their monograph.[15] These principles include the importance of an ideological agenda, capability overmatch, guerrilla tactics and technology, defensive strategies, and employment of attrition tactics. Since my focus in this chapter is Russian military understanding and not contemporary US studies, we should define the types of conflict where nonstate actors are opposing national states that are asymmetric instead of hybrid (whatever means and military technologies each side of the conflict uses to fight it). While usage of "attritional strategies" and "guerrilla warfare" is typical for the weaker actor of asymmetric conflict, it is far from mandatory. Therefore, throughout this chapter I understand *hybrid warfare* as being characterized by the fusion between regular and irregular forces acting in the same battlespace. I use the term *compound warfare* to describe similar yet different forms of combat operations, where irregular forces are used in coordination with the regular military but in a different battlespace and in limited modalities of operations. *Asymmetric conflict* is also used to describe the contemporary understanding of hybrid and insurgency threats by the Russian military.

War in Soviet Military Understanding

Bearing in mind the de facto ban on criticism of ideas and even minor remarks given by Vladimir Lenin in his extensive heritage in the USSR, definitions of *war* used by the Soviet military theorists were in line with those in his works. Lenin, in turn, borrowed the core definition of war from Carl Von Clausewitz, adding various remarks on the character of the war itself, separating imperialistic wars from liberation wars, and specifically noting civil wars as an important part of liberation movements.[16] An important claim introduced by Lenin was the denial of law happening during any kind of armed conflict.[17] Lenin speculated that any kind of war, including civil war, inevitably replaces the law by armed violence. This statement, reflected as one of the ideological dogmas by the Soviet military led to the view of war as a social-political phenomenon, a state of the society characterized by extensive use of armed violence. Hence, the typical Soviet definition of *war* built on Lenin's definitions is even used in schoolbooks:

> War is a social-political phenomenon, a specific state of the society, associated with drastic change of relations between national states, nations themselves, social classes and/or groups. This change leads to implementation of armed violence for obtaining political, economic and other goals. War is a continuation of internal and external politics of warring nations by means of armed violence leading to qualitative changes of all the spheres of social life.[18]

The "social" part in this definition of war appeared as an attempt to fit civil wars and national liberation movements into the same phrase, expanding and at the same time blurring the definition given by Clausewitz. Lenin further speculated that seeing politics as a continuation of the war could be imperialistic or liberational, and this politics can include external and internal reflections. This, in fact, legalized civil unrest if it was ideologically acceptable by the Communist Party, marking it as civil war against an oppressing regime. The definition of the *state of war* in its sociopolitical part was used in propaganda efforts to define insurgencies as liberation wars, thus allowing for providing official even if deniable military advice and assistance to the nonstate actors or regime challengers. This use was in line with the views of Lenin, who thought primarily in terms of political struggle, not applied warfare. The theory of warfare, relatively clear from ideological dogmas, developed independently by relying on the practical experiences gained in fighting numerous conflicts.

The Hybrid Experience of the Russian Army

The hybrid experience in this section does not in fact describe true hybrid warfare. Instead, I briefly review the encounters of the Red Army and Russian army called "hybrid" in various sources. Most of these are not in fact hybrid, according to the criteria introduced in the beginning of the chapter.

Case 1: The Partisan Movement During the Great Patriotic War

In their monograph *Hybrid Warfare,* McCulloh and Johnson chose the Soviet partisan network formed on Eastern Front during World War II as an example to illustrate the theory of hybrid warfare applied on the battlefield.[19] Unfortunately, their analysis is not deep enough and does not explore the roots of the partisan movement in Russia as a whole, and during World War II in particular. The partisan movement in Russia occurred during many conflicts, and this is true for other countries. However, the Russians pioneered the usage of partisan forces as part of a compound military strategy in 1812. The best-known example is Denis Davidov's detachment, initially formed of fifty hussars and eighty Cossacks to operate behind enemy lines, which later grew significantly in numbers due to local volunteers.[20] The experience gained in the forming of such compact diversionary units was largely used later. The principle of using organized partisan forces that developed based on this experience was to detach a small highly mobile unit led by a skilled officer who was assigned to organize local resistance and forces that had been bypassed to fight in coordination with the regular army.[21]

Following the same approach, the formation of Soviet partisan units during World War II was initiated in June 1941 (just days after the German invasion) in Moscow as a number of special detachments of the People's Commissariat for Internal Affairs (NKVD) forces.[22] Those units, typically counting some 100 volunteers, were specifically tasked to fight behind enemy lines. Some ad hoc units were formed of party activists in cities close to advancing German forces. Therefore, the partisan movement was organized by the Soviet government right from the beginning of the war on the Eastern Front, it had an efficient structure and initially acted in a form that we might now call "special operations," and it was under the command of the NKVD's fourth directorate, a part of the Soviet law enforcement and security agency. The fourth directorate was formed under the command of Lieutenant General Pavel Sudoplatov.[23] Russian sources show a clear understanding that Sudoplatov had two brigades under his command, later reinforced with two paratrooper battalions.[24] This was a regular military unit, which later became the core of the partisan movement.[25] While the first partisan operations behind the enemy lines suffered losses up to 93 percent of their personnel, they had become a formidable force by 1942 and the movement was reformed to provide better assistance to the regular army. The fourth directorate focused more on strategic diversions, intelligence, and counterintelligence tasks, and the General Staff of the Partisan Movement was formed in May 1942 led by Army Lieutenant General Panteleimon Ponomarenko.[26] This structure provided operational coordination of partisan units with the regular army and carried out large-scale operations over 750 kilometers in depth and up to 1,000 kilometers wide.

Concerning hybrid warfare, defining the Soviet partisans of World War II as *hybrid warriors* seems incorrect. The close coordination between the units with the regular army, presence of General Staff of the movement led by the Red Army and NKVD officers, and other factors steer to the conclusion that this kind of warfare was in fact compound, according to the definition of *compound warfare* given by Hoffman. Strategically, partisan operations were coordinated with regular army operations even if carried out in a so-called hybrid environment. This kind of warfare clearly reflects the views of Soviet strategists, tending to utilize all means available to fight the existential threat that Nazi ideology represented to the survival of the nation itself.

Case 2: The Soviet Engagement in Afghanistan

The history of Soviet participation in the First Afghan War includes several stages of conflict and demonstrates how the army adapted to the environment. The initial deployment was straightforward and typical for the Soviet military (50,000 personnel and some 8,000 vehicles that reinforced the Fortieth Army were the backbone of the Soviet operational group in Afghanistan because of limited mobilization). While relatively fast, this mobilization was considered to be massive after 1945 and demonstrates the Soviet approach, looking toward yet another deep operation. Soviet troops were initially tasked to only garrison and guard key points on Afghan territory, not to directly engage with the enemy; this task was delegated to the Afghan army. The reality, however, proved that Soviet assumptions were wrong. After the initial takeover of the capital and creating a command and control network, Soviet troops faced armed opposition inside Afghan army corps, so direct combat operations in the form of counterinsurgency raids started just three months after deployment. By August 1980, after the first battalion-level engagement, a local mujahideen organization was considered a significant threat to the deployed forces and Soviet troops quickly found themselves engaged in guerrilla war suffering losses to the poorly armed and trained adversary.

It took approximately one year for the Soviet battle group to adapt and obtain limited success in counterinsurgency operations. This required reinforcements of the core regular force with special operations units from both army structures and security agencies. By 1986, this partly allowed the revival of the initial plan: focusing on fire support of the Afghan local infantry, which had taken the burden of fighting the insurgency with limited use of the special forces for the mission-critical operations and the regular army providing control over strategic points.[27] Different stages of Soviet engagements in Afghanistan represent different modalities of conflict, but it cannot be called "hybrid" at any stage. This was an asymmetrical conflict where regular army troops fought the local nonstate insurgency and guerrillas even if supported from abroad.[28] Interestingly, the war in Afghanistan and the support for the regime fighting a civil conflict was in line with Lenin's definition of *liberational war* while some Western researchers tend to describe it as alien to Soviet ideological dogmas.

Lessons learned from the Afghanistan campaign by the Soviet army did not lead to notable change in the army's structure. Soviet researchers clearly noted the importance of propaganda efforts and changed some approaches to representing the actions of the military forces. Security agencies, in turn, used the experience gained during the Afghanistan engagement to control and divide insurgencies. Both security agencies and armed forces pointed out the importance of special operations units, but this conclusion did not even lead to the creation of a special operations command.[29] Spetsnaz units were detached for specific tasks, not integrated with the army structures. Analysis of the losses distribution demonstrated that most losses were not a result of direct firefights, but an outcome of successful ambushes on the communication lines. This experience was also dropped. Several years later, the Russian army studied it again during the first Chechen campaign.

Case 3: The Chechen Conflicts

The Chechen campaigns of the 1990s and early 2000s are vital for this discussion because not only do these present the hybrid warfare experience, these also demonstrate the concept of the "hybridity-level shift" used by Russian forces during the second campaign. Since Chechnya was not an independent state recognized by the international community, this discussion will stay in the zone of the asymmetric conflict where hybrid warfare principles were used to some extent. The backbone of the Chechen force for the first campaign was some sort of regular army due to the military experience of the Chechens' leader, former Soviet Air Force General Dzhokhar Dudaev. However, the "flesh" of the Chechen army was mainly criminal. With 70 percent unemployment and a volatile status of the republic, the territory was used for money laundering, kidnapping, racketeering, smuggling of all sorts, and many of those who formed the leadership of the hybrid Chechen force had criminal backgrounds.[30] Mercenaries, both native and foreign were used to a higher extent, some without any kind of contract, attracted by the ability to loot the local population and abandoned housing.[31]

Chechen forces during the first campaign were few compared to the opposing Russian army and law enforcement units. The numbers of the regular component were estimated as up to 15,000 personnel plus some 5,000 mercenaries from abroad. Chechens had their own armored forces counting for some 40 tanks and 100 infantry fighting vehicles (IFVs) backed by assorted towed artillery pieces. It initially mimicked the classic military hierarchy forming two brigades, seven regiment-sized detachments, and president's guards.[32] Over 40,000 personnel formed the irregular component of the force. Importantly, the force of the "Chechen Republic" had no clear ideological agenda until 1996 when jihadist ideas became stronger with the new leadership gaining power after Dudaev's elimination. Originally, the main motivation was homeland defense and criminal money. The regular structure established was never used in its original brigade-based form, resorting to small unit operations and relying on attrition tactics.

The first Chechen campaign started using the templates from the Afghanistan deployment. The Russian army mobilized some 40,000 personnel forming three battle groups. Suffering from a lack of coordination, only one of those made it to Grozny in time and started a frontal assault resulting in severe casualties for the attacker. Just a week later, tactics were changed toward using mobile groups supported by aerial and artillery strikes—an experience recalled from the Afghanistan campaign. These new tactics, however, were not effectively employed because of the conscript-based force's poor training and coordination problems between army forces and law enforcement units operating in the same battlespace. In the summer of 1995, the first raid of mass terror was performed by Shamil Basaev's unit outside of Chechen territory.[33] After bloody hostage crises in neighboring Russian regions backed by numerous encounters with Chechen forces on the ground, often unsuccessful for Russian forces, the policy was changed toward negotiations and the conflict was frozen in the summer of 1996. Russian armed forces withdrew from Chechen territory despite the huge advantage in both troops and combat equipment.

The first Chechen campaign was a defeat of the Russian political leadership in facing a new form of threat we might now call "hybrid."[34] The army, in turn, suffered from coordination problems in the core command chain and in coordinating activities with security agencies. The environment was clearly hostile to the Russian forces and there were no psychological operations supporting the advancement of the troops. In fact, the Russian army operated in the form that it was trained for: fighting on hostile territory. It did almost nothing to conquer the sympathies of the local population, resorting to retaliation raids from time to time that only fueled hostilities. Similarly to Israeli forces during the Lebanon wars, it could win battles but not the hearts and minds of the local population. Lessons learned from the first Chechen campaign stressed the necessity of battlespace isolation physically, economically, and in the information domain. Chechens were supported economically and with weapons supplied by foreign organizations, including criminal ones, and this resource flow was never blocked.[35] The Russian government had no clear agenda on how to represent the conflict to its own population, which led to the mixed reception without strong support for the military operation.

The second Chechen campaign was very different, primarily because of a different social context. The population of Chechnya was split in viewing its future as an independent state, and the local government had no control over the territory. Bearing in mind the clan structure of Chechen society, different groups proposed different political and ideological agendas, including the doctrine of Wahhabism that was foreign to the local Islamic tradition. Instead of forming a nation-state, with the growing influence of radical groups the local government drifted toward establishing a theocracy with the Chechen Republic viewed as the core for a future caliphate. Despite several attempts to change the ideological context toward moderate forms, the local government simply did not have the adequate law enforcement structures to fulfill those wishful plans.[36]

While the official starting date of second Chechen campaign is 7 August 1999 (the date of Chechen invasion of Dagestan), the first actions from the Russian side are dated back to March 1999 after the kidnapping of a high-ranking Russian Ministry of Internal Affairs official in Grozny. This led to the economic blockade of the region and de facto military isolation of the Chechen Republic. Attempts to break through the blockade were countered using preventive aerial strikes.[37] Chechen armed groups and foreign mercenaries were not ready to directly engage with the regular Russian army, so initially they focused on insurgency operations against local police forces in mountainous regions on the border between Chechnya and Dagestan, where they were supposed to meet only limited armed response. Unlike the first Chechen campaign, there was no organized regular army structure or even something mimicking it. The core of the fighting Chechen force was formed of radical Islamists and supported by some local criminals while the government-controlled structures initially remained neutral. Despite the total mobilization declared in Chechnya in September 1999, its effect on the progress of the military operations was negligible. Informed about the contradictions on the Chechen territory, Russia chose to implement a strategy of *Chechenization* of the conflict, supporting local moderate groups by providing military and political backing.[38] This term only surfaced in the 2000s, but the elements of this strategy were used starting from October 1999, when Gudermes was surrendered to the Russian army by local warlords. An important factor for further Chechenization was process support from the local religious leaders, who were reluctant about Wahhabist ideology propagated by the militants.[39]

After the initial strikes performed by the Russian regular army, the territory control tasks were delegated to local militias supported by federal law enforcement agencies and special operations forces. In terms of hybrid warfare, the Russian armed forces quickly adopted its elements for fighting the second Chechen campaign. The involvement of heavily armed regular forces was limited while the number of law enforcement agencies controlling the territory and supporting local militias was high. The main military operation of the Russian army in Chechnya had, in fact, finished by mid-2000. Control of the territory forwarded gradually to law enforcement agencies and local authorities in the following years. The changing composition of battle groups participating in the military operations speaks for the intentional hybridity shift performed by Russian combined forces during the second Chechen campaign. It reflects the new approach for the cross-agency coordination when the regular army is no longer seen as a self-sufficient fighting machine. Strategically, however, the second Chechen campaign followed the patterns recalled from the Afghanistan experience. This emphasized the proxy component of warfare, tending to support local militias backed by regular army units evading direct engagement whenever possible and only interfering for mission-critical operations. Therefore, this strategy was not so new in terms of warfare, but saw a clear refinement in its political implementation. Importantly, the strategy implemented was adopted for the local social context, which was studied in depth by the Russian military before armed engagements. This was the part that was missing or misinterpreted for the Afghanistan campaign, at least for its initial phase. Both the Chechen and Afghanistan campaigns demonstrate the desired way of fighting an asymmetric conflict as seen by the Russian military: delegating it to local militias with limited involvement of regular forces. The main difference is the depth of social context understanding and a step away from the ideological dogmas while emphasizing political goals of the conflict, bearing in mind an exit strategy. Regarding whether or not it was hybrid, some operations clearly demonstrated the fusion of regular and irregular forces used in the same battlespace, but it was not an imperative used for operational planning. Some operations met the fluid adversary tending to utilize all means available for winning the battle, but this was the way Russian forces and backed militias were ready to fight themselves: constantly adopting to the context, leaving the hard constraints behind. The experience gained during those complex scenarios was not institutionalized as some dogmas of hybrid warfare. Instead, this led to the transformation of the military structures, command and control, and, importantly, the patterns of cross-agency coordination to bring the art of studying the context of the conflict and battlespace, ever important for the Russian military tradition, to a new level.

Contemporary Understanding of Warfare
in Russian Military Thinking

Military thinking of the late years of the Soviet Union was quite conservative despite the experience gained in Afghanistan and other local conflicts. The predominant concept was a deep operation against a symmetric adversary and its regular armed forces. This, in turn, required gaining superiority on the battlefield and technological advantage of the adversary was reflected as one of the main challenges. The front-scale engagement was meant to gain support from the deliberate use of tactical nuclear strikes and supporting air-mobile operations in the rear formations of the adversary. Yet this was not considered enough to secure the advantage. Massive drills in the 1980s demonstrated problems in command and control hierarchies for such a tremendous force. Attempting to solve this problem, Chief of the General Staff N. V. Ogarkov suggested and promoted the wider use of automated and computerized battlespace management for the Soviets. This is sometimes called the "Russian Revolution" in military affairs, but this estimation is not complete. Ogarkov's doctrine was, in fact, a development of the deep operation concept. It promoted a massive use of non-nuclear missile and aerial strikes to full depth of the enemy formation along with a drastic change in operation tempo. The main innovation was the level of automation of the war machine, allowing it to keep this tempo of decisionmaking in a changing environment and integrating the multitude of data for commanding structures.[40]

After the Soviet collapse, the Russian army was no longer ready to fulfill the requirements for the kind of operations planned by Ogarkov. Furthermore, instead of NATO forces, it faced insurgencies and separatist movements in post-Soviet Russia. Military structures were not trained for such kinds of operations and the army insisted that these threats should be the responsibility of law enforcement agencies. This later led to development of the "agencies fusion" principle used during the second Chechen campaign. Post-Soviet concepts of warfare classification reflected a mix of Western research and local theorizing about the nature of future war, yet remained quite formal. Early post-Soviet military theorists used a multidimensional classification of warfare, operating under the following criteria:[41]

1. Generation: unlike in Western tradition, generations of warfare were associated with generations of weapons used. The modern non-nuclear conflict is classified as fourth generation.[42] The gen-

eration criterion reflects the general technological level of the conflict, allowing fitting wars of the past into the classification.

2. Military and political goals: military and political goals of actors in conflict require differentiation between full-scale wars and local armed conflicts. Political and military goals of an armed conflict are as limited as the use of armed violence is. Generally, an armed conflict is limited in scope to a single military operation even if it is prolonged or frozen.

3. Scale, context, and intensity: *scale* applies to the territory where military operations are taking place, the number of raw forces, and generally correlates with conflict actors' military and political goals. Scale can be regional or global, for example, while *context* describes the number of actors involved. *Intensity* is self-explanatory, having several gradations.

4. Combat means and modalities used: this criterion is reserved for a descriptive dimension. There is no meaningful standard for unfolding it and some researchers use it to describe modality of warfare or general definition of the adversary. If the concept of hybrid warfare existed by the time that this classification was widely used, the word *hybrid* could fit here as a descriptive addendum.

Operation Desert Storm and studies of the US joint perspective concept in the 1990s along with the reflection of modalities of the conflicts with inherent restrictions to use of armed violence, including nuclear weapons, led to the introduction of the sixth-generation warfare concept.[43] It was considered postnuclear and was, in fact, a temporary doctrine suggested to describe full-spectrum operations with restrictions to usage of weapons of mass destruction. The key criteria for the Russian view on sixth-generation warfare were:

- Qualitative change in range of kinetic kill from direct visibility toward intercontinental reach;
- Deep unification of combat systems;
- Full automation of the process of intelligence gathering, targeting, and destruction;
- Wide implementation of unmanned systems;
- A significant rise in kinetic damage thanks to precise guidance and new generation non-nuclear kinetic kill devices;
- Global information awareness in a multifaceted battlespace environment.[44]

This concept clearly inherits some points from late Soviet-theorized approaches of battlefield automation by Ogarkov and bears signs of borrowed US concepts. Moreover, like US concepts of the 1990s, it emphasizes the meaning of technological advantage. However, it was never adopted, primarily because of inability of the Russian economy of the 1990s to support an ambitious military modernization. By this time, Russia could rebuild its outdated army; new doctrines surfaced and those were analyzed in full depth.

Most Russian military theorists received network-centric warfare tenets critically.[45] They were reluctant about the concepts of synergy and self-synchronization, at least in Russian army realities. Further studies and mathematical models challenged the level of training for the sergeant-level military personnel and company-level command structures. Not only was the claimed self-synchronization never achieved, those studies clearly demonstrated degradation in command and control when using these tenets. Criticism toward network-centric concepts rose significantly after studying the results of Millennium Challenge drills, when US Marine Corps general Paul Van Riper who commanded the technologically inferior Red Force managed to inflict significant damage on the Blue Force, which used modern command and control (C2) structures.[46] This led to quite a radical conclusion that the whole concept of network-centric warfare or at least some of its organizational tenets could possibly be part of a disinformation campaign aimed to disrupt the forces trying to implement those principles. Another conclusion was that the reliance on high-tech communication systems was, in fact, generating a new form of vulnerability. As such, Russian military thinking turned toward more classical, yet nonorthodox, principles of warfare.

The concept of "subversion war," mentioned as a precursor of hybrid warfare concepts in Russia, was first theorized by Russian-born Evgeny Messner in 1960, but his original publication went unnoticed by Soviet military theorists for several reasons.[47] First, Messner was an ideological enemy, an officer of the White movement who fought against the Red Army during the Russian civil war and later provided consultations to the Nazi regime in the former Yugoslavia. Second, Messner suggested nothing new from the point of security agencies, describing some of the controlled insurgency technologies and psychological operations already practically implemented in Russia by Lieutenant General Sudoplatov mentioned above. Finally yet importantly, in the 1960s when this work was first published, the USSR was focused on the technological aspects of military buildup, including securing a robust nuclear capability. Social technologies and psychological operations were considered secondary, if not tertiary. Messner emphasized the cultural differences between warring nations and the role of psychological operations to directly attack the opponent's culture while the warfare itself was viewed as supporting activity for the mass insurgency. His works were rediscovered in Russia in 1999 as a part of reflection on the first Chechen campaign. The main proponent of the subversion threat is retired paratroops head of intelligence Pavel Popovskikh.[48] His publications drew attention to the original works by Messner and these were published in Russia by the Military University in 2005.[49] However, by the date of this writing, new works have appeared and influenced Russian military thinking.

Unrestricted Warfare was originally published in China in 1999, but only parts of it were translated into Russian and circulated through military circles.[50] Contrary to the reception in the West, this work was never viewed as original research. It had some impact on the procedures of cross-agency coordination, specifically paying attention to the lawfare and supportive information-psychological operations. This work was primarily received as an addendum to the more thorough concepts. It is also thought to have drawn attention to nonmilitary methods of war deeply studied nowadays as a part of full-spectrum conflict visions.

The concept of fourth-generation warfare (4GW) was here for the US Marine Corps from 1989,[51] but only in 2006 did Hammes rediscover and polish this approach in *The Sling and the Stone*.[52] The Russian military received this work cautiously, viewing it not as stand-alone research, but as the way the US Army is going to fight future wars. As the second Chechen campaign entered its counterinsurgency proxy stage, 4GW studies shifted toward the new forms of controlled insurgency used for fighting full-spectrum or asymmetric conflicts. One of the primary conclusions from studies of 4GW and network-centric warfare along with the Chechen experience was the rise of the studies of complex conflicts in Russia. These studies included new understanding of the conflict context, battlespace domains, and modalities of warfare. It is thought that the introduction of new warfare domains is adding new dimensions to the conflict, where even a militarily superior actor cannot secure the advantage.[53] This imposes a constantly shifting balance between different modalities and domains of warfare, discarding failed approaches that lead to the desired political goal of the armed conflict, an attitude noticed by Roger McDermoth.[54]

In contemporary Russian military studies on the higher level of conflict understanding, the whole multidimensional continuum of a complex conflict, including its political, informational, and social reflections is seen as a battlespace, representing a holistic approach to the studies of war. This holistic understanding of the conflict always bears in mind its political implications, which is distinctive for the Russian military tradition where the deep study of the battlespace has always been seen as the most important part for military planning.[55] This, in turn, permits new levels of freedom of maneuver (including usage of nonmilitary methods) in order to get preferable position or to achieve the desired political goal of the conflict, even facing a superior adversary on the battlefield.[56] The studies of the warfare domains, contexts, and their possible combinations in Russia led to the introduction of new matrix-based classifications[57] that theoretically allow predicting and understanding the context and modalities of warfare used in a conflict. There is no openly available standard for the conflict representation in those matrixes. But judging from some presentations seen during the round-tables and public forums, including those held by the Academy of Military Sciences, *matrix* to describe complex conflicts used in Russian military studies defines inter alia:

1. Grand domains of warfare:
   a. Military
   b. Political
   c. Economical
   d. Informational[58]
2. Character of warfare, subdivided to open and covert (or deniable), direct and indirect (including proxy) operations and distracting activities
3. Means of warfare, subdivided to military and nonmilitary (peace-time), implying usage of:
   a. Conventional weapons
   b. Weapons of mass destruction
   c. Special/nonlethal weapons
   d. Electronic countermeasure (ECM) and cyberweapons
   e. Informational warfare
   f. Disruptive/cognitive methods
4. Forms of warfare, including:
   a. Direct combat operations
   b. Special operations
   c. Psychological operations
   d. Supportive propaganda campaigns
   e. Other nonmilitary means
5. Modalities of warfare, including:

    a. Direct engagement
    b. Demonstrative
    c. Imitational
    d. Supportive
    e. Disinformational
    f. Reconnaissance
    g. Attritional
    h. Hybrid
    i. Disruptive

Interestingly, hybrid warfare is present in this matrix, but only as one possible modality used in concert with others, far from being predominant. It stays on the tactical implementation level, in line with the understanding promoted by Hoffman. Therefore, even a glance on the evolving approach of conflict understanding by the Russian military gives us a clue that hybrid warfare is viewed as one possible option among a multitude of engagement modalities. It is implicitly assumed that the optimal modality or a composition of modalities is chosen after study of the battlespace and context of the conflict, typical for Russian military thinking, while modalities can be switched between each other fluidly or used coherently to achieve the desired political or military goal.

    The most quoted derivative of the matrixes used for conflict mapping in Russia is the so-called Gerasimov's doctrine, a scheme depicting a certain mix of military and nonmilitary means of warfare and stages of conflict escalation. Unfortunately, while Valery Gerasimov's article is often quoted in the context of hybrid warfare, it is completely misinterpreted. "The Value of Science Is in the Foresight" is illustrated with the schemes used for Gerasimov's presentation at the Academy of Military Sciences to represent future forms of conflicts where nonmilitary means, according to his estimation, will quadruple compared to classical armed engagements.[59] In fact, he describes the new threats that the Russian military, along with multitude of security agencies, should be ready to counter. The graph used by Gerasimov in his presentation represented the stages of escalation where an armed violent phase takes only a small part of the scenario. Furthermore, this part of the conflict is not obligatory. He specifically points out the covert initiation, typically not recognized by government structures and leading to internal destabilization.[60] The moment the threat is recognized as immediate and crisis reaction begins, the conflict escalation can pass the point of resolve and the following military reaction be ineffective as commanding structures are disrupted. Further escalation might lead to conventional or even nuclear warfare but this stage, as understood by Gerasimov, is relatively short in modern scenarios and a clear exit strategy should minimize the damage. This approach reflects the understanding of complex threat and, specifically, the risks of color revolutions widely discussed in Russia as a form of controlled insurgency aimed to destabilize and disrupt armed forces and law enforcement agencies.[61]

This form of threat is considered challenging for the Russian military for several reasons, including:

- Military operations initiated by peacetime forces without strategic deployment and battlespace study, which are required by Russian military thinking;
- The warfare itself can exclude the direct contact of regular armed forces of the warring nations shifting toward using of proxy operators, mercenaries, civil activists, and so forth. So the regular army does not actually engage with the enemy, spreading to neutralize distributed or indirect threats instead of fulfilling its primary role of direct engagement;
- The military equipment designed for gradual capture of the territory and tasks of defeating the forces of a symmetrically armed adversary become essentially useless for the highly maneuverable operations while development of the equipment for specific tasks leads to logistical problems.

However, while this form of new threats and the impact of nonmilitary methods are studied in Russia, these are never understood as the one and only definitive image of the future conflict. Furthermore, it is rarely called a hybrid threat,[62] and scholars specifically point out that "this term is counter-productive for the use in professional discourse of the military while focusing too much attention on preparation for 'hybrid war' bears risks of one-sided preparation of the Army and security agencies for the possible conflict."[63] The emphasis on the nonmilitary threats and covert conflict initiation calls for definition of a transitional state of hostilities other than a state of war. This is fulfilled with the introduction of the "hostile activities" stage of escalation, described as follows:

1. Peace: the state of international (intercoalition) and internal relations characterized by the absence of hostile activities against each other;
2. Hostile activities: a form of elimination or suppression of the opponent using induced violence or indirect and covert actions

aiming for the change of policy, social and cultural identity, and peacetime spheres of interest of targeted subject;

3. War: a form of hostile activities, including internal ones, a social-political phenomenon characterized by use of open and direct violence against the subject to force it to withdraw to the demands of other subjects as a result of combat operations (warfare).

The definition of *war* generally remains the same; it is a sociopolitical phenomenon, borrowed from Lenin and Clausewitz. *Hostile activities,* in turn, is quite a vague definition, which could possibly describe any form of political pressure toward a targeted subject. It indirectly refers to the recognized threat of internal destabilization as a part of covert conflict initiation and emphasizes the role of law enforcement and security agencies working in coordination with armed forces to detect and prevent this kind of destabilization at its early stage. Finally, *peace* is defined as an ideal state of international relations without any attempts to influence the decisionmaking and allowing for fully sovereign policy; this is vitally important for contemporary Russian leadership.

Hybrid war is silently omitted as the transitional state of hostile activities still remains below the threshold of recognized armed violence. At the same time, the *state of war* implies the use of any available modality of warfare considered optimal, depending on the analysis of the context, the battlespace, the operation, the political goals, and so forth. *Hybrid threat* is sometimes mentioned as a part of the transitional state of hostilities close to the direct application of armed violence, but it is usually defined as a nonmilitary threat, possibly a form of induced insurgency carried on by the opponent. This kind of threat is discussed primarily in political discourse, not military.

Conclusion

The state of war, without any kind of hybrid understanding, remains imperative for the Russian military while the modalities of warfare may vary depending on the context of armed conflict. The term *hybrid war* is widely used in Russian political discourse as a cliché to describe forms of peacetime hostilities between nations or nonstate actors without introducing a standardized or commonly understood definition. At the same time, military scholars generally avoid using this term, considering it to be counter-productive. Instead, *hybrid warfare* is used in its tactical understanding, which is close to the definition given by Hoffman, limited to describing engagement modality generally associated with a proxy component of warfare in an asymmetric conflict.

Speaking about war, per se, the Russian military stays with the often forgotten concept of "absolute war" given by Clausewitz even if it is just a philosophical abstraction. All of the developments made in the recent years are aimed to minimize the effects of friction of war, thus emphasizing the fusion between political, informational, military, and economical efforts to serve the aim of defeating the enemy on the battlefield.[64] This implies using all means available for fighting, including fluid and deliberate use of irregular militias, shifting balance between domains of warfare, and experimenting and improvising to choose the best methods without institutionalizing any kind of previously theorized predominant form of warfare. Importantly, the vision of the modern Russian military is not constrained by ideological dogmas anymore while the tradition of deep study of the battlespace and context of the conflict, including political and social aspects, is developing. Contemporary Russian understanding of the multimodal full-spectrum conflict in no way emphasizes any warfare modality above other ones. While hybrid warfare is studied as one of the possible applied forms of fighting the war, it is far from being a kind of grand strategy for future conflicts, at least in Russian views.

Notes

1. Wilson Center Digital Archive, "George Kennan on Organizing Political Warfare," https://digitalarchive.wilsoncenter.org/document/114320.pdf (accessed 2 December 2016).

2. Frank Hoffman, "On Not-So-New Warfare: Political Warfare vs. Hybrid Threats," War on the Rocks, 28 July 2014, http://warontherocks.com/2014/07/on -not-so-new-warfare-political-warfare-vs-hybrid-threats/.

3. For a deeper study of the use of the term *hybrid war,* see Chapter 5 of this book.

4. The understanding of "warfare" in Russian military tradition is generally associated with the activities carried out during military engagement. Starting from 2016, the Military University of the Russian Defense Ministry introduced a special course called Social Environments focused on practical implementation of social technologies in warfare. *Rossiyskaya Gazeta,* called its article covering the announcement of those courses "Cadets to Be Taught the Methods of Hybrid Warfare," which is a misleading title that does not reflect the actual article content. See Ivan Petrov, "Kursantov obuchat metodam gibridnykh voyn" [Cadets to Be Taught the Methods of Hybrid Warfare], *Rossiyskaya Gazeta,* 25 November 2015, https://rg .ru/2015/11/25/kursanti-site-anons.html.

5. The very term *cyberwar* is viewed as a media cliché. See "Voyna v kiber- prostranstve: Uroki I vyvody dlya Rossiyi" [The War in Cyberspace: Lessons and

Conclusions for Russia], *Nezavisimoye Voyennoye Obozreniye,* 13 December 2013, http://nvo.ng.ru/concepts/2013-12-13/1_war.html.

6. Depending on the level of the warfare study, the Russian military encyclopedia differentiates between *boyevye deystviya* (military engagement) and *voennye deystviya* (warfare). The first term describes tactical and operational levels of engagement while second term leans toward strategical and logistical aspects of warfare. See *Voenniy Encyclopedichesky Slovar* [Military Encyclopedic Dictionary] (Moscow: Voyenizdat, 1984), http://encyclopedia.mil.ru/encyclopedia/dictionary/list.htm.

7. Makhmut Gareev, "Voyna I Voennaya Nauka Na Sovremennom Etape" [War and Military Science in Their Contemporary Stage of Development], *Voenno-Promyshlennyy Kuryer* 481, no. 13 (2013): 5.

8. Frank Hoffman, *Conflict in the Twenty-First Century: The Rise of Hybrid Warfare* (Arlington, VA: Potomac Institute for Policy Studies, 2007), p. 8.

9. Ibid., p. 4.

10. Ibid., p.5.

11. For understanding of the term *asymmetric conflict* in Russian political discourse, see Larisa Deriglazova, "Asymmetrichny Konflikt v Sovremennoy Amerikanskoy Politilogiyi" [Asymmetric Conflict in Contemporary US Policy Studies], *Mezhdunarodnye Processy* 8, no. 23 (May–August 2010): 51–64.

12. Research Institute of Belorussian Armed Forces, "Assymetriya v vooruzhennom protivoborstve (chast 1), Voenno-politicheskoye obozrenie" [Asymmetry in an Armed Struggle, vol. 1: Political-Military Review], 27 July 2012, www.belvpo.com /ru/15326.html.

13. Ibid.

14. Thomas Hammes, *The Sling and the Stone: On War in the 21st Century* (Saint Paul: Zenith Press, 2006).

15. Timothy McCulloh and Richard Johnson, *Hybrid Warfare* (Tampa: MacDill Air Force Base, Joint Special Operations University Press, 2013), pp. 16–17.

16. Carl Von Clausewitz, *On War,* edited and translated by Michael Howard and Peter Paret (Princeton: Princeton University Press, 1976), chap. 1, sec. 24.

17. Vladimir Lenin, *Polnoye Sobraniye Sochineniy* [Full Collection of Works], vol. 30 (Moscow: Izdatel'stvo politicheskoy literatury, 1973), p. 69.

18. Grigory Osetrov, *Bezopasnost zhiznedeyatelnosti: Uchebnoye posobiye* [Civil Security Basics: Schoolbook] (Moscow: Knignii Mir, 2011).

19. McCulloh and Johnson, *Hybrid Warfare,* pp. 27–33.

20. Evgeni Tarle, *Nashestviye Napoleona* [Napoleon's Invasion] (Moscow: Voenizdat, 1959), p. 667.

21. Andrey Popov, one of the respected researchers of the partisan movement during the 1812 French invasion of Russia points out that the scale of the genuine partisan movement was exaggerated and mythologized by Soviet historians. Instead, resistance was usually formed around regular army detachments. See Andrey Popov, "Partizany i narodnaya voyna v 1812 godu" [Partisans and Patriotic War of 1812], in *Otechestvennaya voyna 1812 goda, Istochniki, Pamyatniki, Problemy: Materialy VIII Vserossiyskoy nauchnoy konferentsii* [The Patriotic War of 1812, Sources, Memorials, Problems: Articles from the VII All-Russian Scientific Conference] (Mozhaysk: Terra, 2000), p. 172.

22. Russian State Military Archive, *NKVD Order 001 as of June 28, 1941;* Russian State Military Archive, *Central Committee of the Communist Party Directive 624 as of June 29, 1941.*

23. Russian State Military Archive, *NKVD Order 00882 as of July 5, 1941.*

24. Russian State Military Archive, *NKVD Order 001108 as of August 19, 1941.*

25. While the military structure of the NKVD special tasks units was established in August 1941, the fourth NKVD directorate was formally instituted in the second NKVD department on 18 January 1942, according to *NKVD Order 00145* issued earlier.

26. Russian State Military Archive, *State Defence Committee Order GOKO-1837 as of May 30, 1942*.

27. Different stages of the Soviet Afghanistan campaign are described by the commander of the Fortieth Army, General Boris Gromov in his *Ogranichenny contingent* [Limited Contingent] (Moscow: Progress, 1994).

28. See Mark Adkin and Mohammad Yousaf, *Afghanistan—The Bear Trap: The Defeat of a Superpower* (Havertown, PA: Casemate, 2001).

29. SpecOps Directorate was only formed in 2009, after the Georgian conflict; it was reformed into SpecOps Command in 2012.

30. See Aleksei Malashenko and Dmitri Trenin, *Vremya Yuga: Rossiya v Chechnye, Chechnya v Rossiyi* [The Time of the South: Russia in Chechnya, Chechnya in Russia] (Moscow: Gandalf, 2002), pp. 17–18.

31. For example, Vassilis Fouskas, ed., *Politics of Conflict* (London: Taylor and Francis, 2007), p. 68.

32. Vladimir Mukhin, "K voprosu o vooruzhennykh silakh I voenno-politicheskoy obstanovke" [On the Question of Military Forces and Military-Political Situation in the Republic], International Humanitarian-Political Institute, April 1994, www.igpi.ru /monitoring/1047645476/apr_94/military_chechn.html.

33. See "Reidy chchenskikh boyevikov" [The Raids of Chechen Militants], *Kommersant,* 8 July 2002.

34. According to Frank Hoffman, "'Hybrid Threats': Neither Omnipotent nor Unbeatable," *Orbis* 54, no. 3 (2010): 443.

35. See S. Gorsky, "Arsenaly prestupnogo mira" [The Arsenals of the Criminal World], *Master-Ruzhyo* 15, no. 3 (1997): 49–53.

36. For a description of the escalation process, see Alexander Cherkasov, "Tango nad propastyu" [Tango Above the Fall], *Polit.ru,* 7 September 2004, www.polit.ru/article/2004/09/07/1999/print/.

37. See "Mesyatsem my zdes' ne otdelayemsya" [We Won't Get Off in a Month Here], *Kommersant-Vlast,* 17 August 1999.

38. The term *Chechenization* itself is a localized Russian version of the Vietnamization concept proposed by the Richard Nixon administration during the Vietnam War.

39. This policy is discussed in Maya Eichler, *Militarizing Men: Gender, Conscription, and War in Post-Soviet Russia* (Stanford: Stanford University Press, 2011).

40. See Makhmut Gareev, *Esli zavtra voyna* [If War Happens Tomorrow] (Moscow: Vladar, 1994).

41. For example, Ivan Kapitanets, *Voyna na more: Aktualnye problemy razvitiya voenno-morskoy nauki* [The War in the Sea: Actual Problems of Naval Science Development] (Moscow: Vagrius, 2001), chap. 2.

42. The fifth generation is reserved for nuclear conflict.

43. First theorized by Vladimir Slipchenko, *Voyny shestogo pokoleniya: Oruzhiye i voennoye iskusstvo budushchego* [The Wars of Sixth Generation: Weapons and Military Art of the Future] (Moscow: Veche, 2002).

44. Ibid.

45. US Department of Defense, *The Implementation of Network-Centric Warfare* (Washington, DC: US Department of Defense, 2005).

46. John Arquilla, "The New Rules of War," *Foreign Policy,* no. 178 (2010): 60; Julian Borger, "War Game Was Fixed to Ensure American Victory, Claims General,"

Guardian Online, 21 August 2002, www.theguardian.com/world/2002/aug/21 /usa.julianborger.

47. Evgeny Messner, *Myatezh: Imya Tret'yey Vsemirnoy* [Subversion: The Name of the Third Worldwide War] (Buenos Aires: South American Division of the Institute for the Study of the Problems of War and Peace named after Professor General N. N. Golovin, 1960).

48. For example, Pavel Popovskikh, "Rossiysky otvet na myatezh-voynu" [Russian Response to Mutiny-War], *Nezavsimoye Voyennoye Obozreniye,* 28 June 2006.

49. Evgeny Messner, *Khochesh mira—pobedi myatezhevoynu* [If You Want Peace—Defeat the Mutiny-War] (Moscow: Voyenny Universitet, Russky Put', 2005).

50. Liang Qiao and Xiangsui Wang, *Unrestricted Warfare: China's Master Plan to Destroy America* (Panama City, Panama: Pan American Publishing, 2002).

51. William Lind, Keith Nightengale, John F. Schmitt, Joseph W. Sutton, and Gary I. Wilson, "The Changing Face of War: Into the Fourth Generation," *Marine Corps Gazette,* October 1989, pp. 22–26.

52. Hammes, *The Sling and the Stone.*

53. Compare to the concept of multidomain battle: US Army Training and Doctrine Command (TRADOC), *Multi-Domain Battle: Combined Arms for the 21st Century,* December 2017, http://www.tradoc.army.mil/multidomainops/docs/MDB _Evolutionfor21st.pdf.

54. Roger McDermoth, "Does Russia Have a Gerasimov Doctrine?" *Parameters* 1, no. 46 (Spring 2016): 104.

55. Ibid., p. 98.

56. Compare to the understanding of "hybrid threat" as defined in NATO documents. See North Atlantic Treaty Organization, *BI-SC Input to a NEW Capstone Concept for the Military Contribution to Countering Hybrid Threats* (Brussels: NATO, 2010), pp. 2–3.

57. For example, Igor Popov, "Matritza vo'in sovremennoi epokhi" [The Matrix of Wars in Contemporary Time], *Nezavisimoe Voennoe Obozrenie,* 22 March 2013, http://nvo.ng.ru/concepts/2013-03-22/7_matrix.html.

58. This also includes cyber domain, as information warfare is studied in its technological aspect (infospace) and in psychological applications (PsyOps).

59. Valery Gerasimov, "Tsennost' nauki v predvidenii: Novyye vyzovy trebuyut pereosmyslit' formy i sposoby vedeniya boyevykh deystviy" [The Value of Science Is in the Foresight: New Challenges Demand Rethinking the Forms and Methods of Carrying Out Combat Operations], *Voyenno-Promyshlennyy Kurier,* no. 8, http://vpk-news.ru/articles/14632 (accessed 18 February 2017).

60. For further discussion, see Valery Gerasimov, "Po opytu Sirii: Gibridnaya voyna trebuyet vysokotekhnologichnogo oruzhiya i nauchnogo obosnovaniya" [According to the Experience in Syria: Hybrid War Requires High-Tech Weaponry and Scientific Foundation], *Voyenno-Promyshlennyy Kurier,* no. 9 (2016), http:// vpk-news.ru/articles/29579.

61. See Chapter 3 of this book

62. Rather than a single entity, a hybrid threat or challenger may be a combination of state and nonstate actors. See Brian Fleming, *The Hybrid Threat Concept: Contemporary War, Military Planning and the Advent of Unrestricted Operational Art* (Fort Leavenworth: US Army Command and General Staff College, 2011).

63. See Alexander Bartosh, "Gibridnaya voyna: Interpretatsii i real'nost" [Hybrid War: Interpretations and Reality], *Nezavisimoe Voennoe Obozrenie,* 16 September 2016, http://nvo.ng.ru/concepts/2016-09-16/1_war.html.

64. Clausewitz, *On War,* chap. 7.

5

A War of Definitions:
Hybridity in Russia and the West

Ofer Fridman

During the past decade, hybrid warfare has become a much-used, yet controversial, term in academic, political, and military discourses. Since the beginning of the Ukraine crisis in 2014, the understanding and conceptualization of hybrid warfare has experienced significant transformations, ultimately becoming one of the most popular concepts to explain the Russian actions in Crimea and Eastern Ukraine. Moreover, almost simultaneously to this Western discourse on so-called Russian hybrid warfare, its Russian counterpart, gibridnaya voyna, has also become popular in professional military and academic discourses in Russia to conceptualize the Western ways to achieve political goals in the twenty-first century. In this chapter I explore the conceptual development of different theories that all fall under the title of "hybrid warfare," showing that the only common ground between them is the name. After discussing each one of the concepts that are defined as hybrid warfare in the contemporary Western and Russian academic and military debates, I critically analyze the conceptual usefulness of the idea of hybrid warfare. In the concluding part of the chapter, I consider the possible contribution of hybrid warfare to the contemporary understanding of strategy making, suggesting that neither of the discussed theories offer anything novel to this process.

While in this chapter I argue that hybrid warfare (in any of its interpretations) is an ambiguous and unhelpful concept, due to its rising popularity in both the Russian and Western contexts an understanding of the essential characteristics of different conceptualizations, as well as different conceptual traps concealed in each one of them, is vital for successful navigation of policymaking in the context of contemporary tensions between Russia and the West.

The Birth of the Theory of Hybrid Warfare

In the Western community of experts, the concept of hybrid warfare is most often associated with US military theorist Frank G. Hoffman, who in the mid-2000s proposed a conceptual bridge between the linear characterizations of regular and irregular types of warfare in the context of the twenty-first-century operational environment. Generalizing the experience of the Israeli Defense Forces (IDF) with Hezbollah in Lebanon in 2006, Hoffman argues that: "The blurring of modes of war, the blurring who fights, and what technologies are brought to bear, produces a wide range of variety and complexity that we call Hybrid Warfare."[1]

While by using the term *hybrid,* Hoffman suggests that "previously separate characterisations of different modes of warfare" are blurring,[2] his conceptualization in fact is a successful hybrid of different strategic ideas and theories discussed in the West in the late 1990s to early 2000s. In addition to the major theories—unrestricted warfare,[3] fourth-generation warfare (4GW),[4] compound warfare,[5]—that influenced Hoffman in his conceptualization, he also acknowledged other scholars, strategists, and military thinkers that captured the trends of blending between different types of warfare. As he states, "Many other analysts have captured these trends, with Russian, Australian, and American authors talking about 'multi-modal' and 'multi-variant' forms of war."[6]

Specifically, Hoffman acknowledges and highlights the importance of the works of John Arquilla, Stephen Blank, Michael Evans, Colin Gray, Bruce Hoffman, and John Robb for their intellectual insights that provided him with useful materials for his conceptualization.[7] Moreover, a closer examination of literature published before the rise of Hoffman's hybrid warfare suggests that even the term *hybrid* was already used to describe the blurring line between regular and irregular forces and capabilities.[8] Nevertheless, it seems right to argue that Hoffman's work was the imperative call that initiated the intellectual debate in the West on contemporary hybrid threats advocating hybrid war as the emerging new conceptualization of conflict in the twenty-first century.

Analyzing different products of strategic thinking from the late 1990s to the early 2000s, Hoffman drew his theory of hybrid warfare on a synergetic combination of different previously suggested observations on modern warfare:

From the 4GW school, it [hybrid warfare] uses the concept of the blurring nature of conflict and the loss of the State's monopoly of violence. The concepts of omni-dimensionality and combinations were crucial ideas adopted from Chinese analysts. From John Arquilla and T. X. Hammes we took in the power of networks. From the proponents of Compound Wars, the concept absorbs the synergistic benefit of mixing conventional and unconventional capabilities, but at lower and more integrated levels. From the Australian experts, we have accepted the growing complexity and disaggregated nature of the operational environment, as well as the opportunistic nature of future adversaries.[9]

As a result of this conceptual synergy between different schools of strategic thinking,[10] Hoffman articulated two definitive and conceptually interconnected terms. The first one is *hybrid war* that "incorporates a range of different modes of warfare, including conventional capabilities, irregular tactics and formations, terrorist acts including indiscriminate violence and coercion, and criminal disorder."[11] And the second is *hybrid threat:* "Any adversary that simultaneously and adaptively employs a fused mix of conventional weapons, irregular tactics, terrorism, and criminal behaviour in the battlespace to obtain its political objectives."[12]

Almost immediately after its first publication, Hoffman's theory spread like wildfire within US military circles, becoming popular and producing a cavalcade of literature. While discussing all of these works is beyond the scope of this chapter, some of the most comprehensive studies deserve to be mentioned. The first wave of military thinkers, writing about hybrid war in the late 2000s, included Colonel Steven Williamson, who made a conceptual transition from 4GW to hybrid warfare;[13] Colonel Margaret Bond, who applied the ideas of hybrid war on stability operations in failing states;[14] Lieutenant Colonel Daniel Lasica, who dealt with the difficult question of victory in hybrid wars;[15] Major Larry Jordan, who analyzed the US Army doctrine through the prism of hybrid warfare, making several constructive recommendations;[16] and Major Sean McWilliams, who produced a useful analysis of the 1976–1989 war in South Africa as an example of hybrid war, thus suggesting that while the concept might be novel, the phenomenon itself is not new at all.[17]

In the years that followed, the professional interest in Hoffman's concept of hybrid war continued to pick up steam, focusing on the additional implications of this theory such as ethical challenges[18] and the increasing role of information warfare.[19] However, the most comprehensive analysis of the subject, since its first introduction, was published in 2013 by two junior officers, Major Timothy McCulloh and

Major Richard Johnson.[20] Simply titled *Hybrid Warfare*, their book not only focuses on a range of historical examples, from World War II to Operation Iraqi Freedom, it also offers an overall assessment of the concept and its relevance to future conflicts.

One of the most important characteristics of Hoffman's definition of *hybrid warfare* is its operational approach in dealing with a mix of regular and irregular threats. Discussing the problem of the emerging hybrid threats, Hoffman and his followers address the problem in pure military terms isolating it at the operational level of military decision-makers. In their eyes, hybrid warfare and hybrid threats describe problems that could be solved by the military, once it has a suitable doctrine, is trained and equipped accordingly, and is supported by the political leadership. From the beginning, Hoffman's conceptualization of hybrid warfare was intended to practically improve the performance of military units on the battlefield because, according to Hoffman: "[If we] simply gain a better understanding of the large grey space between our idealized bins and pristine Western categorizations, we will have made progress. If we educate ourselves about how to better prepare for that messy grey phenomenon and avoid the Groznys, Mogadishus and Bint-Jbeils of our future, we will have taken great strides forward."[21]

Hybrid Warfare Reconceptualized

After several years of intensive and enthusiastic discourse within the US military community, the idea of hybrid wars and hybrid threats started to attract broader attention, exposing itself to criticism and independent interpretations of a wider readership. The main criticism of Hoffman's definition of *hybrid warfare* focuses on three main aspects: the alleged novelty of the described phenomenon, the ambiguous nature of the concept, and its "a-strategic" nature. The first originated with military historians, who claim that there is nothing new in the idea of hybridity proposed by Hoffman; for example, Peter Mansoor, who claims that while "some defence analysts have posited the emergence of a new type of war—hybrid war," a careful examination of history shows that "there is little new in hybrid war as a concept,"[22] and Max Boot, who states that "hybrid warfare is a modern term for an ancient practice" and its origins "can be traced to sometime in the last 5,000 years, before which there were no conventional armies."[23]

The second main criticism of the concept of hybrid warfare comes from the community of military strategists, who claim that Hoffman's concept suffers from an unhelpful ambiguity; as Hew Strachan puts it, "It is unclear whether 'hybrid wars' are those which occupy some middle point in the spectrum between regular and irregular, or whether they are characterised by simultaneous activity on both ends of that spectrum."[24] This leads directly to the third main field of criticism of the concept of hybrid warfare—its "a-strategic" nature, as according to some strategists and military thinkers, "the fundamental problem with the hybrid warfare analysis is that it ignores the role of interaction in strategy."[25] For example, while Bettina Renz argues that hybrid warfare does not represent strategy, but merely an operational approach,[26] Robert Mihara claims that "[the hybrid] threat-based approach makes eminent sense in prioritizing initiatives for developing operational doctrine or in campaign planning, but it makes far less sense when promulgating a strategic plan for an Army institution that is posturing itself for the long term."[27] Either as a result of this criticism, or as a part of the natural development of any voguish concept, the theory of hybrid warfare was reconceptualized, encompassing additional dimensions that were lacking in the original concept. As Lawrence Freedman put it, "As with many similar concepts, [hybrid warfare] once adopted as a term of art, it has tended towards a wider definition."[28]

The most comprehensive and methodological attempt to reconceptualize hybrid warfare and hybrid threats and elevate these concepts to the level of strategy was done by NATO in 2010 in its *Bi-Strategic Command Input to a New NATO Capstone Concept,* which states that: "Hybrid threats are those posed by adversaries, with the ability to simultaneously employ conventional and non-conventional means adaptively in pursuit of their objectives. . . . Hybrid threats are comprised of, and operate across, multiple systems/subsystems (including economic/financial, legal, political, social and military/security) simultaneously."[29]

The task of articulating this new conceptual approach to hybrid threats was assigned to NATO Allied Command Transformation (ACT), which, supported by the US Joint Forces Command Joint Irregular Warfare Center (USJFCOM JIWC) and the US National Defense University (NDU), conducted a series of specialized workshops and experiments aimed to develop this concept further, identifying possible hybrid threats and examining viable and effective strategies to meet them.[30] As an outcome of this collaboration, NATO's understanding of such threats is:

> Admittedly, hybrid threat is an umbrella term encompassing a wide variety of existing adverse circumstances and actions, such as terrorism,

migration, piracy, corruption, ethnic conflict, and so forth. What is new, however, is the possibility of NATO facing the adaptive and systematic use of such means singularly and in combination by adversaries in pursuit of long-term political objectives, as opposed to their more random occurrence, driven by coincidental factors.[31]

And USJFCOM JIWC defines these threats as posed by "multidimensional adversaries [that] employ a complex blend of means that includes the orchestration of diplomacy, political interaction, humanitarian aid, social pressures, economic development, savvy use of the media, and military force."[32] Despite this initial enthusiasm, due to an absence of political willingness among NATO's members to invest additional resources in developing capabilities required to meet hybrid threats, in 2012 NATO decided to halt its work on hybrid threats while encouraging its member states and NATO Excellence Centres to continue working on their own.[33]

The beginning of the Ukrainian crisis 2014, however, served as a catalyst that revived the interest of the Western community in hybrid warfare, as many researchers have noted that the analyses and commentaries on the concept of hybrid warfare, in the context of the Russian reaction to the crisis, have increased exponentially.[34] Moreover, it seems right to argue that within the context of this debate, the West's understanding of hybrid warfare has experienced a significant conceptual transformation. For example, analyzing "the politico-military methods employed by Russia" in Crimea and eastern Ukraine, which are "generally labelled [as] 'hybrid' warfare," the International Institute for Strategic Studies (IISS) concludes that hybrid warfare includes: "the use of military and non-military tools in an integrated campaign designed to achieve surprise, seize the initiative and gain psychological as well as physical advantages utilising diplomatic means; sophisticated and rapid information, electronic and cyber operations; covert and occasionally overt military and intelligence action; and economic pressure."[35]

In analyzing the reconceptualization of the understanding of hybrid warfare that has been developing within the community of NATO's officials and experts, in the context of their interpretation of the Kremlin's actions in Ukraine, it is possible to point to a general direction toward extending the definition of this type of warfare to all possible combinations of military and nonmilitary means. For example, General Philip M. Breedlove, supreme allied commander Europe, stated in 2015, that "what we now commonly refer to as hybrid war" is a "continuum of threat, including unconventional and conventional methods."[36] Diego A.

Ruiz Palmer, an expert in the International Staff at NATO headquarters in Brussels, explains this extended vision of NATO's contemporary interpretation of hybrid warfare, stating that: "In effect, hybrid warfare bridges the divide between the hard and soft power applications that result from the technological and informational revolutions of the last three decades in ways that maximise asymmetric advantages . . . , as well as minimise risks and costs."[37]

As discussed previously, the concept of hybrid warfare was originally developed within the US military as an operational approach, intended to improve the effectiveness of military units on the battlespace. Since then, this term has been significantly developed and transformed, to the extent that the only mutual ground between the original understanding of *hybrid warfare* and the reconceptualized one is their title. While the former describes a mix between conventional and unconventional tactics, capabilities, and technologies on the same battlespace, the latter refers to a combination of hard and soft power in confrontations between two rival political actors. In other words, while the former is limited to the military realm, the latter embraces the whole spectrum of possible combinations of military and nonmilitary means used by an adversary to achieve its desired political goals.

Gibridnaya Voyna: The Russian Theory of Hybrid Warfare

As with many other military concepts, Russia's interest in the theory of *gibridnaya voyna* (hybrid warfare) began with an observation of the West.[38] Russian experts had already taken note of the US debate on hybrid warfare in 2009,[39] and in 2013 even one of Hoffman's original articles was translated and republished in *Geopolitika* (Geopolitics), the journal of the Faculty of Social Sciences at the Lomonosov Moscow State University.[40] Since then, the interest of Russian scholars in the concept has been constantly increasing, creating productive discussions in military and academic circles,[41] including high-profile conferences and seminars organized by the Military University of the Ministry of Defence of the Russian Federation, the Lomonosov Moscow State University, the Financial University under the government of the Russian Federation, and others.[42] However, in analyzing this enthusiastic debate, it is difficult not to notice that the concept of *gibridnaya voyna* significantly differs from the Western understanding of hybrid warfare, either original or reconceptualized.

Since the mid-1990s the Russian conceptualization of war as a sociopolitical phenomenon has been shadowed by the defeat of the

Soviet Union in the Cold War. Analyzing the results of the Cold War and interpreting the causes of the Soviet defeat, Russian strategists and political scientists have emphasized two main aspects that characterize the nature of the confrontations in the post–Cold War era: (1) the aim to break the spirit of the adversary's nation by a gradual erosion of its culture, values, and self-esteem; and (2) an emphasis on political, informational (propaganda), and economic instruments, rather than on physical military force.[43]

In analyzing the scope of literature produced in the past few years by Russian scholars on the phenomenon of *gibridanya voyna,* it becomes clear that the US concept of hybrid warfare focuses chiefly on military tactical and operational activities "directed and coordinated within the main battlespace to achieve synergistic effects";[44] and the reconceptualized idea of hybrid war incorporates a mix of military and nonmilitary means to achieve certain political goals. The Russian concept is completely different; it revolves around more metaphysical ideas and "involves all spheres of public life: politics, economy, social development, culture."[45] For example, underlining the difference between the traditional understanding of war and *gibridnaya voyna,* Konstantin Sivkov, founder of the Academy of Geopolitical Problems (an independent military think tank), stated: "In contrast to the idea of traditional war, which underlines the destruction of an enemy's regular forces and the following enforcement of peace by deposing the existing authority from power . . . the idea of hybrid war is based on . . . first, the disposing of the acting authority, and then the destruction of the military capacity, security system and economy by the establishment of puppet authorities."[46]

Elaborating on this definition, two Russian officers, Colonel (ret.) Sergey Chekinov and Lieutenant General (ret.) Sergey Bogdanov, of the highly influential Center for Military and Strategic Studies of the General Staff of the Russian Federation armed forces, argue that *gibridnaya voyna* is "an element of interstate confrontation intended to realise the national interests of the state by an extensive use of indirect actions, while maintaining the armed forces as a deterrent." Further, according to Chekinov and Bogdanov, "The experience of wars and armed conflicts during the last decade shows that the intensity of the confrontation in spheres, other than the sphere of armed struggle, has significantly increased. This often led to the achievement of the intended aims by non-violent means without the use of military force, i.e., by *gibridnaya voyna.*"[47]

Or, as Russian chief of the General Staff, General Valery Gerasimov, put it in 2016:

In contemporary conflicts, the emphasis of the methods of confrontation is more frequently shifting towards an integrated application of political, economic, informational and other non-military measures, implemented with the support of the military force. These are so-called hybrid methods. Their purpose is to achieve political goals with a minimal military influence on the enemy . . . by undermining its military and economic potential by information and psychological pressure, the active support of the internal opposition, partisan and subversive methods. . . . A state that falls under the influence of a hybrid of aggression usually descends into a state of complete chaos, political crisis and economic collapse.[48]

Consequently, it seems right to argue that, unlike the more traditional concepts of war (regular and irregular, conventional, and unconventional) that first and foremost aim to destroy the political power of an adversary through fighting against its physical power (i.e., armed forces), *gibridnaya voyna* aims to destroy the political cohesion of an adversary from the inside by employing a carefully crafted hybrid of nonmilitary means and methods that amplify political, ideological, economic, and other social polarizations within the adversary's society, thus leading to its political collapse. In this sense, *gibridnaya voyna* is more reminiscent of the US concept of political warfare, rather than hybrid warfare (in any of its Western interpretations), as similarly to *gibridnaya voyna,* "political war is the use of political means to compel an opponent to do one's will . . . [and it] may be combined with violence, economic pressure, subversion, and diplomacy, but its chief aspect is the use of words, images, and ideas, commonly known, according to context, as propaganda and psychological warfare."[49]

In other words while Hoffman's *hybrid warfare* represents the complexity of military threats in the twenty-first century based on a mixture of regular and irregular tactics, technologies, and capabilities, and NATO's reconceptualized definition of *hybrid war* underlines the whole spectrum of activities (military and nonmilitary, covert and overt) combined together to achieve certain political goals, *gibridnaya voyna* focuses on ways that political players undermine their adversaries by eroding their domestic and international political legitimacy and stability by employing a mix of predominately nonmilitary indirect means and methods.

On the Nature of Hybrid War and the Danger of War

The analysis of the discourse on hybrid warfare since its beginning in the mid-2000s until present shows that, in fact, there are three main and completely different phenomena that have been titled as "hybrid war." The first one is the original definition given by Hoffman, according to which, *hybrid war* "incorporates a range of different modes of warfare including conventional capabilities, irregular tactics and formations, terrorist acts including indiscriminate violence and coercion, and criminal disorder."[50] The second definition is a product of NATO's thinking. In an attempt to understand the Kremlin's surprisingly effective actions, which did not fit any of the existing conceptual boxes regarding contemporary conflicts, NATO revived the concept of *hybrid war*, giving it even broader definition than before: "a continuum of threat, including unconventional and conventional methods,"[51] that "bridges the divide between the hard and soft power."[52]

Simultaneous to this development, an independent discourse on hybrid warfare (*gibridnaya voyna*) was occurring in Russia. The term itself became popular in the Russian discourse only after 2014, as a direct answer of the Russian academic community to the politicization of hybrid warfare in the West as something that "Russia allegedly wages in Ukraine."[53] While Hoffman's definition of *hybrid warfare* and its reconceptualized version developed by NATO present different, though conceptually interconnected, views on contemporary conflicts, the idea of *gibridnaya voyna* represents something entirely different, as its purpose is "to achieve political goals with a minimal military influence on the enemy . . . by undermining its military and economic potential by information and psychological pressure, the active support of the internal opposition, partisan and subversive methods."[54]

Following these fundamental differences, especially when they come in the context of the contemporary tension between the West and Russia, it is possible to conclude that the implementation of the term *hybrid warfare* reminds one more of a conceptual salad, in which any ingredient is welcomed, rather than a concept that helps us to understand and interpret the complex reality of contemporary conflicts. Moreover, it seems possible to point to two main reasons that have led to this detrimental situation: (1) the ambiguity of the term *hybrid*; and (2) the misuse of the term *war*. According to its linguistic definition, *hybrid* means "something that consists of or comes from a mixture of two or more other things."[55] In other words, while the term *hybrid* implies that the phenomenon, which it characterizes, consists of different elements, it specifies neither the nature of these elements nor their proportions. On the one hand, the nature of the mixed elements is usually provided by the definition of the phenomenon; for example, *hybrid diesel-electric engine* means that the engine is partly diesel and partly electric. Consequently, it seems right to argue that Hoffman's hybrid warfare is partly conventional and partly irregular means, methods, technologies, and so forth; NATO's hybrid warfare is partly military (partly covert and partly overt) operations and partly nonmilitary (partly informational, cyber, diplomatic, etc.) means and methods; and *gibridnaya voyna* is partly economic, informational, diplomatic, cyber, and so forth. On the other hand, unlike the hybrid diesel-electric engine, which consists of two clearly defined parts, the variety of possible elements and their possible contributions to any of these warfares creates a situation when the term *hybrid warfare* "loses its value and causes confusion instead of clarifying the 'reality' of modern warfare."[56] Hence, a description of warfare as "hybrid" implies any possible combination of all possible means and methods, with no specification of the true nature of the conflict.

Since the beginning of the Ukrainian crisis in 2014, the West has accused Russia of employing hybrid warfare in Ukraine, whether in its original interpretation or the reconceptualized one; and, in its turn, the Kremlin has accused the West of waging in *gibridnaya voyna*. Taking into consideration the fact that, despite their similar titles, these three types of confrontation are completely different, it seems right to argue that in fact both the West and the Kremlin are completely right. First, due to the fact that the separatist movements supported by Russia in eastern Ukraine (regardless the level of support, whether it is political, economic, or even military) employ a combination of conventional and irregular tactics, technologies, and methods of warfare—they present a hybrid threat (according to the original Hoffman definition) to the Ukrainian military force. Second, the combination of military and nonmilitary means and methods employed by the Kremlin in Crimea perfectly answers NATO's definition of *hybrid warfare*. And finally, due to the fact that the West employed nonmilitary subversive means and methods against the USSR during the Cold War[57]—and has continued employing the same methods to extend its influence in the post-Soviet space, thus undermining Russian geopolitical interests[58]—these actions perfectly fall under the definition of *gibridnaya voyna*.

On the one hand, an application of the term *hybrid* perfectly suits any of these interpretations, as all represent a certain combination of different means and methods employed to achieve political goals. On the other, its application seems to be quite useless because instead of describing specific phenomena, "hybrid" simply implies any possible combination, thus meaning everything and nothing. Moreover, it seems right to argue that this conceptual ambiguity has been one of the main reasons for the rising popularity of the term *hybrid warfare*, either in the West or in Russia, as it allows for bringing any hostile action under the same conceptual

umbrella, creating a continuity of a unified political message and allowing different internal political players to close the ranks against an external threat. Despite this political usefulness of the term *hybrid warfare* it
seems that both Russian and Western military professionals have realized
the unhelpfulness of this term in describing the real nature of contemporary conflicts, promoting more specific definitions, such *information warfare* and *cyber warfare,* which are now prevalent in the West,[59] or *new
generation war,* now prevalent in Russia.[60] While each one of these new
terms present a certain hybrid (combination) of different means and methods, the question is whether all of them can be defined as *war,* as according to Carl Von Clausewitz "there is only one means of war: combat"[61]
and, therefore, it seems right to argue that a hybrid of hostile means and
methods without combat is not a war.

One the one hand, the famous Clausewitzian dictum, "War is
merely the continuation of policy by other means,"[62] might be interpreted as a suggestion that a war can be conducted without military
force. On the other, Clausewitz makes it clear that "war . . . is an act of
force to compel our enemy to do our will."[63] Moreover, specifically
referring to the relations between politics and war and what element is
required to transfer hostile diplomacy to war, Clausewitz states: "At the
highest level the art of war turns into policy—but a policy conducted by
fighting battles rather than by sending diplomatic notes."[64] Consequently, it is not surprising that discussing the rising fashion to describe
nonmilitary confrontations as war (i.e., information war or cyberwar,
political war or *gibridnaya voyna*) some scholars rightfully argue that
"there are no wars in history that were won by non-military means, or
by the use of information, alone"[65] because, without using military
force, such confrontations are not wars and to call them as such is "a
dangerous misuse of the word 'war.'"[66] While this danger of misusing
the word *war* in contemporary political discourses has been discussed in
both Russia[67] and the West,[68] General Makhmut Gareev puts it best,
stating: "If an employment of any non-military means is a war, then the
whole human history is war,"[69] as the "over-free employment of such a
word as 'war' devalues the severe [nature of this] concept and dulls its
adequate perception in society."[70]

Conclusion

Concluding this discussion on the conceptual development of the theory
of hybrid warfare, it is important to focus on the novelty (or lack
thereof) that this concept contributes (in any of its three possible inter-

pretations) to the strategy-making process. On the one hand, in an attempt to attract wider attention, researchers frequently tend to give new titles to their creations, proclaiming their conceptualizations as something novel. After all, there is no better way to draw attention to Russian actions during the Ukrainian crisis than to proclaim: "We have witnessed the application of a new type of warfare where dominance in the information field and hybrid, asymmetric warfare are the key elements."[71] On the other hand, it is difficult to disagree with Freedman, who warns against giving new terms to old concepts.[72]

In discussing the potential novelty of any new concept of warfare, it is important to identify whether this concept attempts to describe a new battlefield reality (i.e., on a tactical or operational level) or a new way of strategy making. Since strategy is "the relationship between political ends and (military, economic, political, etc.) means,"[73] it is possible to paraphrase the metaphor used by two Chinese colonels who argue that strategy making is a process of mixing a "cocktail" from these means when "the winner is the one who combined [them] well."[74]

In analyzing the original concept of hybrid warfare, as suggested by Hoffman, it is easy to notice that it attempted to describe a new tactical-operational environment, rather than a new way of strategy making, and the criticism of its a-strategic nature serves as clear evidence of this attempt.[75] Therefore, it is difficult to disagree with Williamson Murray, Peter Mansoor, Thomas Huber, and others, who have claimed that there is little new in the recipe of the cocktail that Hoffman's hybrid warfare deals with—a mix of regular and irregular forces, means and methods.[76] On the one hand, while it is possible to assume that in its attempt to improve the understanding of the transforming tactical-operational environment, Hoffman's hybrid warfare made a significant contribution to this field, its possible impact on strategy-making processes is limited. On the other, in defense of Hoffman's conceptualization, his theory has never intended to suggest a new strategic cocktail.

Following the discourse on the new interpretation of hybrid warfare as a mix of military and nonmilitary means and methods (as suggested by NATO), it becomes clear that it claims to offer a new vision on strategy making. A closer examination of history, however, suggests that strategy-making cocktails of military and nonmilitary means and methods have existed throughout the entirety of the history of war because "anything that might eat away at the enemy is considered worth trying."[77] For example, France employed this cocktail against Britain during the American Revolution by supporting the colonies;[78] Germany did the same by funding the Bolsheviks against the Russian Empire during World War I;[79] and Britain, fighting the Ottoman

Empire, also employed a mix of diplomatic, economic, and other military and nonmilitary means in supporting the Arab Revolt.[80]

Moreover, it seems that the same conclusion applies also to the concept of *gibridnaya voyna,* as it also seems to suggest nothing conceptually new in terms of strategy making. First, the importance of the nonmilitary cocktail for successful strategy making has been known at least since the times of Sun Tzu, who stated that "hence to fight and in all your battles is not the foremost excellence; to break the enemy's resistance without fighting is the foremost excellence."[81] Second, an analysis of human history shows that the nonmilitary cocktails based on "words, images, and ideas . . . [as well as] propaganda and psychological warfare" have being mixed since antiquity.[82]

Keeping this lack of novelty in mind, it is difficult to explain the rising popularity of the term *hybrid warfare* in the both Russian and Western political, academic, and professional discourses. The answer to this question probably rests not in the conceptual strength and novelty of the proposed theories, but in their political usefulness in the context of contemporary relations between the West and Russia. While this question of politicization is crucial for understanding the hybrid warfare–*gibridnaya voyna* debate, the answers are likely to be found more in the political background, rather than in conceptual differences between different interpretations. But that is another story.

Notes

1. Frank Hoffman, *Conflict in the Twenty-First Century: The Rise of Hybrid Warfare* (Arlington, VA: Potomac Institute for Policy Studies, 2007), p. 14.

2. Frank Hoffman, "'Hybrid Threats': Neither Omnipotent nor Unbeatable," *Orbis* 54, no. 3 (2010): 443.

3. Liang Qiao and Xiangsui Wang, *Unrestricted Warfare: China's Master Plan to Destroy America* (Panama City, Panama: Pan American Publishing, 2002).

4. For example, William Lind, Keith Nightengale, John F. Schmitt, Joseph W. Sutton, and Gary I. Wilson, "The Changing Face of War: Into the Fourth Generation," *Marine Corps Gazette,* October 1989, pp. 22–26; Thomas Hammes, *The Sling and the Stone: On War in the 21st Century* (Saint Paul: Zenith Press, 2006).

5. For example, Thomas Huber, ed., *Compound Warfare: That Fatal Knot* (Fort Leavenworth, KS: US Army Command and General Staff College Press, 2002).

6. Hoffman, *Conflict in the Twenty-First Century,* p. 27.

7. Frank Hoffman, "Hybrid Warfare and Challenges," *Joint Force Quarterly,* no. 52 (2009): 35–36; Hoffman, *Conflict in the Twenty-First Century,* pp. 26–28. See also Michael Evans, "From Kadesh to Kandahar: Military Theory and the Future of War," *Naval War College Review* 56, no. 3 (2003): 132–151; Stephen Blank, "The War that Dare Not Speak Its Name," *Journal of International Security Affairs,* no. 8 (2005): 31; Colin Gray, *Another Bloody Century: Future Warfare* (London: Weidenfeld and Nicolson, 2006); John Arquilla, "The End of War as We Knew It," *Third*

World Quarterly 28, no. 2 (2007): 369–386; Bruce Hoffman, "'The Cult of the Insurgent': Its Tactical and Strategic Implications," *Australian Journal of International Relations* 61, no. 3 (2007): 312–329; John Robb, *Brave New War: The Next Stage of Terrorism and the End of Globalisation* (Hoboken, NJ: Wiley, 2007).

8. For example, William Nemeth, *Future War and Chechnya: A Case for Hybrid Warfare* (Monterey, CA: Naval Postgraduate School, 2002); Jerry Morelock, "Washington as Strategist: Compound Warfare in the American Revolution, 1775–1783," in *Compound Warfare: That Fatal Knot*, ed. Thomas Huber (Fort Leavenworth, KS: US Army Command and General Staff College Press, 2002), p. 78.

9. Hoffman, *Conflict in the Twenty-First Century,* p. 30.

10. Frank Hoffman, "Hybrid Threats: Reconceptualising the Evolving Character of Modern Conflict," *Strategic Forum,* no. 240 (April 2009): 2–5.

11. Hoffman, *Conflict in the Twenty-First Century,* p. 29.

12. Hoffman, "'Hybrid Threats': Neither Omnipotent nor Unbeatable," p. 443.

13. Steven Williamson, *From Fourth Generation Warfare to Hybrid War* (Carlisle Barracks, PA: US Army War College, 2009).

14. Margaret Bond, *Hybrid War: A New Paradigm for Stability Operations in Failing States* (Carlisle Barracks, PA: US Army War College, 2007).

15. Daniel Lasica, *Strategic Implications of Hybrid War: A Theory of Victory* (Fort Leavenworth, KS: US Army Command and General Staff College, 2009).

16. Larry Jordan, "Hybrid War: Is the U.S. Army Ready for the Face of 21st Century Warfare?" (master's thesis, US Army Command and General Staff College, 2009).

17. Sean McWilliams, *Hybrid War Beyond Lebanon: Lessons from the South African Campaign 1976–1989* (Fort Leavenworth, KS: US Army Command and General Staff College, 2009).

18. Marty Smith, *Airpower in Hybrid War: Ethical Implications for the Joint Force Commander* (Newport, RI: Naval War College, 2014).

19. Dean Burbridge, *Employing U.S. Information Operations Against Hybrid Warfare Threats* (Carlisle Barracks, PA: US Army War College, 2013).

20. Timothy McCulloh and Richard Johnson, *Hybrid Warfare* (Tampa: MacDill Air Force Base, Joint Special Operations University Press, 2013).

21. Frank Hoffman, "Hybrid vs. Compound Wars," *Armed Forces Journal* (October 2009): 2.

22. Peter Mansoor, "Introduction," in *Hybrid Warfare: Fighting Complex Opponents from the Ancient World to the Present,* ed. Williamson Murray and Peter Mansoor (Cambridge: Cambridge University Press, 2012), p. 1.

23. Max Boot, "Countering Hybrid Warfare," *Armed Conflict Survey,* no. 1 (2015): 11.

24. Hew Strachan, *The Direction of War: Contemporary Strategy in Historical Perspective* (New York: Cambridge University Press, 2013), p. 82.

25. Dan Cox, Thomas Bruscino, and Alex Ryan, "Why Hybrid Warfare Is Tactics Not Strategy: A Rejoinder to 'Future Threats and Strategic Thinking,'" *Infinity Journal* 2, no. 2 (Spring 2012): 27.

26. Bettina Renz, "Russia and 'Hybrid Warfare,'" *Contemporary Politics* 22, no. 3 (2016): 283–300.

27. Robert Mihara, "Beyond Future Threats: A Business Alternative to Threat-Based Strategic Planning," *Infinity Journal* 2, no. 3 (Summer 2012): 25.

28. Lawrence Freedman, "Ukraine and the Art of Limited War," *Survival* 56, no. 6 (2014): 11.

29. North Atlantic Treaty Organization, *BI-SC Input to a NEW Capstone Concept for the Military Contribution to Countering Hybrid Threats* (Brussels: NATO, 2010), pp. 2–3.

30. Michael Aaronson, Sverre Diessen, Yves De Kermabon, Mary Beth Long, and Michael Miklaucic, "NATO Countering the Hybrid Threat," *Prism* 2, no. 4 (2011): 111–124; Sascha-Dominik Bachmann and Håkan Gunneriusson, "Terrorism and Cyber Attacks as Hybrid Threats: Defining a Comprehensive Approach for Countering 21st Century Threats to Global Peace and Security," *Journal on Terrorism and Security Analysis* 9 (Spring 2014): 26–36.

31. Aaronson et al., "NATO Countering the Hybrid Threat," p. 115.

32. Joint Irregular Warfare Center, *Irregular Adversaries and Hybrid Threats, An Assessment–2011* (Norfolk, VA: Joint Irregular Warfare Center, 2011), p. 24.

33. Sascha-Dominik Bachmann and Håkan Gunneriusson, "Hybrid Wars: The 21st-Century's New Threats to Global Peace and Security," *Scientia Militaria, South African Journal of Military Studies* 43, no. 1 (2015): 79.

34. For example, James Wither, "Making Sense of Hybrid Warfare," *Connections* 15, no. 2 (2016): 73–87; Andrew Monaghan, "The 'War' in Russia's 'Hybrid Warfare,'" *Parameters* 45, no. 4 (Winter 2015–2016): 65–74; Renz, "Russia and 'Hybrid Warfare.'"

35. "Editor's Introduction: Complex Crises Call for Adaptable and Durable Capabilities," *The Military Balance* 115, no. 1 (2015): 5.

36. Philip Breedlove, "Foreword," in *NATO's Response to Hybrid Threats*, ed. Guillaume Lasconjarias and Jeffrey Larsen (Rome: NATO Defense College, 2015), p. xxii.

37. Diego Ruiz Palmer, "Back to the Future? Russia's Hybrid Warfare, Revolutions in Military Affairs, and Cold War Comparisons," Research Paper No. 120 (Rome: NATO Defense College, October 2015), p. 2.

38. Vasily Belozerov and Alexey Solov'ev, "Gibridnaya Voyna v otechestvennom politicheskom i nauchnom diskurse" [Hybrid War in Domestic Political and Academic Discourse], *Vlast'*, no. 9 (2015): 5–11.

39. For example, Darya Klimenko and Gennady Nechaev, "Armiya SShA menyayet strategiyu" [The US Army Changes Strategy], *Vzglyad: Delovaya Gazeta,* 24 June 2009, http://vz.ru/society/2009/6/24/300239.html.

40. Frank Hoffman, "Gibridnyye ugrozy: Pereosmysleniye izmenyayushchegosya kharaktera sovremennykh konfliktov," *Geopolitika*, no. 21 (2013): 45–63, translated from Frank Hoffman, "Hybrid Threats: Reconceptualising the Evolving Character of Modern Conflict," *Strategic Forum*, no. 240 (April 2009).

41. For example, Igor Popov, "Matritza vo'in sovremennoi epokhi" [The Matrix of Wars in Contemporary Time], *Nezavisimoe Voennoe Obozrenie*, 22 March 2013, http://nvo.ng.ru/concepts/2013-03-22/7_matrix.html; Vladislav Sayapin, "Sovremennyye vyzovy virtual'nykh voyn" [The Contemporary Challenges of Virtual Wars], *Istoricheskiye, filosofskiye, politicheskiye i yuridicheskiye nauki, kul'turologiya i iskusstvovedeniye: Voprosy teorii i praktiki* 3, no. 12/38 (2013): 180–185; Oleg Bel'kov, "'Gibridnaya voyna': Novaya real'nost' ili novoye slovo o starykh veshchakh?" ["Hybrid War": A New Reality or a New Word About Old Things?], *Bezopasnost' Yevrazii*, no. 1 (January–July 2015): 231–234.

42. Belozerov and Solov'ev, "Gibridnaya Voyna."

43. For example, Alexander Vladimirov, "Gosudarstvo, voyna i natsional'naya bezopasnost' Rossii" [State, War and the National Security of Russia], *Prostranstvo i Vremya* 3, no. 1(2011): 26–38; Mikhail Pavlushenko, Vladimir Zyzin, and Yury Ol'hovnik, "Myatezhevoyna kak forma tsivilizatsionnogo stolknoveniya 'Zapad-Vostok'"[Subversion-War as a Form of the Civilisational Clash "West-East"], *Obozrevatel'-Observer*, no. 5 (2007): 13–19; Alexander Neklessa, "Gibridnaya Voyna: Oblik i palitra vooruzhennykh konfliktov v XXI veke" [Hybrid Warfare: The Armed Conflicts Shape and Palette in the 21st Century], *Ekonomicheskiye strategii*, no. 8 (2015): 78–85; Pavel Zolotoryev, "Global'noe izmerenie voyny: Novye podhody v XXI veke" [The Global Dimension of War:

New Approaches in the 21st Century], *Rossiya v Global'noy Politike* 8, no. 1 (January–February 2010): 45–58.

44. Hoffman, *Conflict in the Twenty-First Century,* p. 14.

45. Pavel Tsygankov, "Gibridnyye Voyny: Ponyatiya, interpretatsii i real'nost" [Hybrid Wars: Definitions, Interpretations and Reality], in *"Gibridnyye Voyny" v khaotiziruyushchemsya mire XXI veka* ["Hybrid Wars" in the Chaotizing World of the 21st Century], ed. Pavel Tsygankov (Moscow: Moscow University Press, 2015), p. 21.

46. Konstantin Sivkov, presentation at the roundtable "Armiya budushchego, vzglyad za gorizont" [The Army of the Future: View Beyond the Horizon] at the International Military-Technical Forum ARMY-2015 (video in Russian), http://journal-otechestvo.ru/kruglyj-stol-armiya-buduschego/ (accessed 28 November 2016).

47. Sergey Chekinov and Sergey Bogdanov, "Evoliutsiia sushchnosti i soderzhaniia poniatiia 'voi'na' v XXI stoletii" [The Evolution of the Nature and the Content of the Concept of "War" in the 21st Century], *Voennaya Mysl',* no. 1 (2017): 39.

48. Valery Gerasimov, "Po opytu Sirii: Gibridnaya voyna trebuyet vysokotekhnologichnogo oruzhiya i nauchnogo obosnovaniya" [According to the Experience in Syria: Hybrid War Requires the High-Tech Weaponry and Scientific Foundation], *Voyenno-Promyshlennyy Kurier,* no. 9 (2016), http://vpk-news.ru/articles/29579.

49. Paul Smith, *On Political War* (Washington, DC: National Defense University Press, 1989), p. 3.

50. Hoffman, *Conflict in the Twenty-First Century,* p. 29.

51. Breedlove, "Foreword," p. XXII.

52. Ruiz Palmer, "Back to the Future?" p. 2.

53. Tsygankov, "Gibridnyye Voyny," pp. 5–6.

54. Gerasimov, "Po opytu Sirii."

55. *Longman Dictionary of Contemporary English,* 6th ed. (Harlow: Pearson Education, 2014), p. 905.

56. "Hybrid War—Does It Even Exist?" *NATO Review,* 7 May 2015, www.nato.int/docu/review/2015/Also-in-2015/hybrid-modern-future-warfare-russia-ukraine/EN/.

57. Smith, *On Political War.*

58. John Mearsheimer, "Why the Ukraine Crisis Is the West's Fault: The Liberal Delusions that Provoked Putin," *Foreign Affairs,* no. 93 (2014): 77–89.

59. For example, Jolanta Darczewska, "The Anatomy of Russian Information Warfare: The Crimean Operation, A Case Study," Point of View No. 42 (Warsaw: Centre for Eastern Studies, Warsaw, 2014); Maria Snegovaya, "Putin's Information Warfare in Ukraine: Soviet Origins of Russia's Hybrid Warfare," Russia Report No. 1 (Washington, DC: Institute for Study of War, September 2015); Rod Thornton, "The Changing Nature of Modern Warfare; Responding to Russian Information Warfare," *RUSI Journal* 160, no. 4 (2015): 40–48; Edward Lucas and Peter Pomeranzev, *Winning the Information War: Technique and Counter-Strategies to Russian Propaganda in Central and Eastern Europe* (Washington, DC: Center for European Policy Analysis, 2016); Ekaterina Kalinina, "Narratives of Russia's 'Information Wars,'" *Politics in Central Europe* 12, no. 1 (2016): 147–165.

60. For example, Sergey Chekinov and Sergey Bogdanov, "O kharaktere i soderzhanii voyny novogo pokoleniya" [The Nature and the Content of a New-Generation War], *Voennaya Mysl',* no. 10 (2013): 13–24; Valery Gerasimov, "Tsennost' nauki v predvidenii: Novyye vyzovy trebuyut pereosmyslit' formy i sposoby vedeniya boyevykh deystviy" [The Value of Science Is in the Foresight: New Challenges Demand Rethinking the Forms and Methods of Carrying Out Combat Operations], *Voyenno-Promyshlennyy Kurier,* no. 8, http://vpk-news.ru/articles/14632, (accessed 18 November 2017).

61. Carl Von Clausewitz, *On War,* edited and translated by Michael Howard and Peter Paret (Oxford: Oxford University Press, 2008), p. 40.

62. Ibid., p. 28.

63. Ibid., p. 13.

64. Ibid., p. 255.

65. Bettina Renz and Hanna Smith, "PART 2: A Dangerous Misuse of the Word 'War'? 'Hybrid Warfare' as a Quasi-Theory of Russian Foreign Policy," in "Russia and Hybrid Warfare—Gong Beyond the Label," ed. Bettina Renz and Hanna Smith, *Papers Aleksanteri* no. 1 (2016): 11.

66. Samuel Charap, "The Ghost of Hybrid War," *Survival* 57, no. 6 (2015–2016): 52.

67. A. Gol'ev, "Voyna kak faktor sovremennogo politicheskogo protsessa" [War as a Factor in the Contemporary Political Process], *Vestnik MGLU* 684, no. 24 (2013): 113–123.

68. Antoine Bousquet, "The Concept of War," in *Concepts in World Politics,* ed. Felix Berenskoetter (London: Sage, 2016).

69. Makmut Gareev, "Voyna i voennaya nauka na sovremennom etape" [Contemporary War and Military Science], *Voenno-Promyshlennyy Kur'er,* no. 13 (2013), http://vpk-news.ru/sites/default/files/pdf/VPK_13_481.pdf.

70. Makhmut Gareev, "Struktura I osnovnoe soderzhanie novoy voennoy doktriny" [The Structure and the Content of the New Military Doctrine], *Voenno-Promyshlennyy Kur'er,* no. 3 (2007), www.vpk-news.ru/sites/default/files/pdf/issue_169.pdf.

71. NATO Strategic Communications Centre of Excellence, *Analysis of Russia's Information Campaign Against Ukraine* (Riga, Latvia: NATO Strategic Communications Centre of Excellence, 2015), p. 26.

72. Lawrence Freedman, "Stop Overestimating the Threat Posed by Russia's 'New' Form of Warfare," World Economic Forum, 4 January 2017, www.weforum .org/agenda/2017/01/stop-overestimating-the-threat-posed-by-russia-s-new-form-of -warfare.

73. Lawrence Freedman, "Strategic Studies and the Problem of Power," in *Strategic Studies: A Reader,* ed. Thomas Mahnken and Joseph Maiolo (Abingdon: Routledge, 2008), p. 32.

74. Qiao and Wang, *Unrestricted Warfare,* p. 117.

75. For example, Mihara, "Beyond Future Threats"; Brett Friedman, "Blurred Lines: The Myth of Guerrilla Tactics," *Infinity Journal* 3, no. 4 (Winter 2014): 25–28; Cox, Bruscino, and Ryan, "Why Hybrid Warfare Is Tactics Not Strategy."

76. Huber, *Compound Warfare*; Williamson Murray and Peter Mansoor, eds., *Hybrid Warfare: Fighting Complex Opponents from the Ancient World to the Present* (Cambridge: Cambridge University Press, 2012).

77. Freedman, "Stop Overestimating the Threat."

78. Jonathan Dull, *A Diplomatic History of the American Revolution* (New Haven: Yale University Press, 1985).

79. George Katkov, "German Foreign Office Documents on Financial Support to the Bolsheviks in 1917," *International Affairs* 32, no. 2 (1956): 181–189; A. Kerensky and George Katkov, "German Foreign Office Documents on Financial Support to the Bolsheviks in 1917," *International Affairs* 32, no. 4 (1956): 534–540.

80. T. E. Lawrence, *Seven Pillars of Wisdom* (Ware, UK: Wordsworth Editions, 1997); David Murphy, *The Arab Revolt 1916–18: Lawrence Sets Arabia Ablaze* (London: Osprey, 2008).

81. Robert Cantrell, *Understanding Sun Tzu on the Art of War* (Arlington, VA: Center for Advantage, 2003), p. 24.

82. Smith, *On Political War,* p. 3.

PART 2

The Information Dimension of Warfare in the Twenty-First Century

6

International Ethics and Information Warfare

Mervyn Frost and Nicholas Michelsen

New technologies have made it possible for new groups (sometimes very small ones) to influence outcomes nearby and distant in world politics using the strategic deployment of information. Previously, this was a potential largely confined to states, large organizations (corporations), and large social institutions such as churches. The reason small groups (such as al-Qaeda, the Islamic State, and al-Shabab) have been able to join more effectively in the global strategic communications (SC) game is that the means for doing so have become cheap and widely available. Particularly important has been the rise of social media.[1]

As has been well documented, the new and rapidly changing media landscape (in particular, the shift from one-to-many to many-to-many online platforms) has wreaked significant transformation on diplomatic practice.[2] One consequence of this development has been that interstate diplomacy now necessitates speaking directly to other societies, as well as to their governments, and requires projecting narratives at home, acknowledging the fact that official messages are rapidly disseminated and reprocessed to these audiences through new media platforms.[3] State to state, and state to nonstate actor collaborative, competitive, or conflictual interactions on the world stage are now widely recognized as heavily, and in some cases exclusively, mediated through new communication technologies.[4] This suggests that a good deal has changed since the characteristic ideological struggles of the Cold War era.

Foreign states and nonstate actors, large and small, are now able to much more easily participate clandestinely in the internal politics of other states (e.g., meddling in their electoral and party political processes). The implications of this are significant inasmuch as the proliferation of strategic communicators leads to considerable information overload and uncertainty, rendering official messages insecure. In attempt to gain control of their message, governments and other actors have increasingly turned to expert private consultants.[5] As the scope for private, secret, and unattributable strategic communications of various kinds has increased in recent years, the problem of accountability has become acute.[6]

The world has become envisioned as beset by irreconcilable clashes of interpretations, which may be settled only through mastery of techniques of strategic communication. One notable concern that arises here is that the criteria for identification of one's international political and military opponents widen to include anyone who threatens an actor's command of the informational space (including, for example, legitimate domestic pressure groups). Amid rising geopolitical tensions and public anxiety associated with campaigns by hostile state and nonstate actors seeking to shape public opinion and attitudes in pursuit of their own strategic objectives, in this chapter we seek to shed light on the unavoidable ethical dimensions that arise in this information war. We aim to elucidate the ethical dimensions of acts of strategic communication, within which are included those acts referred to as *information war,* by reference to the global practices within which they take place.

The argument that we present is an exercise in practice theory understood in holist terms. A key feature of practice theory is that it is presented from the internal point of view, from the viewpoint, that is, of all of us who are participants in the global practices being analyzed. The point of departure is that in the contemporary world all actions, including the strategic deployment of information, take place within two overarching international practices: the international society of sovereign states and the global civil society of individual rightsholders (which we call global civil society [GCS]). An understanding of the ethics of information war, we argue, requires that the global practices in which all strategic communication takes place must be better understood. What this means for international relations is that the sense of any act of information war needs to be recognized as wholly defined within these two global practices and the settled ethical norms embedded in them. Such an understanding will clarify how a diverse field of actors, including private corporations, public institutions (states and international organizations), and nonstate actors (from the Islamic State to Amnesty International) are constituted as such, within those global practices. The ethical debates, which arise for these different actors when they engage in contestation at the informational level, are internal to the overarching global practices that define world politics today.

International Truth Telling and Strategic Communication

In both democratic and authoritarian states, in global civil society within which corporations operate, and in communications between individual men and women (and children), it has become difficult to determine who is using various forms of communication to do what, to whom, and for what reason. As opportunities for (legitimate and illegitimate) intervention into the communicative field have proliferated at the global level, and become available to a wide range of actors, a sense of confusion has arisen about what these strategic communications mean for international actors, particularly as they relate to international contestation or international conflict. Associated debates around hybrid warfare have been accompanied by calls for new integrated responses from Western states and international organizations such as NATO that seek to unify military with informational strategies.[7] However, what might be involved in such responses has tended to be conceptualized under frames that assume we are entering a new Cold War–like clash between ideological or communicative formations that are deemed to lack a common register that might facilitate adjudication between their contrasting claims about the world. Our suggestion here is that success in international political or military contests is increasingly determined by mastery over techniques of narrative construction, or mastery over the material networks that govern communication flows.[8]

Given the sense of geopolitical crisis attached to contemporary debates around Russia's hybrid warfare or the Islamic State's propaganda, and the inherently covert nature of much SC in practice, it is perhaps unsurprising that there is widespread skepticism about the possibility of developing an overarching ethical framework for evaluating SC. This skepticism arises against a background in which the clash of such communications is seen simply as a naked power struggle in which notions of right and wrong or truth and falsehood have no role.[9] We contend that this view of SC as a naked power struggle is incoherent. We set out to demonstrate this by showing that all SC actors and the SC actions they carry out are constitutively embedded in a set of ethical norms that characterize the international metapractices in which we all are participants. A greater understanding of this constitutive architecture that makes SC possible will provide critical insights for SC practitioners and will shed light on the ethical puzzles arising from technological advances in this field.

This argument's foundation may be stated quite simply: all actors and their actions get their meaning, point, and purpose from the social practices within which they are located. For example, consider a diplomat from State X who presents credentials in State Y. We can only understand what a diplomat is and what "presenting credentials" involves (what it means) once a substantial amount about the practice of diplomacy is known as a whole. Analogously, a move in a game can only be understood (e.g., chess) once the game as a whole is understood. Included in what should be known about practices to understand actors and their actions are the ethical values embedded in them. In the practice of diplomacy, one of the core values is the value of open channels of communication. In the practice of chess, one of the values involved is that of not cheating. In like vein in the international arena, SC actors and the acts of communication they perform can only be understood in the global practices within which they are constituted as such. The actors, their actions, and the global practices are all internally related to one another.[10] Crucial to understanding these global practices is the requirement to understand their ethical dimensions. Participants in these practices (and we all are participants) interpret one another's actions, including their SC, in the light of these ethical values.

The arguments used in social practices to support one interpretation of an action (or of many actions that together constitute the "state of play" within a practice), as opposed to another interpretation, are rhetorical arguments rather than formal proofs. Such arguments make appeal to what is accepted and settled within a given practice, including the ethical values intrinsic to it. The planks of such arguments either support, or refute, a given conclusion. SC in international relations are themselves interpretations of actions and states of play in the international domain; as such, they, themselves, are rhetorical arguments. A feature of these is that the components of the argument can be manipulated in many different ways. For example, they may rely on appeals to emotions that are relevant to a given narrative, but that highlight only a part of a story rather than the whole, or may hide the implications of a given narrative or effectively silence other relevant arguments that ought to have been aired. In some cases, they rely on photographs or videos that carry an emotional charge.

There is a panoply of rhetorical devices used by strategic communicators to support the narrative story line or framing of events. This might potentially lead to the imputation that all SC are nothing but propaganda. This would imply that SC simply amount to a clash of voices between opposed groups (states or communities) who have, between them, no agreed way of determining the truth of any of their communications. On this view, the clash of SC should then be understood simply as an aspect of a general struggle for power in the international arena. SC, here, dissolve all international political dialogue into discursive coercion, or "information war." Although there is no formal procedure, analogous to an academic peer review, by which to test the logic or truth of international actors' claims, we contend that to communicate in international relations, whether strategically or not, is nonetheless to make claims that have an ethical dimension arising within an existing global architecture of intelligibility. A global architecture of norms determines the conditions under which the rhetorical claims put forward by strategic communicators in international relations are received as persuasive or not. Ethical judgment is thus at the very heart of success and failure in strategic communication. That is to say, to practice SC is always to propose judgments (offer interpretations) about the communications put forward by others.

Regularly in such judgments the claim is made that the rival actor-communicators have been unethical, in manipulating data, in supplying disinformation, telling lies, or engaging in other ethical wrongdoing. Ethical terms are transparently central to the justifications, rationales, narratives, and explanations that make up all SC actions. For such terms to make sense to interlocutors, whether states or publics, they must be rooted in a common or shared architecture of meaningfulness. Effective SC seek to persuade domestic and foreign audiences that their account is the most legitimate, vis-à-vis their competitors. To do this, they necessarily have to reference a set of already existing and well-settled normative formations that give structure to the contesting ethical claims and interpretations going back and forth between the rival strategic communicators. The mere fact that SC seek to intervene, rhetorically, in the ethical interpretation of an act or event, reveals them to be actions that are tightly bound up with settled norms already contained in international metapractices.

It is self-evident that all actions are constitutively related to the ethical components of the practices within which actors are participants. To be an actor in international relations is to be an entity that makes certain ethical claims for itself and recognizes such claims that come from others. To be a state is to claim, for oneself and one's citizens, sovereignty, which is an ethical claim for a certain kind of autonomy. To claim this is to hold that those who infringe this sovereignty are guilty of ethical wrongdoing. A fortiori to claim this is to recognize that other states have a right to a similar ethical standing. In the practice of sovereign states, besides sovereignty, there are many other ethical requirements states are required to uphold. These include the upholding of the value of communication between sovereign states by respecting the elaborate rules of diplomacy (key among these, of course, is the requirement to be truthful in one's dealings with other states), upholding the values protected by international law, upholding the values protected by the International Law of Armed Conflict and also International Humanitarian Law, respecting the value of *pacta sunt servanda* (the assumption that treaties or agreements between states will be honored), a prohibition against empire and colonialism, and many others. Respecting and protecting these values is a fundamental requirement of what is involved in being a state in the practice of sovereign states. Wrongdoing erodes a state's standing in this practice, just as being caught cheating in a game undermines a player's standing or, at the limit, results in his or her expulsion from the game altogether.[11]

It follows from the above that states, in all that they do, including their SC actions, must have regard to the ethical constraints operative on them by virtue of their standing as states in the global society of states. Individual citizens in states are similarly constrained by the requirements of citizenship. To make matters more complicated, states and individuals are also actors in global civil society, a key component of which is the global market. As such, they have to pay attention to the constraints operative on them in GCS. These include ethical constraints. The SC of actors in GCS (whether they be states, corporations, or individual men and women) have traction only when they appeal to the ethical norms that are constituted and settled in that practice. In GCS, once again, a key requirement of all actors is that they be truth tellers. If it becomes known that they are consistently untruthful, then their standing in the practice will be seriously eroded. This is particularly important in GCS because core to all activity in this practice is contract making. For a state, corporation, or individual to flourish in GCS, it is important that the other participants are able to take their word that they will honor their contracts. Once this ethical standing is eroded, an actor's future in the practice will be a dim one.

As indicated, the two social practices in which strategic communication is carried out are the international society of states and global civil society. These practices are identifiable as social arrangements within which agents of a certain kind are constituted. In the former the key agents are sovereign states, and in the latter they are individual rightsholders. These practices determine who the actors are, what claims they may make for themselves and what claims from others they have to respect, what actions are available to them (what moves they can make), and what would count as a case of ethical wrongdoing (what would count as a foul). These, taken together, are, one might say, "the rules of the game."

These rules of the game are not static, but have been constructed over time. They have a history that reveals a degree of flexibility, openness to contestation, and a propensity to change over time. Such changes occur within the rules of many games; for example, the "offside rule" was introduced in professional football to remove an action allowed under the previous rules that resulted in regular interruptions to the flow of the game. But in all practices, including our international ones, the rules must hang together in a more or less coherent way for the game or practice to exist at all, and for there to be identifiable players or participants in it. This limits the degree to which the rules of any given practice are vulnerable to extensive change.

The society of sovereign states has existed for several centuries now. In this practice, states justify their actions in terms of the values internal to them, and criticize those who do not honor them. Like all actions within this practice, the subcategory of action known as *strategic communications* can be read as meaningful only in the context of this practice and the ethical values embodied in it. GCS is a practice that has emerged comparatively recently. As outlined earlier, *global civil society* may be defined as that society within which individuals recognize one another as holders of first-generation rights. The core values constituted and protected within GCS are those of freedom of the individual and the overall accommodation of diversity in GCS as a whole. Among the rights protected within GCS are the rights of the person not to be killed or tortured, and the rights to free speech, to association, to freedom of conscience, and to own property. The list of rights is not static, but under constant review within the practice itself. The role of nongovernmental strategic communicators in this process of review has been well documented,[12] and they always appeal in one way or another to GCS's core values. For example, while communications from the Islamic State often depict the United States and its allies as guilty of military action that kills innocent civilians (thus not respecting their right to life), SC from the United States and its allies often depict the Islamic State as flagrantly abusing the human rights of its victims. Similar allegations about torture are issued from both sides. Nongovernmental organizations also mount SC campaigns that hinge on claims about human rights abuses committed by a number of parties involved in conflicts in general, and the one that taking place in Syria in particular.

The society of sovereign states and GCS are multiactor practices and both are what we might call "superpractices" in that they contain within them a host of other social practices. They are practices of practices. They are highly interdependent. For example, a state seeking to give priority to free trade in its relations with other states implicitly commits itself to endorsing within those states the establishment of conditions that would allow business representatives to conduct themselves as rightsholders within an effective legal architecture. That is to say, it assumes their recognition as actors within GCS. Most people, wherever they happen to be, are participants in both overarching practices, as citizens of sovereign states and as rightsholders in GCS. In these practices, most actors make regular use of SC. One such use relates to contestation over the relative significance of international norms. This contestation is an ongoing process within the two practices we have outlined. While the international practices we have described are not immune to dissolution, and their rules can and do change over time, the architecture of interdependent norms that they constitute is elastic. This is exploited by strategic communicators in international relations, so as to frame their actions as more in line with international norms than the actions of their rivals, but such norm contestation does not itself offer evidence of an incremental breakdown in the architecture of international ethical norms.[13] What we see, rather, is analogous to the mechanism by which case law develops in response to disagreements within a legal system. Hard cases are resolved through sophisticated debates between jurists who make their cases before learned judges.[14]

There is regularly an element of competition involved in international SC. Actor X seeks to communicate a message that is significantly at odds with the message Actor Y is advancing, with respect to the significance attached to one or other settled international norm (say, an individual's accepted right to be free from torture, and a state's accepted right to self-defense). This is the world of "spin." It should be highlighted in this chapter that the spinners cannot escape the ethical criteria that constrain action in the practice in which they are doing their spinning. In spinning a message, the risk of discovery is always present. There is one particular maneuver that is central to competitive spinning: the activity of *ethical trapping*.

The superpractices we have described, like all social practices, include a certain category of action that we call "ethical fouls." Such fouls include a wide range of actions that are not permitted by the rules constitutive of the practice (the rules of the game). In football, players are not permitted to punch the referee or commit a handball infringement. Repeated infringements result in the player being sent to the bench or, at the limit, excluded from the game altogether. Similarly, in the Olympics, to take certain performance-enhancing drugs is to violate settled ethical norms within the practice (Olympic competition). To be caught doping would result in exclusion. Perhaps the defining *foul* in international relations is to be caught out lying. This is particularly clear in the act of declaring war. While it may be, as Sun Tzu argues, that "all war is deception,"[15] if a state is recognized to have embarked on a war for reasons other than the declared reason, it is likely to suffer considerable damage to its standing in world politics.

The UK experience of strategically communicating the rationale for the Iraq War provides a useful illustration of the commission of a foul and of the consequences that follow from such an action. Whereas Tony Blair was successful in strategically communicating to Parliament that Saddam Hussein represented a clear and present danger to the United Kingdom, over time widespread skepticism developed. Indeed, many came to believe that the communicators had deliberately fabricated a story about the severity of the threat. What followed was that the British government suffered a loss of credibility. This, in turn, has constrained subsequent governments that have sought to frame British foreign policy as ethical. For example, it has had implications for the credibility of UK appeals to humanitarian values as a justification for military interventions abroad. The UK's credibility as an upholder of human rights has been discredited in the eyes of both domestic and international publics. Here, we see a successful (short-term) SC campaign resulting in major (long-term) costs to UK credibility as a strategic communicator. The costs of this perceived foul have been significant for Britain's claim to an ethical role in both the society of sovereign states (SOSS) and GCS. What we see here is that SC actions appeal to the architecture of settled ethical norms, in an attempt to convince others of their validity. To engage in SC is always to make an appeal to certain shared assumptions about what constitutes ethical and unethical action. To be viewed as having lied or misled audiences in the past makes future exercises of SC more difficult or even impossible, as it damages an actor's credibility as a communicator within the confines of the broader practice. In international relations, severe costs are associated with being found out as the author of duplicitous communications. Potentially such exposure inflicts fatal harm on an actor's capacity strategically to communicate in the future. For this reason, no SC actor in international relations admits to lying, deceiving, or, indeed, spinning the truth, as SC actors of all kinds (state and nonstate) go to elaborate lengths to conceal or deny lying. This is true of weak states and nonstate actors, such as the Islamic State or al-Qaeda, and of strong states such as the United States or the United Kingdom.

There is a further point worth noting, which is that there are sometimes greater costs to the credibility of liars that are strong than there are to liars that are relatively weak. Clearly states, as well as nonstate actors (e.g., terrorist groups), can and do lie in their SC. Their duplicity often goes undiscovered and they succeed in securing their goals. Here, their actions may be seen as analogous to what often happens in football where it is possible to get away with a foul, perhaps even score a goal using a hand, or by pretending to have been fouled to get a penalty, and by doing so one may win a particular contest. These, one might say, are tactical fouls. But in the long run, gaining a reputation as a serial fouler carries a cost to a player's standing in the game. If a pattern of cheating were to be sustained, it is likely that a player (or the whole team) will no longer be recognized as a player in the game (by suffering a ban from Olympic competition, for example).

In international relations, the crucial cost is a loss of credibility and, at the limit, being pushed into holding the status of a pariah state. From such a position, the SC of a pariah state would no longer be given any credence whatsoever—this is a position in which North Korea currently finds itself. Because one's appraisal by others as deceitful carries the high cost of incredulity with respect to all future statements about one's own actions, it is the first principle of competitive SC practice to seek to identify the points of empirical weakness or ethical flaws in the accounts one is trying to oppose.[16] Actors possessing high credibility have the most to lose, but settled norms against lying tend over time to reassert themselves among strategic communicators of all kinds. For both weak and strong actors in international relations, there are benefits to being recognized as a reliable communicator—that is, as a legitimate participant in the SC game. There is no mileage in becoming the Lance Armstrong of international politics. For weak actors, such as al-Qaeda or the Islamic State, seeking recognition as a credible enunciator of statements of fact about world politics is a foundational aim. These groups seek credibility as strategic communicators. The central role of appeals to justice and attempts to draw attention to Western duplicity in their public diplomacy and propaganda effort show that appeals to a shared regulatory architecture for ethical dispute are recognized as of great value on the road to achieving such status.

Truth telling, as an ethical norm, is a fundamental requirement for the mutual constitution of participants in any given social practice. It is only as truth tellers that participants are able to make sense of themselves to relevant audiences, as practitioners within the two most important and interconnected international practices: global civil society and the society of sovereign states. SC that in the short term might be effective, but that are not truthful and thus not ethical, create ethical traps for the user who becomes a permanent hostage to fortune. Since untruthful communications become traps, which other actors can spring, we argue the ethics of information war has clear practical significance. Highly effective information operations (in the short term) can create opportunities that empower even weak hostile actors and undermine the basic structural conditions on which even the strongest actors' credibility is rooted.

Ethical Puzzles and Information War

Having argued that recognition as a truth teller is not established solely through one's technical mastery of storytelling methods (such as priming, framing, or narrative mode), within an open global discursive field, but rather may be established only by reference to the ethical architecture of the two international metapractices, we now move forward to illuminate specific ethical challenges relating to information war.

As noted above, the peculiar challenge that arises today is derived from the proliferation of new SC actors, as a direct consequence of new communications technologies. In most cases, new actors remain bound by the standard constraints inherent in the global practices in which they operate. However, there is one factor that greatly complicates the overall picture: the nonattributable nature of many communications via the new media. It often is not possible for ordinary members of the public to determine who the authors of a particular communication are. There are huge difficulties in determining who authored an item on social media, or who is responsible for a leak from a government through such media. In such cases, although one can determine in the normal way that a given communication is partial, biased, spun, or even false (and thus unethical), it is not clear whose ethical standing in the practice is damaged by such discoveries.

The anonymous authors seem to be immune to the normal consequences of such conduct. Revealing the flaws in the message leaves the author untarnished because the identity of the author is not known. One potential implication of this is communicated in the claim that the very currency of truth telling is being eroded within contemporary international practices and in national politics.[17]

This sense that some contemporary information warriors have impunity from loss of standing is only apparent. The author of such cases of SC, even if known only as "Anon," will still be perceived as an actor, as the source of the message, whose ethical standing in the practice can go up and go down following good or bad ethical conduct. Such sources will soon be branded as reliable or not.[18] Anonymity does not shield a voice from judgment; it only hides the identity of the speaker. Huge efforts will be directed to uncovering the identities of states and other actors who seek to hide their real identities and bring them to the bar of international ethical judgment. A recent example of such an endeavor has been the tracking down of the hackers who hacked the files of the Democratic Party in the US presidential election campaign and published some of the stolen material to embarrass Hillary Clinton. Once Russia was revealed as the source, ethical blame for meddling in the sovereign affairs of a foreign state could be allocated.

The identities of some new actors in international relations are known, groups such as al-Qaeda and the Islamic State who, on the face of the matter, do not confront the same sanctions as those applied to established international actors, state or nonstate, for lying or otherwise committing ethical fouls. Such actors are, from the outset, seen to be illegitimate players in the global practices of sovereign states and GCS. In a sense, they are widely construed as outlaws, unconcerned by the judgment of other actors. An implication that has been drawn from this is that such actors also contribute to a generalized devaluation of truth telling, in that this status would seem to give them a free hand to flout the ethical requirements of the global practices. It would seem to allow them carte blanche to exploit all of the devices used in strate gic communication, including spinning, playing on emotion, giving biased interpretations of action, fabricating "facts," and presenting outright lies as "truths." Such carte blanche would surely be infectious. If it is perceived as creating an unlevel playing field, it might lead to the corruption of other competitors in the SC game. This is analogous to what those who were caught cheating in cycling argued had occurred in their sport as a whole.

This view of such actors as unconstrained by the ethics of the global practices, and thus a source of structural risk, is also misconceived. To make the case, readers are invited to consider the role that ethical trapping plays in the search for power by such groups. In the formation of such groups, the following trajectory of action is common. Prior to the establishment of groups such as al-Qaeda and the Islamic State, the involved people were citizens of some state and rightsholders in civil society and, therefore, were participants in the global practice in the normal way. By establishing the group, they became wrongdoers and violators of the norms internal to the global practices. Their activities such as suicide bombings, public executions, and other terrorist deeds reinforce their status as unethical actors. Subsequently, though, such groups start making use of a different and more reliable source of power. They find this in the reactions of other global actors to their unethical deeds. This happens when great powers are provoked by al-Qaeda and the Islamic State to respond in particularly brutal ways that themselves flout the ethical basis of the global practices relating to human rights, state sovereignty, the laws of armed conflict, and international law more generally.

International actors, by doing these things, may be understood to have fallen into an ethical trap. They have acted in ways that can be criticized by al-Qaeda and the Islamic State in the conventional way. These maverick groups are then able to use SC to present themselves as less bad than the major international actors, and to recruit people to their cause on the grounds that they are legitimate actors. Subsequently, a pattern of conduct emerges that starts with the commission and communication of a bad deed by a terrorist group with a view toward provoking a worse one by the target state and the international community more generally. Part of the ethically obnoxious response sought might be to have foreign great powers put boots on the ground in a sovereign state in an act that could be portrayed as aggression, to make use of assassination methods that result in collateral damage, or to start using intelligence-gathering methods that include the use of torture. These wrongs can then be advertised to recruit more people to the side of al-Qaeda and the Islamic State and also to shore up their legitimacy. This ethical trapping soon becomes the major source of power for such groups, far outstripping any power derived from the use of terrorist methods alone.

As indicated, ethical trapping can be carried out only from inside the global practices within which all participants understand the ethical game being played. Furthermore, such ethical trapping also, in the long run, traps the trapper. To realize the power available to them from ethical traps, the outlaw group has to use SC to communicate the turpitude of the major actors to the international community. In response, the major players in world politics (states and international organizations) ramp up their SC portraying, and drawing attention to, the evil deeds of the terrorists. What develops is a fight for the ethical high ground. The terrorist groups have to appeal to the normal ethical bases of the global practices. To not undermine their own SC, it then becomes important for such groups to be seen as upholding the ethical standards to which they appeal when springing the ethical trap. This requires that future actions be more closely aligned with the core values of the global practices. Indeed, this is precisely what has transpired in the conduct of both al-Qaeda and the Islamic State.

After their initial savagery and the SC that made use of it, the Islamic State sought to show how they provide welfare services to those over whom they rule and how they keep order where others have failed. Our point is that when involved in SC, actors of any kind (even the most violent) will seek in the long run to acquire and hold rhetorically stronger positions within common structures of ethical intelligibility established by global metapractices. In 2005 al-Qaeda's Ayman al-Zawahiri, among others, publicly criticized Abu Musab al-Zarqawi for his attacks on Shia civilians in Iraq, explicitly referencing mounting reputational costs for the group in the judgment of wider Muslim populations. What we see in this competitive SC is the attempt by a participant in international relations to acquire communicative authority by displaying their actions as more in line with the ethical standards of the global practices than those of their opponents. A key implication of the above is that powerful states making use of SC must be careful not to fall into the ethical traps laid by hostile SC actors.

Ethical traps appear for powerful international actors even without their deliberately making statements that are known to be untrue. In the complex practices of world politics, telling "the whole truth," as any actor understands it, is always difficult. Any given international state of play is always complex; there will be ambiguities in any interpretation, and there might be things that have been accidentally overlooked. SC are driven by the urge to persuade others about one's ethical status. The essential nature of SC requires events to be packaged, in narrative or other forms, so as to be convincing, by caveating and simplifying the matters of fact as they are perceived by the strategic communicator. As demonstrated, there are, however, significant costs to being recognized as spinning or fudging the truth for political ends. Since the aim of SC is to present oneself as a participant in the global practices who is in good ethical standing, and to present the opponent in a dark ethical light, there is always a risk associated with using the methods of SC, for if they are discovered they will undermine this very standing. For this reason, parsimony is a core feature of successful SC campaigns, in the attempt to anchor the sense of an SC action as unambiguously as possible in relationship to the settled norms of international metapractices.

Successful SC campaigns in international relations often seek to tap into the settled norms of international metapractices through symbolic images or actions. Russia's hosting of a classical music concert in the ruins of Palmyra in Syria, after its recapture from Islamic State forces, provides an example. Here, an attempt was made to establish the validity of an ethical interpretation of the Russian intervention in Syria. This account represented the intervention as an action in defense of global cultural resources. Combined with Russia's highlighting of its intervention as authorized by the sovereign government of Syria (and so legitimate under international law), a powerful strategic communication of Russia's legitimacy, as an actor in this conflict, was effected that appealed to the ethical structures of the international society of states and global civil society. This action constructed an ethical trap for Western strategic communicators in the Syrian conflict, as any attempt to reframe the concert as an example of Russian propaganda would likely have incurred the inverse perception.

Likewise, groups such as al-Qaeda and the Islamic State seek to articulate ethical diagnoses of the contemporary world that are credible by publicizing evocative images of collateral damage from Western drone strikes. In doing so, they appeal to the settled architecture of international ethics that Western states claim to uphold. A claim propounded by al-Qaeda has been that many Muslim individuals live with significant injustice, and that Western states have simultaneously failed to respect the sovereignty of Islamic majority states in conducting such strikes and failed to protect the rights of individual victims.[19] These actors appeal directly, in their SC, to ethical claims that are constitutive of international metapractices, and seek to justify their actions as legitimate by reference to these same shared norms, in the light of an accusation of Western hypocrisy.

This is not, of course, to suggest that such information campaigns are necessarily persuasive (though they clearly have purchase with some audiences). Neither is it to imply that what is called for here is simply a better or more efficacious narrative contestation. Rather, the role of existing settled norms, in governing the legibility of certain ethical claims, shows that even those actors who are widely deemed illegitimate or nonplayers in the game are, in fact, operating with it. The appeal to the common structures of intelligibility embedded in international metapractices shows that SC are best understood as a global forum for international ethical arguments. SC actors are participants in a practice that is defined by putting to the test others' truth claims. SC interlocutors hope to present the other as a hypocrite, liar, or disseminator of half-truths. SC involve an appeal to mutually acknowledged rhetorical grounds for legitimacy. SC actors seek to provide an ethical gloss, which will be appraised in relation to the settled rules of the game of international practices; indeed, by reference to the coherence of these actors' actions with those practices. This applies no less to those trying to change the rules of the game such as al-Qaeda or the Islamic State.[20]

A final concern, emerging from new technologies and the consequent proliferation of effective SC actors, is that the scope for international ethical discourse and appraisal might be increasingly constrained by the complexity of the new media ecology. In this environment, surely what information warriors argue is less important than their ability to establish their authority in the cacophony of voices that proliferate online. This is facilitated by the manner to which a self-selective electronic autism characterizes online media consumption patterns.[21] We have argued that authority can spring only from a track record of telling the truth. This has traditionally been the strength of established media organizations such as the BBC, but established platforms are increasingly vulnerable to the imputation of partiality or bias. A trend toward decline of faith in established platforms is linked to the rapid proliferation of alternative outlets.[22]

An option that is newly available to international actors is that of drenching the online media space with conflicting accounts, narratives, and interpretations, rendering it highly difficult to identify sources or adjudicate the matters of fact. This is facilitated by the manner in which user content-driven news websites borrow content from each other, and thus appear to provide multisource corroboration for claims. An argument has been promoted by new media outlets, including RT (formerly Russia Today, a Russian state-funded media outlet), that there are multiple truths and that giving air to this multiplicity (regardless of content) establishes conditions for open dialogue.[23] There is clearly potential, within this democratizing process, for SC actions that do not make a rhetorical argument that can be proven credible or not, but that operate in relation to the communicative field in general, creating an atmosphere of distrust of specific official messaging (by disseminating multiple contradictory stories).

Actions of this variety put enormous pressure on targeted governments, and construct ethical traps for their victims. The ethical traps that arise here relate to how states respond to conditions of pervasive distrust with regard to their official messaging. It is central to the efficacy of SC that these messages are not interpreted as explicit propaganda, yet nonetheless that they influence the conditions of possibility for audience interpretations. As a wide range of new actors (including private companies) engage in SC, this power to influence operates outside traditional structures of democratic accountability and attribution.

The difficulty of attributing accountability with regard to the complex weaves of narrative, facts, or interpretations that circulate online plays into this condition and fosters public distrust in most national contexts. The proliferation of new media platforms means that political communicators can now directly access their target audiences,[24] but traditional methods for assessing the credibility of their SC (reputation, political status or role) have increasingly lost their purchase, precisely where and when they are most needed. This opportunity space clearly carries the potential for covert manipulation of interpretations on a global scale through acts of communicative disruption (e.g., the anonymous dissemination of multiple, contradictory, and knowingly false stories, or comment board stuffing). It should be clear that democratic states, as SC actors with a particular stake in the sustainability of the metapractices of international order, must ensure their SC actions do not contribute to eroding their own conditions of possibility. In this area, new media technologies, combined with a new set of market dynamics associated with the field of professional SC contractors, might impart a corrosive seduction to leverage online communicative disorder for strategic ends.

This danger should not be overstated; actors who engage in this kind of ethical foul will continue to incur long-term costs. For example, Russian communications around the Syrian conflict are seen to have been effective in supporting its strategic aims. These successes have precisely centered on diversion, disruption, and confusion, rendering it difficult to attribute responsibility for particular acts, such as air strikes, before news cycles have moved on. Whereas these actions have led to short-term successes in winning tactical contests around the Syrian negotiations, such successes have clearly resulted in real costs to Russian credibility. Russia's standing in international practices has been damaged. Much for the same reasons as the Iraq War damaged Western states' capacity to strategically communicate, Russia's credibility as a player in negotiations has been degraded.

While SC are a necessary feature of all political and diplomatic practice, repackaging events in narrative and other forms by caveating, obfuscating, and simplifying the matters of fact, they cannot function effectively without a strategic sensitivity to the ethical rules that determine one's standing in international metapractices. Obfuscatory narratives, or other rhetorical ploys that may have tactical value within a particular informational contest, are subject to the criteria pertaining to truth that we have set out. State and nonstate actors' leveraging of new technologies for the purpose of disruption (within particular operational contexts) presents little threat to the maintenance and sustainability of international metapractices since such ethical fouls will result in longer-term costs for the actors' standing.

Conclusion

In this chapter we argued that all actors in international relations, even rogue communicators such as the Islamic State, suffer costs from lying and other kinds of ethical wrongdoing. This is because all strategic communicators must seek to establish ethical validity for their claims by reference to existing shared rhetorical architectures of intelligibility. As actors within international practices they can establish their credibility, and engage in competitive rhetorical contestation, only by aligning words and deeds to the ethical norms that are internal to the two international metapractices, the international society of sovereign states and global civil society. Contestation in the informational realm, or information war, takes place within these two practices and is determined as meaningful by the ethical constraints that operate on all strategic communications.

The only communication that may be properly termed *strategic* is one that establishes its rhetorical validity by reference to the identifiable rules of the game constituted within international practices and that seeks to align an actor's actions and words so as to support its preferential standing as a player within those international practices. Communications that do not align with a strategic sensitivity to an actor's long-term standing, and seek to tactically counter hostile communications or narratives only in the short term, will invariably carry long-term costs to that actor's standing within international practices. Thus, they will tend to be self-defeating. An implication here is that widespread anxieties regarding the potential for an incremental unraveling of the international normative regime constructed during the past century, in the face of recurrent tactical ethical fouling by state and nonstate actors engaged in information war (e.g., lying or hacking), are not warranted.

Notes

This chapter is based on an article published as "Strategic Communications and International Relations: Practical Traps and Ethical Puzzles," *Defence Strategic Communications* 2 (Spring 2017): 9–34. It is published here in revised form with kind permission of the journal.

1. Kirk Hallahan, Derina Holtzhausen, Betteke Van Ruler, Dejan Verčič, and Krishnamurthy Sriramesh, "Defining Strategic Communication," *International Journal of Strategic Communication* 1, no. 1 (2007): 3–35; Craig Hayden, *The Rhetoric of Soft Power: Public Diplomacy in Global Contexts* (Lanham, MD: Lexington Books, 2012).

2. Manuel Castells, *Communication Power* (Oxford: Oxford University Press, 2013).

3. Alister Miskimmon, Ben O'Loughlin, and Laura Roselle, *Strategic Narratives: Communication Power and the New World Order* (New York: Routledge, 2014); Tom Fletcher, *Naked Diplomacy: Power and Statecraft in the Digital Age* (London: William Collins, 2016).

4. Richard Halloran, "Strategic Communication," *Parameters* 37, no. 3 (2007): 4; John Owen IV, *The Clash of Ideas in World Politics: Transnational Networks, States, and Regime Change, 1510–2010* (Princeton: Princeton University Press, 2010); Joseph Nye, *Soft Power: The Means to Success in World Politics* (Washington, DC: Public Affairs, 2004); Castells, *Communication Power.*

5. For example, nation-branding consultants provide support to both highly developed and developing states. For a range of examples, see Keith Dinnie, *Nation Branding: Concepts, Issues, Practice* (New York: Routledge, 2015).

6. Ben Mor, "Credibility Talk in Public Diplomacy," *Review of International Studies* 38, no. 2 (2012): 393–422.

7. John Arquilla and David Ronfeldt, *Networks and Netwars: The Future of Terror, Crime, and Militancy* (Santa Monica: RAND, 2001); Hallahan et al., "Defining Strategic Communication"; Dennis Murphy, "In Search of the Art and Science of Strategic Communication," *Parameters* 39, no. 4 (2009): 105; Severin Peters, "Strategic Communication for Crisis Management Operations of International Organisations: ISAF Afghanistan and EULEX Kosovo," Diplomacy Paper No. 1 (European Union, January 2010), p. 34; David Betz, "Communication Breakdown: Strategic Communications and Defeat in Afghanistan," *Orbis* 55, no. 4 (2011): 613–630.

8. Miskimmon, O'Loughlin, and Roselle, *Strategic Narratives.*

9. Matthew Kroenig, "Facing Reality: Getting NATO Ready for a New Cold War," *Survival* 57, no. 1 (2015): 49–70; Cristina Archetti, "Terrorism, Communication and New Media: Explaining Radicalization in the Digital Age," *Perspectives on Terrorism* 9, no. 1 (2015), www.terrorismanalysts.com/pt/index.php/pot/article/view/401/html.

10. Mervyn Frost and Silviya Lechner, "Understanding International Practices from the Internal Point of View," *Journal of International Political Theory* 12, no. 3 (2016): 299–319.

11. As those, such as Lance Armstrong, who have been caught cheating in professional cycling have discovered.

12. Martha Finnemore and Kathryn Sikkink, "International Norm Dynamics and Political Change," *International Organization* 52, no. 4 (1998): 887–917; Charlotte Epstein, *The Power of Words in International Relations: Birth of an Anti-Whaling Discourse* (Cambridge, MA: MIT Press, 2008).

13. The interdependent architecture of norms carries significant though not unlimited resilience. Just as pulling on a metal spring then releasing it will result in it returning to its initial form, until a certain limit is reached when the spring will lose this capacity to return to its original state.

14. See Ronald Dworkin, "Justice for Hedgehogs," *Boston University Law Review* 90, no. 2 (2010): 469–478. Indeed, law is thus, for Dworkin, a "branch of morality," or interpretative moral reasoning.

15. See Sun Tzu, *The Art of War,* translated and with an introduction by Samuel B. Griffith (New York: Oxford University Press, 1963).

16. James Farwell, *Persuasion and Power: The Art of Strategic Communication* (Washington, DC: Georgetown University Press, 2012), p. 6.

17. Benjamin Tallis, "Living in Post-Truth," *New Perspectives: Interdisciplinary Journal of Central and East European Politics and International Relations* 24, no. 1 (2016): 7–18.

18. The anonymous source of information to Bob Woodward and Carl Bernstein in the Watergate scandal soon earned high standing for the truthful quality of his communications.

19. Faisal Devji, *The Terrorist in Search of Humanity: Militant Islam and Global Politics* (New York: Columbia University Press, 2008).

20. It is worth noting that, just as precedent can be overruled through legal challenge, changes to settled international norms can occur, as they did regarding the acceptability of colonial rule. Our claim is not that international norms are essentially stable, only that they change in a procedural manner through deliberation within international practices. See Jeremy Waldron, "The Rule of Law as a Theatre of Debate," in *Dworkin and His Critics: With Replies from Dworkin,* ed. Justine Burnley (Oxford: Blackwell, 2004), p. 326.

21. Castells, *Communication Power,* p. 154.

22. Miskimmon, O'Loughlin, and Roselle, *Strategic Narratives,* p. 164.

23. Ilya Yablokov, "Conspiracy Theories as a Russian Public Diplomacy Tool: The Case of Russia Today (RT)," *Politics* 35, nos. 3–4 (2015): 301–315.

24. Castells, *Communication Power;* Fletcher, *Naked Diplomacy.*

7

The Politics of Information Warfare in the United States

Matthew Armstrong

As resolutions do, Senate Resolution 74 opened with a declaration of fact: "Whereas the first weapon of aggression by the Kremlin is propaganda designed to subvert, to confuse and to divide the free world, and to inflame the Russian and satellite peoples with hatred for our free institutions."[1] While these words sound familiar, this resolution is not of recent vintage. It passed in June 1951 to launch congressional investigations into a perceived failing response by the United States to an expanding nonmilitary war. This was a "cold war," not yet the institutionalized Cold War it would become the next decade, and the "weapons" were not guns, tanks, or planes, but ideology and narratives. The battlefield was the minds and wills of the public as all sides assiduously avoided going "hot" in the aftermath of World War II. Even the outbreak of the Korean War in 1950 did little to affect the ideological cold war in Europe and elsewhere.[2]

History provides context to understand the present, but misunderstood history misleads the present. Today is not the yesterday of the Cold War's bipolar order, but of the ideological struggle of the cold war of propaganda and subversion across permeable borders. Testifying before the Senate Armed Services Committee in January 2017, James Clapper, director of national intelligence, recommended the United States reestablish a United States Information Agency (USIA) "on steroids" in response to Russian efforts to subvert Western stability and interests. Clapper may as well have included China, the so-called Islamic State, Iran, and others while invoking the romantic image of the Cold War–era agency designed to centralize the US government's international public affairs programs.[3] Clapper was not alone, as I have frequently heard suggestions of a new USIA in conferences, meetings, and other conversations in and around the US government. References such as Clapper's expose how little is remembered about the early years of the cold war before the walls went up, the borders were set, and the "war" shifted from ideological and political to being firmly anchored in military terms.[4] Underlying such calls is not just an indictment of an aloof State Department charged with leading US efforts to counter the Kremlin's political warfare, but the hope that an organizational fix will compensate for the failure of leadership and doctrine in responding to and even preemptively neutralizing adversarial influence operations.

Despite modern suggestions, USIA was not a kind of Captain America's shield against political warfare. The concerns raised in the preamble of the 1951 Senate resolution continued well beyond the first decade of USIA as the information agency, the State Department, and various foreign aid activities failed to anticipate, or adapt to, the Kremlin's tactics. Reasons for this failure ranged from a lack of training, to bureaucratic lethargy, to a failure to align and coordinate overt and covert activities. The nature of political warfare changed as the cold war became the Cold War and US failure to arm itself for the free-for-all was forgotten. Even today, small reactive programs such as the Active Measures Working Group are held out as exemplary responses to the Kremlin's propaganda, and yet they provide incidental tactical responses in a struggle fought in the margins.[5] The United States never properly armed itself, and especially not with USIA, for the cold reality of the political warfare it was embroiled in. Any interest and capacity to defend against Russian political warfare declined from the 1960s to virtually no organized response by the mid-1970s, with only a resurgent blip right before the Soviet Union collapsed.[6] The result is that, outside the limited covert use of private organizations, primarily through the intelligence community, the United States lacks a historical precedent to draw on today.

Public Opinion Matters: The Origins of USIA

Labels such as "psychological warfare," "information warfare," "hybrid warfare," "political warfare," and "cognitive warfare" have appeared in recent years to reflect attempts to understand and frame how an adversary attempts to shape the minds and will of people toward a political end. This is not new to the United States. Consider the examples from the American Revolution: the work of Paul Revere (see, e.g., the engraving about the Boston Massacre), pamphleteers such as Thomas Paine, sending privateers to the shores of England to influence the merchant class against the Crown's war, and the Declaration of Independence's purpose of mobilizing support, at home and abroad, for the Revolution.

Though rooted in many of the discussions around the aforementioned labels, it is a false assumption that military power has only recently been undermined by the role of information in understanding national power. One hundred years ago, the United States government first officially grasped that national power was expressed across four high-level domains—diplomatic, informational, military, and economics (collectively referred to as DIME in modern discussions).[7] An April 1918 report by the US Army General Staff recognized that in the "strategic equation" of war there are "four factors—combat, economic, political, and psychologic—and that the last of these is coequal with the others."[8] The psychologic factor, loosely equivalent to "information" in today's taxonomy, appeared in the writings of Giulio Douhet's advice on the strategic effect of bombing civilian populations to E. H. Carr's landmark work on the interwar years.[9] A July 1945 report prepared for the State Department declared that the "nature of present day foreign relations makes it essential for the United States to maintain informational activities abroad as an integral part of the conduct of our foreign affairs."[10] Two years later, a congressional report elucidated on the nature of the cold war: "Europe today has again become a vast battlefield of ideologies in which words have replaced armaments as the active elements of attack and defense. The USSR and its obedient Communist Parties throughout Europe have taken the initiative in this war of words against the western democracies."[11]

Emphasizing the nonmilitary nature of the conflict, General Dwight D. Eisenhower testified in 1947 in support of a government-led postwar information program. Eisenhower stated that "real security, in contrast to the relative security of armaments, could develop only from understanding and mutual comprehension."[12] Clearly, the United States understood the importance of the psychologic factor and its role with policy: information was not separate from, but in a complementary relationship with policies. These policies included developing economic and political security. Local insecurity led to vulnerabilities and opportunities. Communists aggressively exploited gaps, perceived or real, between Western policies and understanding while offering promises of a better future laden with acrimony toward democracy, its institutions, and prospects. The United States thus recognized the role of foreign aid as a counter to the Kremlin's political warfare. Following a narrow effort aimed at Greece and Turkey, in June 1947 Secretary of State George Marshall announced a recovery program for Europe directed against "hunger, poverty, desperation and chaos."[13] The European Recovery Program, commonly referred to as the Marshall Plan, was to facilitate "the emergence of political and social conditions in which free institutions can exist." In a classified memo a few weeks later, George Kennan expanded on Marshall's comments to describe the goal of the program as providing:

> a sense of political security, and of confidence in a future marked by close association with the Western Powers, [that] would itself release extensive recuperative forces in Europe which are today inhibited or paralyzed by political uncertainty. In this sense, we must recognize that much of the value of a European recovery program will lie not so much in its direct economic effects, which are difficult to calculate with any degree of accuracy, as in its psychological political by-products.[14]

The White House and Congress accepted that targeted foreign aid could be an effective tool of national security. Not merely a gesture of goodwill, properly structured aid was fundamental to positively influencing the political, economic, and societal future of nations. Like any other policy, foreign aid required complementary information efforts to deny the Communists from owning the narrative of the source and purpose of the aid. The Sunday, 9 November 1947, edition of the *New York Times Magazine* looked at international assistance as a counter to the ideological threat posed by Communism. One author argued that aid should be predicated on a nation's democratic values and not its economic organization because forcing a certain political structure was undemocratic.[15] The head of the UN's Food and Agriculture Organization wrote about the ripple effects of a severe drought in 1946 that led to food shortages in Europe and around the globe. "Apart from the humanitarian aspect of the problem," wrote Sir John Boyd Orr, "there is a real danger that the food shortage will prevent a return to stable, peaceful conditions." Orr continued, "People will not support a Government which cannot provide food. Widespread and continued hunger, with the resulting social and political unrest, will undermine the foundation of governments."[16]

Congressman Karl E. Mundt (R-SD) argued in the same magazine that foreign aid must be directly tied to US foreign policy interests and that it must be properly supported and integrated with broader efforts. Mundt's article, entitled "We Are Losing the War of Words in Europe," made the case for focused aid as well as sharing information and developing local capacity through exchanges as a means to counter Soviet subversion: "We may help avert starvation in Europe and aid in producing a generation of healthy, physically fit individuals whose bodies are strong but whose minds are poisoned against America and whose loyalties are attached to the red star of Russia. If we permit this to eventuate it will be clear that the generosity of America is excelled only by our own stupidity."[17]

The following month, the recently established National Security Council called for coordinated information programs "to influence foreign opinion in a direction favourable to U.S. interests and to counteract effects of anti-U.S. propaganda"[18] in response to the "intensive propaganda campaign" and "coordinated psychological, political and economic measures designed to undermine non-Communist elements in all countries."[19]

The foundation for these efforts was authorized by President Harry S. Truman when he signed the Smith-Mundt Act into law on 27 January 1948. Originally introduced in March 1943 by Mundt, it was broadened in October 1945 following requirements laid out by President Truman in an Executive Order issued a few months earlier on 31 August, which repeated the recommendations found in the State Department's report of July of the same year.[20] The act provided permanent (i.e., not annual) authorization of a consolidated global engagement program run by the State Department that included libraries, posters, books, filmstrips and movies, radio programming, speakers tours, funding US experts to help foreign governments and civil society rebuild, and exchanges spanning the breadth of technical, educational, and cultural affairs. Prior to Truman's 31 August 1945 Executive Order, most of these programs were in the Office of War Information (OWI) and some resided in the State Department during or before OWI was established in 1942. The purpose of the Smith-Mundt Act was clearly articulated in a congressional report that accompanied the legislation:

It is the responsibility of the United States to affirm without reserve the ideas and ideals which motivate our course of action in the world. In this way, we can help Europe steer hers. . . . United States foreign policy should be explained not only to the citizens of this country but to those of other countries as well. During recent years our power and influence has grown to greater proportions than even we realize. At the same time the world has shrunk to a point which brings forcibly before the nations the fact that this new and unpredictable intimacy can benefit man, or it can destroy him. As the most powerful nation in the world today, our motives are often misunderstood. It is quite natural that the smaller nations, particularly those so situated in Europe as to be most affected by Soviet Russia, are eager to know the facts of our foreign policy and what motives are inherent in them. Are we intent on expansion and control in Europe to offset Soviet aggression? Are the aid-for-Europe proposals of Secretary Marshall just an economic smoke screen to blind the nations of Europe to our true and carefully hidden designs? There is doubt in many minds, especially in the face of the deluge of Soviet propaganda flooding Europe today. It is essential to clarify this issue. We have nothing to hide. To fail to tell the truth effectively is to risk defeat for our policy abroad.[21]

The State Department would, however, ultimately reject two key roles that it was charged with. One was global engagement through its vast public affairs operation that was embedded in foreign lands that ranged from face-to-face activities to radio broadcasting. The other was as the central agency for intelligence for the US government leveraging its network of foreign posts and contacts with foreign governments and local populations. The two functions were mutually supporting, but both were outside the traditional bounds of diplomacy as envisioned by the State Department. In his 1969 book, Dean Acheson, secretary of state 1949–1953 and undersecretary of state 1945–1947 (when he championed for the Smith-Mundt Act), described the department's rejection with frustration:

> The Department muffed both of these opportunities. The latter, research and intelligence, died almost at once as the result of gross stupidity. . . . When, therefore, in 1947, the Central Intelligence Agency was proposed as part of the armed services unification bill, the State Department had abdicated not only leadership in this field but any serious position. Information and public affairs had a better chance and were well served by several devoted assistant secretaries. . . . In all these cases, either the Department was not imaginative enough to see its opportunity or administratively competent enough to seize it, or the effort became entangled in red tape and stifled by bureaucratic elephantiasis, or conflict with enemies in Congress absorbed all the Department's energies.[22]

In 1948, John Foster Dulles, who would follow Acheson as secretary of state, was among those who believed another organization was necessary. Dulles wrote that a cabinet-level information organization independent of the State Department, and an equal peer of the State and Defense Departments, was needed: "We need an organization to contest the Communist Party at the level where it is working and winning its victories. We ought to have an organization dedicated to the task of non-military defense, just as the present Secretary of Defense heads up the organization of military defense. The new department should have an adequate personnel and ample funds."[23]

The need for a nonmilitary response was clear, but the responsibilities placed in the State Department fell short and Senate Resolution 74 of 1951 would be penned. Soon, two recommendations for new organizations would surface. One would come to pass and be mythologized as something it was not while the other would be blocked and forgotten. In 1952, as a candidate for president, Eisenhower was frustrated with how the government was failing the needs of the United States. He chastised the Departments of State and Defense, as well as the Mutual Security Administration, the agency managing US foreign aid:

> We shall no longer have a Department of State that deals with foreign policy in an aloof cloister; a defense establishment that makes military appraisal in a vacuum; a Mutual Security Administration that, with sovereign independence, spends billions overseas. We must bring the dozens of agencies and bureaus into concerted action under an overall scheme of strategy. And we must have a firm hand on the tiller to sail the ship along a consistent course.[24]

As president the following year, Eisenhower introduced Reorganization Plans No. 7 and No. 8 to restructure US foreign policy around the same DIME model laid out by the Army General Staff thirty-five years earlier. These two plans addressed two "very urgent needs," as Under Secretary of State Walter Bedell Smith, previously the head of the Central Intelligence Agency and retired four-star general, explained in congressional hearings that began in June 1953. The first was the "clear assignment below the President for primary responsibility in foreign policy . . . is the Secretary of State." The second, Smith continued, was "the elimination of what [the Eisenhower administration believes] to be an insufficient scattering within the executive branch of overseas assistance and information programs."[25]

Reorganization Plan No. 7 consolidated government operations aimed at the "cooperative development of economic and military strength among the nations of the free world" under one organization, a hybrid agency that brought together programs by Treasury, Defense, and State, largely under the State Department's direction as the lead in "control and formulation of [US] foreign policy." This lasted two years.[26] Reorganization Plan No. 8 created USIA, centralizing US public affairs operations under one agency, one leader, and one congressional appropriation. Considering this was the model that Dulles, then secretary of state, proposed in 1948, it is not surprising that the State Department backed this plan. The creation of USIA, like the passage of the Smith-Mundt Act, was not a singular effort but part of a larger reorganization. The so-called Bedell Smith paragraph of the reorganization plans established a leadership and accountability regime for US foreign affairs:

> The Secretary of State, the Secretary of Defense, and the Secretary of the Treasury as appropriate, shall review plans and policies relative to military and economic-assistance programs, foreign-information programs and legislative proposals of the Foreign Operations Administration and the United States Information Agency to assure that in their conceptions and execution, such plans, policies, and proposals are consistent with and further the attainment of foreign policy, military policy, and financial and monetary policy objectives.[27]

At its most aggressive, USIA was a tool of information warfare while the Russians waged political warfare across all nonmilitary fronts. It was a singular agency with a limited mandate of countering propaganda and sharing liberal concepts of rights, accountability, and governance. Overall, USIA was at best reactive to Russian psychological and political aggression, especially the Kremlin's subversion. There was little to nothing in the way of training or support for USIA employees, or other government agencies, to identify, mitigate, or counter political subversion encouraged by Moscow. USIA had several lines of effort, all of which were centrally directed. The public affairs sections at embassies and consulates were under the authority of USIA, not the local ambassador or the State Department. USIA also oversaw a massive information division that managed libraries and reading rooms; produced and distributed movies, books, pamphlets, and posters; and hosted talks by and exchanges among academics, scientists, technicians, entertainers, and even bureaucrats.[28] By fostering understanding of the United States and its policies USIA aimed to disrupt disinformation campaigns but, equally important, the agency was developing local capacity to develop the political security and confidence in a future of economic and political relations between nations. While Voice of America (VOA) is recalled as a primary resource for USIA, radio was secondary to this "ground game" as Edward R. Murrow later described it in 1963: "The real art in this business is not so much moving information or guidance or policy five or 10,000 miles. That is an electronic problem. The real art is to move it the last three feet in face to face conversation."[29]

That real art was not initially focused on nations behind the iron curtain. In 1956, for example, based on budget and personnel allocations, USIA's top markets were Germany, India, Japan, Pakistan, France, Italy, Thailand, Austria, South Vietnam, and Korea.[30] The "electronic problem" became more pronounced as Russia and its satellites began closing their borders as the Kremlin relied on force to compensate for disaffection and defection. VOA, under the State Department, had a diplomatic voice of "restraint and dignity." The platform permitted the government to speak directly to "peoples in crucial areas overseas."[31] The US intelligence community wanted something more. Within a year of Truman signing the Smith-Mundt Act into law, Radio Free Europe was launched, and soon followed by Radio Liberty and Radio Free Asia. These and similar covert programs by the US intelligence community were richly funded, but lacked accountability, leadership, and strategic focus.[32]

Amateurs Versus Professionals

With the State Department abrogating its responsibility to understand how the Kremlin was undermining the West, and the intelligence community operating in the shadows with little to no oversight or integration with broader policy goals and the efforts of various government agencies, the gap between US capabilities and requirements grew. In 1950, the National Security Council issued NSC 59/1, a report on the "Foreign Information Program and Psychological Warfare Planning."[33] This established the Psychological Operations Coordinating Committee to provide a structure for "information programs" in "periods of peace" and for psychological warfare programs during "periods of national emergency or war." Replaced by Eisenhower with the Operations Coordinating Board in 1953,[34] the intent remained the same: to better align resources and accountability. However, rewiring the organizational chart with these boards, and USIA, did not create the capability to understand and anticipate in Washington or in the field the tactics, techniques, and procedures used by the Kremlin. A private initiative evolved to fill this gap.

In 1950 Alan Grant, an attorney in Orlando, Florida, realized there were virtually no studies in the United States about the history, methods, and the political techniques used by the Communists. A paratrooper during World War II, he had taught a course at Harvard on the subversive tactics of then little known Mao Tse-tung. Russian interventions in Europe, Chinese activities, and the Korean War convinced Grant that the United States was in a long war where the real battleground was not fought with military weapons, but in the minds of men. "Military weapons are not enough. Man is the ultimate weapon."[35] Following the outbreak of war in Korea, Grant organized a committee called "Know Your Enemy Speakers," which claimed that:

> as an absolute minimum our high school seniors should be given a broad survey course on world communism (in addition to courses in American history and civic courses to show the advantages of an open society) so they could understand something of the frightful challenge—political, scientific, economic, and military—facing their Nation, and as a result would better understand the unique obligations of American citizenship.[36]

The US education system, the committee charged, "was being run as if the Soviet challenge did not exist."[37] Grant persuaded the local school board to sponsor a "Know Your Enemy" series for the committee's speakers—young lawyers, businessmen, and educators—to engage high school students. For five months, they researched Communist and Soviet history, case histories of communist coups, riots, strikes, guerrilla movements, communist strategy, party organization, and recruiting and training methods. They reached an interesting conclusion:

> All our reading and study pointed to the central fact that the Soviets were winning the cold war, because they had systematically prepared themselves over many decades to wage total political war, while the West had not. To the Soviets, political warfare or psycho-political warfare is an all-encompassing concept which gives direction and orientation to everything they do. They consider it the most important of the sciences. In the West it has been a neglected stepchild.[38]

Moscow's concentration on political warfare, according to the committee, focused on four elements. First, their view of political warfare, or psychopolitical warfare, was that of a "true operational science": "The Soviets have meshed their psychopolitical warfare into their overall long-range strategy of protracted conflict, in which we are never given a sufficient provocation to use massive retaliation, but where, nevertheless, our overall position gradually weakens in relation to the Soviets."[39]

Second, the Russians had a vast educational system to develop a political warfare cadre. Third, they had the holistic view and organizational agility to bring together Russian and local resources to operate by, with, and through the local population to "take full advantage of the infinite variety of organisational possibilities inherent in a total political war, whether setting up a front to organise and manipulate a previously unorganised sector of a given society [or] infiltrating an existing institution."[40] Fourth, the Kremlin employed a comprehensive approach to political warfare that included language training incorporating "the numerous languages and dialects of Asia and Africa, and in the training of engineers and technicians beyond internal needs" to "flatter and impress" their target nations. They also provided developmental aid and produced educational materials in local languages.[41] This was the first systemic effort to understand how to respond to Moscow's political warfare as an operational science incorporating diplomatic, information, military, and economic methods. In 1952, a Georgetown University professor captured the failure of the United States to understand and learn from the Soviets: "Only fools refuse to learn from their enemies": "There is no reason why we should not pick up some of the Communist tricks and use them, if and when they fit into the framework of our own requirements and morality. If only for defensive purposes, we must understand Soviet procedures. The Western World must urgently develop a new synthesis of the operational art."[42]

In 1953, with the ink still wet on Reorganization Plans Nos. 7 and 8, Grant's group reorganized as the Orlando Committee to raise awareness of the dire difference in attention and capabilities between Russia and the United States. The new committee soon produced Freedom Academy and Freedom Commission concepts. The academy, initially to be a privately financed operation, was to be overseen by a bipartisan oversight commission. The Freedom Academy was to be a research and education institute. Its students were to include civil society and government employees involved in the cold war to rectify the imbalance of "well meaning amateurs competing with fully committed professionals."[43] Eisenhower's Psychological Operations Coordinating Board reviewed the proposal late in 1954, but the board separated policy from its information component and, thus, failed to recognize the need for the academy. Subsequent outreach to the private sector also went nowhere, likely because of the Army-McCarthy hearings in 1954.[44] Meanwhile, criticism of USIA increased. Congress, unclear about USIA's mission, its impact, and allegations that USIA was competing with US media companies operating overseas, cut the agency's funding.[45] Eisenhower's second USIA director, Arthur Larson, was actively opposed by congressional Democrats, from the chairman of the appropriations subcommittee responsible for USIA, to Senators Lyndon B. Johnson (D-TX), who in 1957 would propose USIA be moved into the State Department, and J. William Fulbright (D-AR). They declared USIA ineffective and charged the director with wasting money.[46] Larson would not be the only director whose antagonistic relationship with Congress would have detrimental effects on the agency. In the late 1950s, the Freedom Academy proposal was resurrected. Congressman Alfred Sydney Herlong Jr. (D-FL) introduced, in early 1959, a bill to establish the Freedom Academy and Freedom Commission. A foundational pillar was the establishment of an "operational science" of countering political warfare that closely integrated the range of government and private capabilities. A single organization—the Freedom Academy—was to "consider all aspects of this infinitely complex and sophisticated problem."[47] Ultimately, the bill remained focused on a research and training center that would analyze, document, and provide training on the tactics, techniques, and procedures of Russian nonmilitary conflict.

The government remained deficient in responding to Russian political warfare, which it acknowledged in an early 1959 appropriations hearing. Under Secretary of State C. Douglas Dillon testified that the State Department erred by compartmentalizing the analysis, planning, and execution of programs to counter Soviet psychological, political, and economic warfare. Herlong's bill picked up eager bipartisan support in both chambers, including Representative Walter Henry Judd (R-MN) to cosponsor the bill in the House. Vocal supporters in the Senate included liberals and conservatives, including Paul H. Douglas (D-IL),[48] Clifford Case Jr. (R-NJ), Thomas J. Dodd (D-CT), Barry Goldwater (R-AZ), William Proxmire (D-WI), Bourke Hickenlooper (R-IA), George Smathers (D-FL), and Karl E. Mundt (R-SD). Mundt, along with Case and Douglas, introduced the Senate version of the Freedom bill in the Special Subcommittee to Investigate the Administration of the Internal Security Act and Other Internal Security Laws under the Senate Judiciary Committee. Others, like Lev Dobriansky, Georgetown University professor and chairman of the Ukrainian Congress Committee of America, threw their full support behind the measure. Dobriansky wrote a letter of support for the Senate bill declaring that the bill "points to the most essential course open to us in combating successfully the conspiratorial and subversive inroads made by

Moscow in the free world." He continued by explaining the enduring nature of the Russian threat:

> The passage of this bill would make possible concentrated studies of Russian cold war operations in terms of indispensable historical perspectives which would deepen our insights into the basic nature of the enemy. Careful analyses along these and primarily substantive lines would reveal that what we classify today as Moscow's cold war techniques and methods are essentially traditional totalitarian Russian diplomacy. Contrary to rather superficial opinion, they are not the created products of so-called Communist ideology and operation. It can be readily demonstrated, for example, that methods now employed by Moscow in the Middle East, particularly in Iran, were in essence used by the white Tsars of the old Russian Empire. Except for accidental refinements, many of the techniques manipulated by the rulers of the present Russian Empire can be traced as far back as the 16th century.[49]

The academy was to be the equivalent to the National War College, but focused on nonmilitary conflict. Students would fall into three general categories: US government officials whose agencies were involved in the effort to resist communism abroad; leaders from US civil society, including management, labor, education, social, and fraternal and professional groups; and leaders and potential leaders in and out of government from foreign countries. The Freedom Academy was to be strictly a research and educational institution and would not engage in any operational activities. An editorial in the *Saturday Evening Post* explained the need for the academy in simple terms: "We don't have amateur military officers. Nor do amateurs manage our huge industries. Yet we have thousands of amateurs who are trying their untrained best to resist attacks of the highly trained professional Communists."[50]

The Freedom Academy never came to be, despite a Gallup poll showing a remarkable 70 percent of the public knew of and supported the proposal. The *New Republic* magazine denounced the proposal as a vehicle to "propound dogma" while the *Washington Post* feared the academy would be subverted by the far right. The State Department strongly objected to the initiative primarily because it viewed the Freedom Academy as infringing on its primacy in foreign affairs. It also argued that its Foreign Service Institute (FSI) could do the job, though it never did and a limited proposal to expand FSI was quickly dropped after the Freedom Academy bill died. Ambassador Charles Bohlen, then in the State Department's Policy and Planning Office, added the argument that private universities already performed the proposed mission of the academy. Asked by Congress to square the Freedom Academy proposal with the State Department's arguments, Grant eloquently described the bureaucratic resistance in 1963:

> Professional diplomats through the centuries have been trained observers, reporters, negotiators. They feel that a good liberal education and grounding in history, economics, and languages followed by active experience will provide the diplomat with all he needs to know. Faced by an enemy who fights in all dimensions, using a broad range of nondiplomatic weapons and a revolutionary world situation, our career people have been slow to adjust and often reluctant to master or even think about the new methods by which we must make things happen and control and guide the currents of history. They have seen their exclusive control whittled away as other agencies have moved into the expanding fields of aid, technical assistance, informational programs, and military assistance and seem to resist almost instinctively the development of new tools and methods which go far beyond conventional diplomacy.[51]

Ultimately, however, the Freedom Academy bill failed to pass because of Fulbright, chairman of the Senate Foreign Relations Committee, who successfully pulled the bill out of the Judiciary Committee, where it was introduced as a matter of domestic security, and into his committee to let it die.

Fulbright rejected that Communism and the Soviet Union posed an existential threat to the United States and the West. Peace with the Kremlin would come, Fulbright argued, if we could develop mutual trust. "I refuse to admit that the Communist dogma per se is a threat to the United States,"[52] he told his Senate colleagues while arguing to relax trade with Russia. For Fulbright, even USIA was unacceptable. In 1953, Fulbright supported establishing USIA if it would be shuttered within 3 years, or "maybe 10."[53] By 1967 Fulbright was actively opposing the agency,[54] and by 1972 he was waging an all-out war against USIA, including requiring the agency's authorization be renewed, and thus reviewed, annually.[55] Radio Free Europe and Radio Liberty also faced Fulbright's ire. During a Senate meeting, he argued that "Radio Free Europe has done more to keep alive the cold war and prevent agreement with Russia and improved relations than good."[56] As if his view was unclear, Fulbright restated his goal: "These radios should be given an opportunity to take their rightful place in the graveyard of cold war relics."[57] That same year, Fulbright would score another blow on

US public diplomacy. Senator James L. Buckley (I-NY) showed a USIA film about Czechoslovakia on his monthly television show for his constituents. Fulbright complained that the USIA film should not have been available to US audiences. Since Buckley had requested the film from USIA, the US attorney general declared the showing to be permissible under the Smith-Mundt Act.[58] Fulbright responded by successfully amended the Smith-Mundt Act to block US citizens—including the press and Congress—from accessing USIA material.[59] No longer would the material be available "by request," regardless of requestor.[60] In 1985, a Democratic senator amended the Smith-Mundt Act to "close the loopholes" left by Fulbright following questions about nepotism at the agency, and the USIA director's use of tens of thousands of agency dollars for a home security system, among other issues. This amendment led directly to a US Federal Court ruling that USIA material was exempt from Freedom of Information Act requests.[61] The impact of Fulbright's deleterious amendment was twofold. First, it insulated US "public diplomacy" from Congress, academia, and the public, thereby limiting awareness of the practice and, equally important, understanding its utility. Second, it reframed the Smith-Mundt Act as an "antipropaganda" law as many have thought of it since. This twist tainted nearly every international information effort by the US government as propaganda and led to many in government to invoke the act to limit or fail to engage foreign audiences, from the most benign activities to counterpropaganda to information warfare.

By blocking the development and deployment of civilian and overt activities, Fulbright's actions on the Freedom Academy and the Smith-Mundt Act have done more to militarize US foreign policy than any other single act by denying Congress, policymakers, and practitioners critical experience, methods, and historical precedent to properly defend the nation through nonmilitary means. Further, it denied what would have been a shove to the State Department to lean into modern foreign policy of the twentieth and twenty-first centuries.

Conclusion

Since its establishment, USIA was constantly fighting for resources for a role that was misunderstood, unclear, or simply rejected. Congress questioned its tactics, how it spent US tax dollars, and whether it was supporting or undermining the United States. In 1999, USIA was abolished and ceremoniously sent to the graveyard of Cold War relics. In reality, it was split in two. The broadcast operations were spun out into an independent federally run news organization while the bulk of USIA—the libraries, exchanges, and other information programs—returned to the State Department as they existed forty-six years earlier. The public affairs sections of the embassies and consulates, however, were now under the direction of the ambassador and no longer centrally directed.

In 2016, Congress, after considering various options to push the White House to act more aggressively, settled on what is essentially an effort to create a cross between USIA and the Psychological Operations Coordinating Board. Responding to the growing informational and psychological threat from Russia, the Islamic State and al-Qaeda, and others, Congress established the Global Engagement Center (GEC) inside the State Department. The GEC is authorized to develop, plan, and synchronize "in coordination with the Secretary of Defence, and the heads of other relevant Federal departments and agencies" programs to identify and counter foreign propaganda and disinformation directed at "United States national security interests."[62] Suggestions to recreate USIA continue, as if updating the organizational chart will compensate for absent leadership and strategy. Forgotten is that USIA, like the Smith-Mundt Act before it, was part of a larger realignment of agency missions and accountability in support of an overarching strategy. Also forgotten is that a new wire diagram does not suddenly result in trained personnel capable of anticipating and countering the Kremlin's political warfare.

The stakes today are higher than before since the cost of failure has increased as public opinion, influenced by both increased transparency and disinformation, enjoys an increasing influence on domestic and foreign policy. Societal, economic, and political disruption no longer require the resources of a national government, as terms such as *self-radicalization* mask the effectiveness of foreign (ideological, geographical, cultural, or political) influence. "If a country is lost to communism," George Gallup wrote in 1962, "through propaganda and subversion it is lost to our side as irretrievably as if we had lost it in actual warfare."[63] Through political warfare, the enemy not only gets a vote in the success of its foes' policies, but it can rig the public opinion against them. The United States covered this ground before and the solution was found in a new agency.

In their 1963 surrender letter following Fulbright's "success" in killing the Freedom Academy bill, the Orlando Committee held out hope that over fifty years later remains unfulfilled: "Someday this nation will recognize that global non-military conflict must be pursued with the same intensity and preparation as global military conflicts."[64] That day has yet to come.

Notes

This chapter is based on an article published as "The Past, Present, and Future of the War for Public Opinion," War on the Rocks, 19 January 2017, https://warontherocks.com/2017/01/the-past-present-and-future-of-the-war-for-public-opinion. It is published here in revised form with permission.

1. US Congress, *Overseas Information Programs of the U.S.: Hearings Before the United States Senate Committee on Foreign Relations, Subcommittee Under S. Res. 74 on Overseas Information Programs of the U.S., Eighty-Second Congress, Second Session* (Washington, DC: US Government Printing Office, 1952), p. 1.

2. A nonscientific review of contemporary material, including newspapers, magazines, and books, shows the noncapitalized "cold war" was dominant if not exclusive in the 1940s through early 1950s. By about 1962 cold war apparently fell into disfavor and by 1967, according to Google's Ngram Viewer, the capitalized "Cold War" became dominant. See https://books.google.com/ngrams/graph?content =Cold+War&case_insensitive=on&year_start=1940&year_end=2008 (accessed 1 June 2017).

3. Carlo Munoz, "Clapper Calls for U.S. Information Agency 'On Steroids' to Counter Russian Propaganda," *Washington Times,* 5 January 2017.

4. See, for example, Mathew Armstrong, "No, We Do Not Need to Revive the U.S. Information Agency," War on the Rocks, https://warontherocks.com/2015/11/no-we-do-not-need-to-revive-the-u-s-information-agency/ (accessed 12 May 2017).

5. For a detailed history of the Active Measures Working Group, see Fletcher Schoen and Christopher J. Lamb, *Deception, Disinformation, and Strategic Communications: How One Interagency Group Made a Major Difference.* Institute for National Strategic Studies Strategic Perspectives (Washington, D.C.: National Defense University Press, 2012). Schoen and Lamb explain that it took three years to launch the AMWG and that its effective operational life was only about one year, 1986–1987, at what would become the very tail end of the Cold War.

6. Ibid., 12.

7. It is interesting that the DIME model, which originated in the 1980s in the United States, closely resembles the 1918 report. As of yet, I have been unable to determine whether the US military authors cribbed from the General Staff report, but considering the parallels, I think it is safe to say they did so without attribution.

8. This report is referenced in James Robert Mock and Cedric Larson, *Words that Won the War; the Story of the Committee on Public Information, 1917–1919* (Princeton: Princeton University Press, 1939), p. 238. The same framework is found in Alexander Powell, *The Army Behind the Army* (New York: Charles Scribner's Sons, 1919), pp. 331–334. Powell's book, commissioned and supported by the secretary of war, described how the organization of the US Army's wartime Military Intelligence Directorate incorporated the "four factors." The structure and operation was based on "the investigation of active and potential enemies, allies, and neutrals; their military, political, and economic condition; their state of mind," among other areas.

9. The use of "information" instead of "psychologic" is significant. The first is neutral without action or intent, while the second reflects the purpose to influence. In

the 1940s and 1950s, Presidents Truman and Eisenhower referred to the "struggle for minds and wills" when describing the contemporary foreign policy challenges. The underlying principle was to affect the will to act in some way, either in support of a cause or, at minimum, not in opposition to the cause in a dynamic environment. It is also worth noting that in a foreign policy plank speech when he was running for president in 1952, Dwight D. Eisenhower said of "psychological" that "we need to stop being afraid of that five-dollar, five-syllable word." Contrast all of that with both the modern use of the sterile word "information" and the phrase "the battle for hearts and minds." A book can, and should, be written on this but for now consider the implication that a "battle" has a definitive start and end, unlike an enduring struggle, and instead of affecting the will to act, the goal is to be liked. Numerous anecdotes can be shared regarding how hearts were won but supported by adverse actions, including the bomb maker in southern Afghanistan selling his wares to kill British and US soldiers because he was trying to make enough money to move to the United States.

10. Arthur Macmahon, *Memorandum on the Postwar International Information Program of the United States* (Washington, DC: US Government Printing Office, 1945).

11. US House of Representatives Committee on Foreign Affairs, *The United States Information Service in Europe* (Washington, DC: US Government Printing Office, 1948), p. 1.

12. Samuel Tower, "House Group Votes to Keep U.S. Radio; Sanctions State Department's Information Work After an Urgent Plea by Eisenhower," *New York Times*, 21 May 1947. General Dwight D. Eisenhower testified in support of what is now known as the Smith-Mundt Act.

13. Charles Mee, *The Marshall Plan: The Launching of the Pax Americana* (New York: Simon and Schuster, 1984).

14. George Kennan, *Top Secret Supplement to the Report of the Policy Planning Staff of July 23, 1947. Certain Aspects of the European Recovery Program from the United States Standpoint,* Library of the U.S. Adversary Commission on Public Diplomacy, Washington, DC, www.state.gov/pdcommission/library/178673.htm (accessed 12 May 2017).

15. James Angell, "Shall We Say: 'No Aid for Socialism'?" *New York Times,* 9 November 1947.

16. John Boyd Orr, "Program to Meet the World's Food Crisis," *New York Times,* 9 November 1947.

17. Karl Mundt, "We Are Losing the War of Words in Europe," *New York Times,* 9 November 1947.

18. Frank Ninkovich, *The Diplomacy of Ideas: U.S. Foreign Policy and Cultural Relations, 1938–1950* (Cambridge: Cambridge University Press, 1981), p. 135.

19. Nicholas Cull, *The Cold War and the United States Information Agency: American Propaganda and Public Diplomacy, 1945–1989* (Cambridge: Cambridge University Press, 2008), p. 39.

20. For the text of the Executive Order, see Harry Truman, *Executive Order 9608—Providing for the Termination of the Office of War Information, and for the Disposition of Its Functions and of Certain Functions of the Office of Inter-American Affairs,* in Gerhard Peters and John T. Woolley, *The American Presidency Project,* www.presidency.ucsb.edu/ws/?pid=60671 (accessed 31 May 2017). For Truman's statement on Executive Order 9608, see "Statement by the President," 31 August 1945, Truman Library, WHCF, Box 166, OF 20-E.

21. US House of Representatives Committee on Foreign Affairs, *The United States Information Service in Europe,* pp. 2–3.

22. Dean Acheson, *Present at the Creation: My Years in the State Department* (New York: Norton, 1969), p. 127. The department's rejection of the intelligence role is more interesting when compared to the department's position before and during World War I when then-Secretary of State Robert Lansing aggressively sought to make the department the nation's central domestic and foreign intelligence agency. At the time when the War and Navy Departments were establishing their first offices for press and public relations, Lansing placed the department's press relations office inside his counterintelligence office.

23. US Congress, *Freedom Commission and Freedom Academy: Hearings Before the United States Senate Committee on the Judiciary, Subcommittee to Investigate the Administration of the Internal Security Act and Other Internal Security Laws, Eighty-Sixth Congress, First Session, on June 17–19, 1959* (Washington, DC: US Government Printing Office, 1959), p. 49. The idea of a separate agency for this function was not entirely new. In June 1945, a bill in the House of Representatives called for a Department of Peace, a cabinet-level agency coequal with the Departments of State and Defense. See also House Resolution 3628 to establish a "Department of Peace," introduced 29 June 1945.

24. Lori Lyn Bogle, *The Cold War,* vol. 2 (New York: Routledge, 2001), p. 147.

25. US Congress, *Reorganization Plans Nos. 7 and 8 of 1953 (Foreign Operations Administration) (United States Information Agency): Hearings . . . Eighty-Third Congress, First Session on H.J. Res. 261 and H.J. Res. 262. June 22, 23, and 24, 1953* (Washington, DC: US Government Printing Office, 1953), pp. 30–31.

26. Ibid., p. 7. See also Dwight D. Eisenhower, "Letter to Secretary Dulles Regarding Transfer of the Affairs of the Foreign Operations Administration to the Department of State," 17 April 1955, in Gerhard Peters and John T. Woolley, *The American Presidency Project,* www.presidency.ucsb.edu/ws/?pid=10454 (accessed 31 May 2017).

27. Ibid., p. 32.

28. USIA's authorities were derived primarily from the Smith-Mundt Act of 1948. A report by the Senate Committee on Foreign Relations that accompanied the final bill described the "main purpose" of the pending legislation as follows: "to enable the Government of the United States to promote a better understanding of the United States in other countries, and to increase mutual understanding between the people of the United States and the people of other countries. Among the means to be used in achieving these objectives are: (1) an information service to disseminate abroad information about the United States, its people, and the policies promulgated by the Congress, the President, the Secretary of State, and other responsible officials of Government having to do with matters affecting foreign affairs; and (2) and educational exchange service which would enable the United States to cooperate more effectively with other nations in (a) the interchange of persons, knowledge, and skills; (b) the rendering of technical and other services; and (c) the interchange of information and developments in the field of education, the arts, and sciences." Senate Committee on Foreign Relations (1948), Report 811 to Accompany H.R. 3342, 1. In 1946, amendments were made to the 1944 Surplus Property Act. The United States has been using educational institutions to further political goals since 1908 with the use of the Boxer Indemnities to fund scholarship programs of Chinese in the United States under President Theodore Roosevelt. As was pointed out by the chair of the Surplus Property Subcommittee of the Senate Committee on Military Affairs while discussing an amendment to the Surplus Property Act, legislation that would become known as the Fulbright Act: "Some 2,000 Chinese were educated in our schools. That may be one reason why the democratic movement became so vigorous

in China, because so many of those young Chinese came over here and were educated, and adopted points of view in this country." US Senate, Committee on Military, *Foreign Educational Benefits and Surplus Property: Hearing before a Subcommittee of the Committee on Military Affairs, United States Senate, Seventy-Ninth
Congress, Second Session, on S. 1440, a Bill Authorizing Use of Credits Established
through the Sale of Surplus Properties Abroad for the Promotion of International
Good Will through the Exchange of Students in the Fields of Education, Culture, and
Science; and S. 1636, a Bill to Amend the Surplus Property Act of 1944 to Designate
the Department of State as the Disposal Agency for Surplus Property Outside the
Continental United States, Its Territories and Possessions, and for Other Purposes*,
February 25, 1946 (Washington, DC: US Government Printing Office, 1946).

29. Edward R. Murrow, quoted in Gregory Tomlin, *Murrow's Cold War: Public
Diplomacy for the Kennedy Administration* (Lincoln: Potomac Books, an imprint of
University of Nebraska Press, 2016), p. xv.

30. Kenneth Alan Osgood, *Total Cold War: Eisenhower's Secret Propaganda
Battle at Home and Abroad* (Lawrence: University of Kansas, 2006), pp. 92–93.

31. US House of Representatives Committee on Foreign Affairs, *The United
States Information Service in Europe*, p. 421.

32. An interesting thought experiment is if the radio operation, with its news and
information programming, had been moved from the State Department, where it was
temporarily placed following the closing of the Office of War Information on August
31, 1945, by an executive order of the president, to a private entity wholly funded by
the US government. This was the intent of the State Department and Congress from
October 1945 through early 1947. However, what became known as the Smith-
Mundt Bill, and later the Smith-Mundt Act, was modified in 1947 to accede to the
bill's eventual cosponsor Senator Alexander Smith's (R-NJ) demand to keep the
radio operation, commonly referred to as the Voice of America, in the State Department. If VOA had been moved into a private entity, would the CIA have then used
VOA instead of creating Radio Free Europe and Radio Liberty, and later Radio Free
Asia? Details of nonprivatization of VOA are found in my forthcoming book.

33. National Archives, RG 59, S/S–NSC Files: Lot 66 D 148, Psychological Warfare. Secret. NSC Action No. 283 recorded that the National Security Council approved
NSC 59 as amended by memorandum action of 9 March. The report in its approved
form was circulated as NSC 59/1 under cover of a 9 March note from Lay and submitted to the president for consideration. NSC Action No. 283 is ibid., S/S–NSC Files: Lot
66 D 95, Records of Action by the National Security Council. A memorandum from
Lay to the National Security Council, March 10, indicates that the president approved
NSC 59/1 on 10 March. Ibid., S/P–NSC Files: Lot 62 D 1, 1935–62, Box 115. Office
of the Historian of the Department of State website, https://history.state.gov/historical
documents/frus1950-55Intel/d2 (accessed 31 May 2017).

34. Osgood, *Total Cold War*, p. 85.

35. Eugene Methvin, "Let's Demand This New Weapon for Democracy," *Reader's
Digest*, May 1963.

36. US Congress, *Freedom Commission and Freedom Academy*, p. 11.

37. Ibid., p. 13.

38. Ibid., p. 14.

39. Ibid., pp. 14–16.

40. Ibid.

41. Ibid.

42. Stefan Thomas Possony, *A Century of Conflict; Communist Techniques of
World Revolution* (Chicago: H. Regnery, 1953), p. 418.

43. US Congress, *Freedom Commission and Freedom Academy,* p. 18.

44. Senator Karl Mundt (R-SD), formerly Congressman Mundt, chaired these televised hearings that looked at accusations by the US Army and Senator Joseph McCarthy (R-WI) over alleged pressure on the army to hire Roy Cohn, a former aid to McCarthy.

45. Cull, *The Cold War and the United States Information Agency,* p. 136.

46. For greater detail on this, see Cull, *The Cold War and the United States Information Agency,* chap. 2 (for details on Eugene McCarthy and the United States Information Agency [USIA]) and chap. 3 (for Larson's relationship with Congress).

47. US Congress, *Freedom Commission and Freedom Academy,* p. 22.

48. Senator Paul H. Douglas was married to Congresswoman Emily Taft Douglas who, during and after her time in office, was an active supporter of the bill that became known as the Smith-Mundt Act.

49. US Congress, *Freedom Commission and Freedom Academy,* p. 160.

50. "The Freedom Academy Bill Should Pass," *Saturday Evening Post,* 18 February 1961.

51. "Training of Foreign Affairs Personnel," Senate Foreign Relations Committee, 88th Congress, 1st Session, 1963, p. 353.

52. US Congress, *Government Guarantees of Credit to Communist Countries. Hearings, Eighty-Eighth Congress, First Session, on S. 2310, a Bill to Prohibit Any Guaranty By the Export-Import Bank or Any Other Agency of the Government of Payment of Obligations of Communist Countries. November 20–22, 1963* (Washington, DC: US Government Printing Office, 1963).

53. See the statement by Robert Johnson, administrator of the International Information Administration, Department of State, referring to conversations he had with Senator J. William Fulbright in US Congress, *Reorganization Plans Nos. 7 and 8 of 1953,* p. 178.

54. See, in particular, p. 91 onward in US Congress, *U.S. Informational Media Guaranty Program. Hearings, Ninetieth Congress, First Session on S.1030, March 21, and April 25, 1967* (Washington, DC: US Government Printing Office, 1967).

55. Previously, USIA enjoyed, as most federal agencies do, a "permanent" authorization. Public Law 92-226, enacted February 7, 1972. For a description, see p. 19 of Library of Congress, *Programs and Activities Within the Jurisdiction of the Committee on Foreign Affairs Scheduled to Terminate During the 93d Congress Submitted in Accordance with Section 321(a) of the Legislative Reorganization Act of 1970* (Washington, DC: US Government Printing Office, 1970).

56. US Congress, *Departments of State, Justice, and Commerce, the Judiciary, and Related Agencies Appropriations for Fiscal Year 1972. Hearings Before a Subcommittee of the Committee on Appropriations, United States Senate, Ninety-Second Congress, First Session, on H.R. 9272* (Washington, DC: US Government Printing Office, 1971), p. 1081.

57. Bernard Gwertzman, "Funding Near End for U.S. Stations Aimed at Red Bloc," *New York Times,* 21 February 1972. Leopold Labedz, testifying before a Senate committee to comment on what he described as Fulbright's "semantic blackmail": "Looking at the voting record of the junior Senator from Arkansas on the Negro rights, I wonder why nobody refers to him as a 'relic of the Second Zulu War.'" See US Congress, *Negotiation and Statecraft Hearings, Ninety-Third Congress, First Session. Pursuant to Section 4, Senate Resolution 46, 93d Congress [and Section 4, Senate Resolution 49, 94th Congress]* (Washington, DC: US Government Printing Office, 1973), p. 66.

58. John Finney, "Kleindienst Says Buckley Can Show U.S.I.A.'s Film," *New York Times,* 1 April 1972. In 1953, both the US Advisory Commission on Information and

the president's Jackson Committee recommended removing the "by request" language from the Smith-Mundt Act, which was the real barrier to domestic access to the State Department and USIA. This was reiterated in a 1967 hearing in which the chairman of the US Advisory Commission on Information reemphasized the recommendation to Fulbright, which the senator rejected.

59. John Finney, "Vote in Senate Gives Fulbright Another in a Series of Rebuffs," *New York Times*, 26 May 1972.

60. The original "by request" language in the Smith-Mundt Act was to keep costs down. Congress was initially interested in the State Department making all of its foreign language programs authorized under what would be the Smith-Mundt Act immediately available in English to facilitate oversight by the Congress, the press, and the public. When told by the department this would require substantial additional staff for translation and filing, in addition to additional facilities for storage, Congress determined "by request" would be an adequate solution. The language was thus never intended to prohibit access to the material.

61. *Essential Info., Inc. v. USIA*, 134 F.3d 1165, 1168 (D.C. Cir. 1998).

62. See S. 2943, sec. 1287—National Defense Authorization Act for Fiscal Year 2017. The Global Engagement Center (GEC) was already operational under Executive Order 13721 signed by President Barack Obama. An Executive Order can be ended by the president at any time; legislation has its own sunset or requires an act of Congress to end any authorized activities.

63. John Boardman Whitton and Princeton University, *Propaganda and the Cold War; a Princeton University Symposium* (Washington, DC: Public Affairs Press, 1963), p. 55.

64. Senator Karl Mundt, "The Freedom Academy and Foreign Aid," *Congressional Record* 109, no. 16 (8 November 1963): 20413.

8

The Politics of
Information Warfare in Russia

Radomir Bolgov

In Russia today, information warfare and information security
are topics in demand. More than 5,000 articles on "information security"–
related topics are already in the bibliometric database Russian Scientific
Citation Index, and the publication activity continues to grow. To clarify
the thematic focus of the articles, we analyzed the dynamics of publication activity broken down into two periods: 2000–2008 and 2009–
2016. On average, the number of published articles in the second period
is more than three times higher than those in 2000–2008. This indicates
an increase of interest by the Russian academic community, with many
of these publications focusing on the legal aspects of information security.[1] Thus, Roger Hurwitz considers the efforts of states to create legal
norms in the field of cybersecurity. In addition, some authors present
their ideas from the perspective of practitioners.[2]

Several areas within the framework of this subject are worth high-
lighting:

- Theoretical aspects of information security;[3]
- Activities of international organizations in the provision of infor-
mation security;[4]
- Russia's position on this issue;[5]
- Russia's activities in ensuring information security in the frame-
work of international organizations.[6]

Nevertheless, there is no consensus in the Russian academic community on key issues of the subject: What is information warfare? How
has information technology (IT) changed the nature of warfare? What

is the future of information warfare? In this chapter, I provide an overview of the approaches to information warfare in the Russian political and expert community. I analyze the legal and doctrinal framework of information warfare policy in Russia, including the Doctrine of Information Security, Military Doctrine, National Weapons Program, and a set of federal laws, as well as cybersecurity strategy drafts and principles of state policy of the Russian Federation in the field of international information security until 2020. I also consider the government authorities, security agencies, and so forth. This study would be incomplete without an understanding of the enforcement and implementation of the information warfare laws and programs. I analyze the practical activity of actors in charge of information warfare policy in Russia, especially the Russian military, and discuss the international aspects of the Russian information security policy to draw conclusions for designing future works.

Key Terms and Concepts

Information security can be defined as the state of society, which provides reliable and comprehensive security of individuals, society, and government in the information space from the impact of a special type of threat acting in the form of organized or spontaneously emerging information and communication flows. The components of information security are:

1. Security of the information domain, which ensures its formation and development in the interests of citizens, organizations, and the state;
2. Security of information infrastructure, in which information is used strictly for its intended purpose and does not adversely affect the system (object) when it is used;
3. Security of information per se, in which the violation of its properties (e.g., confidentiality, integrity, accessibility) is excluded or significantly hampered.

The UN defines *international information security* as the state of international relations, excluding the violation of world stability and creating a threat to the states' security and the world community in the information domain.[7] In accordance with the Russian Doctrine of Information Security (2000), *information security* is the security of national interests in the information sphere. National interests in the information sphere are determined by a combination of balanced interests of the individual (constitutional human and citizen rights to access to information), society (strengthening democracy, creating a legal social state, achieving and maintaining public harmony), and the government (creating conditions for the development of information infrastructure, ensuring the inviolability of the constitutional order, ensuring sovereignty and territorial integrity, ensuring law and order, etc.).[8] However, there are differences in approaches to the definition of information security. In Russian legislation, the concept of *information security* is reduced to "the security of the information environment of society."[9] In foreign doctrines and strategies (particularly those of the United States), *information security* implies not only a protection of the information environment, but the ability of a network or system to withstand the required level of reliability of accidents or malicious acts that can disrupt accessibility, integrity, and confidentiality of stored and transmitted information.[10]

Scientific research and open discussions on these issues have led in recent years to a significant part of the work being split into two main poles. Representatives of the first pole (technological), such as Richard Hundley and Robert Anderson, discuss in their works the problems of information warfare and information protection in computers and networks.[11] The representatives of the second pole (in particular, Joseph Nye and William Owens) focus on the political and ideological context of the ongoing informatization processes. Information strategy is viewed as a way of expressing the soft power of ideals to spread its influence on the leadership and the population of foreign countries.[12] Moreover, it is worth noting that these two approaches to information security, are conventionally called "realistic" and "liberal."

The realistic approach focuses on:

1. Increasing the level of security of information systems within the country;
2. Creating a large number of internal networks, independent of each other and from global networks;
3. Regular monitoring of the level of information security of potential opponents as well as a targeted search for vulnerabilities in their software;
4. Control over the dissemination of information and related technologies;
5. Development of means of conducting information warfare;

6. Reducing the interdependence and openness of foes in the information sphere.

The realistic approach, in fact, reflects the modern policy of ensuring information security, conducted in China, the United States, and, to some extent, Russia. The concepts of "information superiority" and "information deterrence" accepted in the United States are a clear illustration of the application of such an approach.

The liberal approach is more idealistic, and can be reduced to the following: (1) increasing the interdependence of states in the information sphere; (2) ensuring general security through the creation of a network of international structures and treaties; and (3) liberalization of information relations and the information market.[13] This concept assumes that relations between states should be built primarily through mutual trust and strict adherence to concluded treaties. A priori, it is expected to reduce restrictions on the dissemination of information. The liberal approach can also include the adoption of international agreements on the problems of information security (e.g., the Okinawa Charter of Global Information Society).

As for *information warfare,* the term was entered into circulation in the academic and expert community in the mid-1980s in connection with new tasks of the US armed forces after the end of the Cold War. Later, the wave of interest in information warfare was related to Operation Desert Storm in 1991 in Iraq, where new information and communication technology (ICT) was widely used for military purposes; there is currently no definition of this term in international law. Various security agencies in their policy papers emphasize the military-political aspect of this concept.

Information Warfare Studies in Russia

Research on the Information Revolution's impact on the military began in the Russian expert and academic community in the late 1990s. There were objective reasons for that; after the collapse of the USSR, Russia has been inferior to the US in conventional weapons and information superiority. The concept of "information dominance" implied asymmetric threats to the enemy, where information technology was designed as an efficiency multiplier. In addition, some authors (e.g., Vladimir Slipchenko) treated these concepts in terms of opportunities to go beyond the conventional battlefield. That is, being behind a potential enemy in conventional weapons, one can negate its superiority through the creation of asymmetric threats, including information threats. In Russia, the discussion of these issues was pictured to the fullest extent in journals such as *Military Thought, Independent Military Review, Foreign Military Review, International Trends, Information Wars,* and in the publications of such think tanks as the Russian Institute of Strategic Studies and the PIR Center. While a large number of publications on the subject is the characteristic phenomenon for the initial stage of any discourse, research on this subject can be divided into two large groups. The first group includes works that recognize the fundamental transformation of the nature of war.[14] The second group consists of works that also recognize the influence of the Information Revolution and its influence on the characteristics of conflict, but not on the essence of the conflict, its motivations, and its means, which remain unchangeable.[15] The early period of study of this problem in the Russian academic, military, and political communities is also characterized by an isolated consideration of the different aspects (computer, organizational, psychological, etc.). Discussions are focused on the following issues related to the revolution in military affairs and the Information Revolution:

1. Changing the nature of war. Here, questions raised include: Is it possible to consider war a continuation of politics today? Or, do politics and war not correlate anymore? Or, do changes affect only certain aspects of military affairs (control of the armed forces, electronic warfare)?
2. The problem of the role and effectiveness of information technology in conflicts. Researchers are trying to answer questions such as: What is the role of IT in conflicts? How can IT be used effectively and in what areas? What are the conflicts categorized as: only armed conflict or political, social, ideological? How can the effectiveness of information technologies in armed conflicts be assessed: In terms of increasing the number of casualties and the destruction of the enemy's infrastructure, or, on the contrary, from the point of view of "sterilization" of the war—that is, to achieve victory provided by new technologies in bloodless "humane" war with a minimum of casualties from the enemy?

An attempt to answer this set of questions ultimately leads to several additional questions concerning the transformation of the nature of war. That is, is it correct to consider the information war and information weapons in the framework of traditional military science? Is the information war a war? Is the use of the term *information war* correct? A negative answer to this question is possible in two situations. The first is that the nature of war is not changed (i.e., use of the term *information war* is incorrect); the information war is not a war but rather wordplay. The second is a more interesting situation: it is understood that the nature of war is changing, but the use of the term *information war* is still incorrect because it does not reflect a fundamental change in the nature of conflict. Information war is not a war in the traditional sense and, therefore, we need a new specific conceptual apparatus. A positive answer to the question of the correct use of the term *information war* also leads to two situations. First, the term adequately reflects the fundamental transformation of the essence of war, underlining that information not only supports a military action, but it creates an opportunity to conduct a separate information war, which is apart from the armed conflict. Second, the nature of the conflict is not changed, and the use of the term is possible, but only based on traditional military science. This term may be used only for the informational and psychological support of military action.

3. Terminological and methodological problems. This deals with the question: What terms can be adequately studied to identify the phenomenon? How justifiable is borrowing the military terminology from other fields of knowledge (in particular, the term *information technology*), as well as the crossing of categories of military science (war, warfare, weapon) with the epithet "information"? What kind of methodological basis can be carried out in this area, at the junction of military, political, and social sciences? We must consider the impact *on* information or impact *with* information (the problem of objects and subjects).

4. Recognition of the possibility of further changes. If the modern conflict is transformed under the influence of the revolution in military affairs and the Information Revolution, then how long will these changes continue? Where is the ultimate development of a point (if it exists)? Are these changes reversible? Is it possible to return to what it was before? If changing the nature of war is not recognized, can changes come in the future? A number of scholars agree that the war ceases to be the continuation of the policy. Some researchers go further and agree that the war is no longer a political tool that would allow us to achieve a victory in the fight between the two states. Thus, Sergey Konopatov and Vladimir Yudin believe that modern war is a substantially new

phenomenon, and discuss the need to revise and clarify these concepts as well as to conduct interdisciplinary research. New wars, according to these authors, have a "velvet" hidden nature, as they are more violent, more intense and more "fast."[16]

However, a large part of the Russian military community does not consider modern warfare as a qualitatively new phenomenon. Thus, Oleg Kalinovsky says that, indeed, today the information component in the military is becoming more significant. An information struggle does not fit within the scope of military terminology and, therefore, requires the development of its concepts.[17] However, causes of the Soviet collapse do not lie in the information dimension, and the information war cannot be called "war" because it is not comparable to the "hot" war on the scale of impact on the nation and society. Therefore, a more suitable term is *information warfare*. In addition to the difference in scale, there are also legal differences of information war from the hot war because information war is not declared, does not lead to a peace treaty, and does not require the imposition of martial law. However, if we focus on the development of cheaper and more fashionable information weapons, we can fail to address the main challenges of national security. Yurii Gorbachev believes that the new concept of military development—in particular, the concept of network-centric warfare (NCW)—reflects the new way to control the military, but does not change the system of views on the war and the war per se.[18] However, Gorbachev believes that in the future changes in the forms of military organization may lead to the transformation of the nature of war as a whole. Information technology itself is unlikely to lead to any changes in the military-political sphere. One can cite the example of the situation during World War I, when there also were numerous technological innovations (radio, telephone, tank, airplane), but the nature of war did not change. Obviously, the need for the transformation of the war is not just a technological revolution, but also political, social, cultural, and moral change. Oleg Belkov believes that war is inseparable from the physical armed violence by the state. Any other meanings of *war* are only a metaphor ("chicken war," "war on corruption," etc.).[19] Vladimir Orlyansky considers unreasonable compound categories of military science (war, warfare, weapons) with the epithet "information." However, in this case, it seems an unreasonable borrowing of terms by military science, as it may further confuse the situation with terminology. As Orlyansky writes, psychological warfare (i.e., propaganda) should be separated from information warfare. Psychological warfare, unlike information, is directly related to the armed struggle.[20] In this approach, simplification of the term *information* is clear. The refusal of the complexity of the information warfare concept, dominating today in Russian military thought, is due to the fact that in the process of military training, such a complex understanding can "unleash the fog" in the education of officers. On the issue of the effectiveness of new information weapons, points of view differ among Russian researchers. Orlyansky believes that the effectiveness of such weapons is low. Information does not exist without a material carrier. It still cannot influence a person as effectively as conventional weapons.[21]

Legal and Doctrinal Framework

Currently, Russia has more than 40 federal laws in the field of information, more than 80 presidential acts, and about 200 government acts. However, Russia does not yet have a separate information warfare strategy in the form of a policy paper. One of the key papers in this field is the Doctrine of Information Security, the first version of which was adopted in 2000. A new version was only adopted in December 2016. The adoption of this doctrine was preceded by a series of events throughout the 1990s. Until the 2000s, Russia had practically no clear government attitude toward the problem of information security. Unlike the US approach, in the Russian doctrine the provision of information security for individual, group, and public consciousness is in the forefront. Today, a set of agencies is engaged in the development of the national idea of information warfare; particularly, the Ministry of Defence, FSB, and Department "K" of the Interior Ministry, which is investigating crimes in the high-tech field of information technology.

At the beginning of the 1990s, the situation with information security in Russia was quite difficult. On the one hand, the liberal media was constantly criticizing information security per se, using the analogy of the Orwellian "Big Brother." On the other, some politicians and experts began to adhere to the obscurantist positions, believing that ensuring Russia's national interests in the information space requires the rejection of an open society and participation in globalization. Two stages prior to the adoption of Doctrine of Information Security can be identified:

The first is 1991–1996: the formation of the prerequisites and the legal framework. During this period, the federal law On Information, Informatisation and Information Protection (1995) and a number of other laws were adopted. The accumulation of the positive experiences of cooperation with Russian participation in the international arena was associated with the acquisition of a new identity as a participant in international relations and media interest in the information domain. This period is characterized by discord in the role and place of Russia in estimates in the information domain, noticeable in the statements of different political parties, institutions, and interest groups. The utopian idea of Russia's long-term inclusion in the global information space dominated. It has been challenged by the need to protect Russia's information resources from the technological point of view and as a form of national identity (traditions, customs, and mentality).

The second is 1996–2000: the formation of agencies to ensure information security. During this period, an interdepartmental commission for information security was formed as part of the Security Council with the participation of the Ministry of Internal Affairs, Federal Security Service, and others. Through the activities of these agencies, a draft Doctrine of Information Security was prepared in 1997. However, the power vacuum and intensification of the contradictions within the ruling elites did not allow for acceptance of the doctrine. The financial and economic crisis in 1998 also delayed its adoption. The doctrine was finally approved in 2000; it is a set of official views on the goals, objectives, principles, and main directions of ensuring information security of the Russian Federation. It serves as a basis for the formation of government policy in the realm of national information security; the preparation of proposals to improve the legal, methodological, technical, and organizational sides of Russian information security; and the development of targeted programs to ensure information security. The Doctrine of Information Security is considered that of national interests in the information sphere, determined by a combination of balanced interests of the individual, society, and government. The doctrine spelled out the threats, sources of threats to the national interests, as well as the ways of international cooperation in the field of information security. It allocated four types of threats: (1) threats to constitutional order and human rights in the information sphere; (2) threats to information security policy of the government; (3) threats to development of the domestic IT industry; and (4) threats to security of information systems and networks. However, since 2000 there have been many changes. The appearance of Web 2.0 and social media dramatically changed national security, as demonstrated by the protests in the Arab countries in 2011 (the so-called Twitter revolutions). In addition, the appearance of new phenomena, such as smartphones, the Internet of Things, smart city, cryptocurrency, and blockchain technology, have also forced a rethink of cybersecurity. Sanctions against Russia led to a policy of localization of the IT industry.

New policy papers have been prepared that are related to the development of information technologies in Russia. The new version of the Doctrine of Information Security adopted in 2016 was an attempt to better reflect the changes that had occurred in the past sixteen years. The new doctrine paid greater attention to the use of computer technology to influence Russia's critical infrastructure. In addition, there is a component associated with the risks of using social media to influence public opinion. These are risks not only of extremist and criminal content, but in general any content that represents a threat to political and social stability. As for *information warfare,* this term was mentioned twice in the doctrine of 2000. The doctrine of 2016 does not contain any mention of the term.[22] Russia's intention to develop a code of conduct in the field of international information security under the auspices of the UN is reflected in the Russian Foreign Policy Concept.[23] In addition, as one of the directions to counter threats in the information sphere, the policy paper "Fundamentals of the Russian Federation's State Policy in the Field of International Information Security for the Period Up to 2020" calls for "the promotion of preparation and adoption of the UN international regulations governing the application of the principles and norms of international humanitarian law in the field of ICT usage."[24]

Information Warfare in the Russian Military

So far, Russia has no separate strategy for military information and technological modernization in policy. The cyber modernization of the Russian military is not moving fast. The main objective of the IT application in military affairs is to provide combat capability for alertness, quick communication, and interaction between troops; personnel training; and effective control systems, operational management, communications, surveillance, reconnaissance, and so forth. According to some researchers, not all of this will be implemented over the next ten years.[25] In practice, this resulted in the focus of Russian military and political leaders on old military equipment and conventional military force during the conflict in South Ossetia and Georgia in August 2008. It showed a certain efficiency but, at the same time, problems with interactions between military units were revealed during this conflict. This was largely due to the inadequate provision of communications and outdated equipment, especially on a tactical level.[26] After the conflict, then president Dmitry Medvedev set a task to the Ministry of Defence to establish a training center fitted with equipment for information warfare.[27] *Information warfare* is defined here as propaganda to influence public opinion, psychological operations, and so forth. In September 2008, Defence Minister Anatoly Serdyukov presented the president with an action plan for a new image of the Russian armed forces. However, optimization did not provide additional funding, leading to a limited reduction in the number of officers while increasing the number of soldiers. Technological modernization in these conditions has received little attention. However, the situation changed in 2010 with the adoption of a new Military Doctrine and a discussion of the draft of a National Weapons Program for 2011–2020. High-precision weapons and command and control (C2) systems were in second and third place, respectively (after nuclear weapons), in the list of the draft's priorities.[28] Attempts were made to reduce the gap from the leading countries of the West in unmanned aerial vehicles (UAVs) and individual ammunition.

In accordance with the new Military Doctrine of the Russian Federation (2014), among the characteristic features of modern military conflicts were strengthening of the role of information warfare without the use of military force to achieve political goals, the transition from a strictly vertical system for automated control on troops and weapons, and the massive use of weapons systems and military equipment based on new physical principles. One of the main weapons problems was "the development of forces and means of information warfare . . . the creation of new high-precision weapons, . . . C2 information systems, . . . qualitative improvement of the means of information exchange through the use of modern technologies and international standards, as well as a joined information field of the Armed Forces and other troops of the Russian Federation as part of the information domain."[29] At a special meeting in Voronezh in early 2010, then prime minister Vladimir Putin called for the creation of a joined C2 system for troops. An order for the development of such system was signed in 2000, but nobody was appointed to be responsible for the project. The Scientific Research Institute of Communications (the part of "Sozvezdiye" consortium) was in charge of the project. This project is not the first; even in 1983, the C2 system "Maneuver" was adopted. As a result of the simulation exercise with the use of this algorithm, the simulated Warsaw Pact army defeated NATO in three days. After the collapse of the USSR, the algorithm of "Maneuver" became known to the US armed forces.[30] However, in 2009 the Taman Brigade held exercises with the test of a joint tactical control system. During the exercise, about 140 failures were found. The main technical problem was the insufficient development of the foundations of the Global Navigation Satellite System

(GLONASS), a comprehensive constellation of satellites, which at the time included only seventeen units.[31]

The Russian president tasked the Defence Ministry to digitize military C2 systems. In this aspect, the ministry was working with business; the Zelax company participated in the execution of orders for the digitization of the communications structures in the navy. There are projects for introduction of nanotechnology in military information and communication systems. The comprehensive program "Nanoelectronics 2010" provides for the establishment of molecular transistors and transistors on carbon nanotubes. At the same time, a problematic point is the parallel development and lack of cooperation between the enterprises that produce telecommunications equipment for the army. Especially worrisome is the need for development and production of electronic components for the Russian defense industry. Today, more than 60 percent of the electronic components Russia uses are manufactured abroad. From 1990 on, one of the main topics for discussion in the Russian security structures has been the issue of potentially harmful hardware and software from abroad. This issue is still open, despite the fact that the Russian government reached an agreement with Microsoft to open a Windows operating system code for Russian authorities. However, Smirnov and Zhitnyuk believe that, in case of a potential conflict with NATO, Russia should be prepared for the fact that "the cellular communications will suddenly stop working."[32] This problem is not unique to Russia; even the United States could become a potential victim of "bookmarks." Today, there is not a fully government-controlled cycle of IT production, so information systems are designed on the basis of Chinese or Taiwanese hardware.[33]

After the military operations in August 2008 in South Ossetia and Georgia, from time to time the media have reported about the Defence Ministry's intentions to create informational troops, whose functions should include all aspects of information warfare: from psychological operations and propaganda (including the Internet) to security of computer networks and cyberattacks on the enemy's information systems.[34] It should be noted that the formation of a special kind of troops seems to be inappropriate for propaganda. It is worth leaving this for security services and business, if they interact intelligently. As Aleksey Smirnov and Pavel Zhitnyuk believe, the technical aspects of cybersecurity are under monopoly of the Federal Security Service (FSB) since all structures are obliged to use means of information protection that are certified by the FSB.[35] At the same time, it would be advisable to create a joint regulatory authority in this field on the basis of representation of various departments. The Chinese experience is an interesting one to consider, where the government interacts with business more actively than Russia.

International Aspects of Russian Information Security Policy

The use of information weapons is regulated by the following treaties: Malaga-Torremolinos International Telecommunication Convention (1973) and International Maritime Satellite Agreement (INMARSAT) (1976), adopted under the auspices of the specialized agencies of the United Nations, respectively, the International Telecommunication Union and the International Maritime Organization. Article 35 of the International Telecommunication Convention defines that all stations, regardless of their purpose, must be installed and managed so as not to harm radio services or communications of other members. As such, the convention prohibits the use of a satellite station for destruction of or collision with communications of other states. Yet Article 38 agrees that states retain complete freedom with regard to the military radio stations of their army, naval, and air forces.[36] Thus, the convention recognizes that it is possible to use the satellite system for military purposes; however, most of the military information flows of developed countries pass through civilian communication systems. Therefore, in this convention there is a contradiction between Articles 35 and 38, which is just one example to illustrate the weak development of international law on information security.

Russia has consistently emphasized the legal regulation of cybersecurity issues at the national level; especially in recent years, if we consider the number of adopted policy papers. This adheres to the same approach at the international level: cybersecurity issues need to be regulated, as soon and as detailed as possible. Russia has adhered to this approach for fifteen years, offering its projects within the UN (in particular, the proposal to establish a special international court for cybercrimes). Russia was supported by China, India, and Brazil, but this approach countered the position of the United States, European Union (EU), and Japan, who believed that cybersecurity issues need not be overregulated in bias against the freedoms of citizens and business. They proceeded from the priority of developing information security measures with regard to terrorist and criminal threats. At the same time, the threat of creating information weapons and the emergence of information warfare was viewed more as a theoretical one. Accordingly, the disarmament aspect of the problem of international information security also came to naught. Further discussion of this problem was proposed to be divided into regional and thematic forums such as the EU and Group of 7 (G7). The representatives of this approach have offered to move the discussion within the UN from the military-political dimension to legal and economic ones. They believe that the issue of international legal regulation of the military and political aspects of information security has not yet been relevant. It seems necessary to first accumulate sufficient practical experience in regulating such problems.[37]

These approaches were manifested in the discussion on the Okinawa Charter of Global Information Society (2000). During the fifty-third session of the UN General Assembly, Russia put forward a draft resolution on *Developments in the Field of Information and Telecommunications in the Context of International Security,* adopted by consensus in 1998.[38] Another success, but a later one, is the UN General Assembly resolution *Creation of Global Culture of Cybersecurity and Taking Stock of National Efforts to Protect Critical Information Infrastructure.*[39] Some convergence of positions on these issues emerged at Munich Security Conference in February 2011, where most politicians and experts spoke in favor of the need for international legal regulation of cyberspace. Although no specific binding decisions were made, a joint Russian-US report entitled *Working Towards Rules for Governing Cyber Conflict: Rendering the Geneva and Hague Conventions in Cyberspace* was prepared. The report points out the following problematic issues, for which the United States and Russia still do not have a common position, but on which the parties undertake to agree: it is possible to legislatively and technically "isolate" protected infrastructure from the "cloud" of unprotected objects in cyberspace in the way that civil facilities are protected by international agreements during war. In addition, the parties must decide whether cyberweapons (viruses, worms, etc.) are similar to weapons banned by the Geneva Protocol (e.g., poisonous gases). The conference also agreed to develop an international convention on cyberwar and establish an international tribunal on crimes in cyberspace. The parties will have to resolve these issues within these structures.[40] Russia's failure to conduct initiatives on cybersecurity through the UN (since 1998) spurred it to include these issues on the agenda of the Shanghai Cooperation Organization (SCO). Since 2011, China and Kazakhstan have also viewed this organization as a tool for cyberspace monitoring. During the Russian presidency of the SCO in

2014, information security was one of the priorities of the agenda that Russia defined in this organization. Among the main projects and initiatives on cybersecurity within the framework of the SCO, the following are worth mentioning:

- Discussion of strengthening of state control over the Internet as a consequence of protests in Arab countries.
- The creation of cyberpolicy (in 2011, this initiative was not implemented).
- Strengthening of cooperation on Internet security.
- Fighting the financing of terrorism through the Internet.
- Drafting a Code of Conduct in the field of international information security (in the letter of the SCO to the UN on 12 September 2011).

Another format for promoting Russia's interests in cybersecurity is Brazil, Russia, India, China, and South Africa (BRICS). Within the framework of this informal organization, the fight against cyber threats is called one of the four spheres of perspective cooperation. Ideas for the creation of a BRICS cyber threat center as well as a hotline for informing and warning about cyberincidents have been discussed.

Conclusion

The discussion of the prospects for the aforementioned cyber command in Russia has shown that the establishment of this agency would face not only objective difficulties such as lack of funding. The cyber command was planned to be formed according to the US model, which has not yet been created. The troops of information operations were established in 2014, but their formation was forced and not always rationalized. According to the media, formation of the troops was completed in February 2017. As for future works, it is worth elaborating on a list of criteria for information warfare effectiveness assessments: herewith it is necessary to differ between assessment of information warfare per se and information warfare policy effectiveness. The existing indexes or rankings of information warfare potential do not consider the aforementioned difference. Concerning the differences in the approaches of Russia and the West to the information war, we should consider more than the different level of openness for innovations in such a conservative sphere as the military one. This means that Russian experts should not focus only on information and psychological aspects; US experts consider the whole spectrum of this concept, including technical aspects. Furthermore, the department that drives information security (the Air Force in the United States vs. the FSB in Russia) matters.

Israeli author Dima Adamsky offers an interesting point of view; he conducted a comparative analysis of the latest military concepts of some of the world's most powerful countries militarily (the United States, Russia, and Israel). The starting point of Adamsky's theorizing is that cultural factors affect the military capabilities of leading powers, especially in the context of the Information Revolution. The military and political leaders of each state have their own cultural patterns that determine the views and the policy resulting from them in the field of military technology. Adamsky defines them with the term "cognitive style."[41] This is not so much about the national style of developing some military equipment as much as the mechanisms for circulating military information and control algorithms which, of course, in each country have their own specifics. This factor plays a key role in the fact that the concepts of modernization of the armed forces in Russia, the United States, and Israel are very different from each other. The style of knowledge is determined by a number of factors: geographical, historical, economic, and even religious and psychological. The military and political leaders of Protestant America are more open to innovation in such a conservative sphere as the military one. However, Adamsky notes that the pioneer in the sphere of the "military and technical revolution" was nevertheless the Soviet military, led by Marshal N. Ogarkov, and this was due to the prevailing technocratic approach in the USSR in the 1960s to 1970s including, inter alia, the active engagement of cybernetics into the national economy. Adamsky believes that this concept emerged as a reaction to the development of NATO doctrines of a deep blow to the advancing echelons of the Soviet troops in the case of war in Europe.[42] In practice, not all of Ogarkov's ideas were implemented in the USSR. Adamsky explains this by the prevalence in Russian culture of a holistic cognitive style aimed at creating a coherent picture, sometimes even at the expense of technical details.[43] In US culture, the logical and analytical cognitive style is dominant, emphasizing certain details and practical activities. Therefore, the development of information systems and high-precision weapons already took place in the United States in the 1970s to 1980s, but original theoretical developments appeared only in the 1990s (i.e., ten years later than in the USSR). However, it is worth noting that, according to the Soviet military newspaper *Krasnaya Zvezda* (Red Star), there were prototypes of the first UAVs in the USSR already in the early 1980s.[44] Thus, there is no need to overemphasize the cultural differences that affect the information warfare policy, and there are a number of common problems for all states implementing the information warfare. Technical aspects of ICT are almost the same everywhere because the connection of parts in telecommunication networks does not depend on the cognitive style. A number of armies have similar mechanisms for circulating information. Therefore, the cognitive style cannot be unequivocally regarded as something characteristic of the entire national or regional culture.

Notes

1. For example, Roger Hurwitz, "The Play of States: Security and Norms in Cyberspace," *American Foreign Policy Interests* 36, no. 5 (2014): 322–331; Tim Maurer, *Cyber Norm Emergence at the United Nations: An Analysis of the UN Activities Regarding the Cybersecurity* (Cambridge, MA: Harvard Kennedy School's Belfer Center for Science and International Affairs, 2011).

2. For example, Sergey Boiko, "Gruppa pravitelstvennyh ekspertov OON po dostizheniyam v sfere informatizatsii i telekommunikacii v kontekste mezhdunarodnoyj bezopasnosti: Vzglyad iz proshlogo v budushcheye" [UN Group of Governmental Experts on Developments in the Field of Information and Telecommunications in the Context of International Security: A View from the Past to the Future], *Mezhdunarodnaya zhizn*, no. 8 (2016): 53–71; Angela Kane, "The Rocky Road to Consensus: The Work of UN Groups of Governmental Experts in the Field of ICTs in the Context of International Security, 1998–2013," *American Foreign Policy Interests* 36, no. 5 (2014): 314–321.

3. For example, Radomir Bolgov, "Informacionnye tekhnologii v sovremennyh vooruzhennyh konfliktah i voennyh strategiyah (politicheskiye aspekty)" [Information Technology in Contemporary Armed Conflicts and Military Strategies (Political Aspects)] (PhD diss., Saint Petersburg State University, 2011); Sergey Komov, ed., *Mezhdunarodnaya informacionnaya bezopasnost: Diplomatiya mira* [International Information Security: Peace Diplomacy] (Moscow: Voeninform, 2009).

4. For example, Irma Kvantaliani, "Rol' mezhdunarodnyh organizaciy v dele obespecheniya bezopasnosti informacionnogo prostranstva" [The Role of International Organizations in the Security of Information Domain], in *Aktualnye problemy sovremennogo mezhdunarodnogo prava* [The Actual Problems of Contemporary International Law], ed. Aslan Abashidze and Ekaterina Kiseleva (Moscow: Peoples' Friendship University of Russia, 2012), pp. 26–30; Natalya Romashkina, "OON i mezhdunarodnaya informacionnaya bezopasnost" [The UN and International Information Security], in *Bezopasnost i kontrol nad vooruzheniyami 2015–2016: Mezhdunarodnoe vzaimodejstviye v borbe s globalnymi ugrozami* [Security and Arms Control 2015–2016: International Cooperation in Fighting Against Global Threats], ed. Alexey Arbatov and Natalia Bubnova (Moscow: IMEMO RAN; ROSSPE, 2016), pp. 273–286.

5. Elena Zinovieva, "Analiz vneshnepoliticheskih iniciativ RF v oblasti mezhdunarodnoy informacionnoy bezopasnosti" [An Analysis of Russia's Foreign Policy Initiatives in the Field of International Information Security], *Vestnik MGIMO-Universiteta*, no. 6 (2014): 47–52; Sergey Shirin, "Rossiyskie iniciativy po voprosam upravleniya Internetom" [Russian Initiatives on Internet Governance], *Vestnik MGIMO-Universiteta*, no. 6 (2014): 73–81; Oleg Demidov, "Obespecheniye mezhdunarodnoy informacionnoy bezopasnosti i rossiyskie nacionalnye

interesy" [Ensuring International Information Security and Russian National Interests], *Indeks Bezopasnosti,* no. 104 (2013): 129–168.

6. For example, E. Lobanova, "Nekotorye iniciativy RF v OON po resheniyu problemy mezhdunarodnoy informacionnoy bezopasnosti" [Some Russian Initiatives in the United Nations to Address the Issue of International Information Security], in *Globalizaciya i problema vojn v sovremennom mire* [Globalization and the Problem of War in the Contemporary World], ed. Victor Barabash (Moscow: Peoples' Friendship University of Russia, 2011), pp. 29–35; Boiko, "Gruppa pravitelstvennyh ekspertov OON."

7. UN General Assembly, *Report of the Human Rights Committee,* vol. 1 (New York: UN, 2000).

8. Presidential Decree, "The Doctrine of the Information Security of the Russian Federation," Moscow, 5 December 2016 (in Russian).

9. State Duma, "Federal Law N 2446-1: On Security," Moscow, 1992 (in Russian).

10. US Congress, "Federal Law N 107-347: The Federal Information Security Management Act of 2002," Washington, DC, 2002.

11. Richard Hundley and Robert Anderson, *Security in Cyberspace: An Emerging Challenge for Society* (Santa Monica: RAND, 1994).

12. Joseph Nye and William Owens, "America's Information Age," *Foreign Affairs* 75, no. 2 (1996): 20–36.

13. Radomir Bolgov, Natalya Vasil'eva, Svetlana Vinogradova, and Konstantin Pantzerev, *Informacionnoye obshchestvo i mezhdunarodnye otnosheniya* [Information Society and International Relations] (Saint Petersburg: Saint Petersburg State University, 2014).

14. For example, Aleksandr Dugin, "Mir ohvachen setevymi voynami" [The World Is in the Network War], *Nezavisimoe voennoe obozrenie,* no. 44 (2005): 453; Vladimir Slipchenko, *Voyny shestogo pokoleniya: Oruzhiye i voennoye iskusstvo budushchego* [The Wars of the Sixth Generation: Weapons and Military Art of the Future] (Moscow: Veche, 2002).

15. Makhmut Gareev, "O nekotoryh harakternyh chertah voyn budushchego" [Some Characteristics of Future Wars], *Voennaya mysl,* no. 6 (2003): 53; Vladimir Orlyansky, "Informatsionnoe oruzhiye i informatsionnaya borba: Realnost i domysly" [Information Weapons and Information Warfare: Reality and Fiction], *Voennaya mysl,* no. 1 (2008): 62–70.

16. Sergey Konopatov and Vladimir Yudin, "Traditsionnyj smysl ponyatiya 'voyna' ustarel" [The Traditional Meaning of the Concept of "War" Is Obsolete], *Voennaya mysl,* no. 1 (2001): 53–57.

17. Oleg Kalinovsky, "Informatsionnaya voyna—Eto voyna?" [Is Information War a War?], *Voennaya mysl,* no. 1 (2001): 57–58.

18. Yurii Gorbachev, "Setetsentricheskaya voyna: Mif ili realnost?" [Network-Centric Warfare: Myth or Reality?], *Voennaya mysl,* no. 1 (2006): 67.

19. Oleg Belkov, "Ponyatiye 'voyna' i yego aberratsii v otechestvennom diskurse" [Concept of "War" and Its Aberrations in Domestic Discourse], *Vlast',* no. 9 (2009): 6–7.

20. Orlyansky, "Informatsionnoe oruzhiye i informatsionnaya borba," p. 70.

21. Ibid., p. 64.

22. Presidential Decree, "The Doctrine of the Information Security of the Russian Federation," 5 December 2016.

23. Presidential Decree, "The Foreign Policy Concept of the Russian Federation," Moscow, 30 November 2016 (in Russian).

24. Presidential Decree, "Fundamentals of the Russian Federation's Policy in the Field of International Information Security for the Period Up to 2020," Moscow, 24 July 2013 (in Russian).

25. Valeri Maskin, "K voprosu o soderzhanii soedineniy i voinskih chastey v kategorii postoyannoy gotovnosti" [The Question of the Maintenance of Military Formations and Units in a Permanent Readiness], *Voennaya mysl,* no. 1 (2010): 26–30.

26. "Kak slyshno? Priem! Intervyu s E.R. Meichikom" [Do You Copy? Over! Interview with E.R. Meichik]," *Krasnaya Zvezda,* no. 190 (2008): 1.

27. "Minoborony RF podgotovit specialistov dlya vedeniya kibervoyny" [The Russian Defense Ministry Will Prepare Professionals for Conducting Cyberwar]," *IT Security,* 14 October 2009, www.itsec.ru/newstext.php?news_id=61879.

28. Vladimir Putin, *Statement at a Meeting on the Priorities of National Weapons Programme for 2011–2020,* Moscow, 17 February 2010, http://archive.premier.gov .ru/events/news/9426/.

29. Presidential Decree, "The Doctrine of the Information Security of the Russian Federation." Moscow, 25 December 2014 (in Russian).

30. Victor Myasnikov, "Putin natselil armiyu na Internet" [Putin Directed the Military Towards the Internet], *Nezavisimoye voennoye obozreniye,* 19 January 2010, www.ng.ru/nvo/2010-01-19/2_sozvezdie.html.

31. Ibid.

32. Aleksey Smirnov and Pavel Zhitnyuk, "Kiberugrozy realnyie i vyduman-nyie" [Cyber Threats, Real and Imaginary], *Rossiya v globalnoj politike,* no. 2 (2010): 190.

33. Ibid.

34. "Tsyganok: Sobytiya v Yuzhnoy Osetii sozdali neobhodimost informatsion-nyh voysk v armii RF" [Tsyganok: The Events in South Ossetia Have Created a Need for Information Troops in the Russian Military], *Kavkazskiy uzel,* 23 June 2009, www.kavkaz-uzel.ru/articles/155755.

35. Smirnov and Zhitnyuk, "Kiberugrozy realnyie," p. 190.

36. International Telecommunication Union (ITU), *International Telecommunication Convention,* Malaga-Torremolinos, 1973, www.itu.int/en/history/Pages/Con-stitutionAndConvention.aspx.

37. Alexander Fedorov and Vitali Tsygichko, eds., *Informatsionnye vyzovy nacionalnoy i mezhdunarodnoy bezopasnosti* [Information Challenges to National and International Security] (Moscow: PIR Center, 2001).

38. UN General Assembly, *Resolution A/RES/53/70—Developments in the Field of Information and Telecommunications in the Context of International Security,* New York, 4 December 1998, www.un.org/ru/documents/ods.asp?m=A/RES/53/70.

39. UN General Assembly, *Resolution A/RES/64/211—Creation of a Global Culture of Cybersecurity and Taking Stock of National Efforts to Protect Critical Information Infrastructures,* New York, 17 March 2010, www.un.org/ru/documents/ods .asp?m=A/RES/64/211.

40. Karl Frederick Rausche and Andrey Korotkov, *Working Towards Rules for Governing Cyber Conflict: Rendering the Geneva and Hague Conventions in Cyberspace* (New York: EastWest Institute, 2011).

41. Dima Adamsky, *The Culture of Military Innovation: The Impact of the Cultural Factors on the Revolution in Military Affairs in Russia, the US, and Israel* (Stanford: Stanford University Press, 2010), p. 9.

42. Ibid., p. 31.

43. Ibid., p. 41.

44. Nikolai Rogachevsky, "Letayuschiye roboty" [Flying Robots], *Krasnaya Zvezda,* no. 205 (1984): 3.

9

Using Information:
Methods and Cases from Russia

Oxana Timofeyeva

The concept of "exposure" has a complex structure and includes a number of other concepts such as influence, persuasion, suggestion, manipulation, and inculcation. All of these categories have semantic differences but, in the modern public discourse in Russia, they all often boil down to the notion of *information warfare* (IW). In this chapter, I explore the multitude of Russian views on the IW concept, as the most aggressive form of information exposure. Despite those evolved views, there still is no consolidated opinion on the definition of IW and there are reasons for ambiguous interpretation of the term. Some of the causes are general, but others are specific to Russia. This allows for some narrowing of the field of consideration and discussion, and greater simplification. At the same time, all of these increase the terminological chaos and obstruct the comparison of various studies for several reasons.

The first reason is that the terminology usage is time dependent, being influenced by internal and external contexts. For example, the Western term *information warfare* was strictly extraneous in the USSR while *ideological struggle* was a substitute bearing a close meaning. Without a homegrown theory, some Russian authors tend to reflect foreign research, speculating on the "true" nature of Western concepts. Those speculations are evolving, and definitions of IW are changing to reflect this evolution. The problem of a clear definition is getting worse due to the absence of translation standards. Terminology is often borrowed from different foreign sources. Therefore, terms and definitions used in Russian studies rarely resemble the Western understanding. Second, the understanding of IW in Russia has two dimensions, technological and social. The *technological* dimension is genuine for the security domain, steering to certain secrecies and limitations of academic discussions of the topic. Thus, most of the public discussions related to IW happen from the *social* standpoint. Yet security-related research papers seemingly operate with the same terminology implying radically different or complex meanings. Finally, the concept of IW is controversial because of its interdisciplinary nature; it covers a broad range of actions and objects. IW is studied by many sciences, where different approaches appear and can produce new definitions in each case.

Perhaps the biggest problem surrounding the discussion about the Russian dimension of information warfare is the different discourses that contain references to IW. For example, there is an official one presented in the Doctrine of Information Security. The problem, however, is that there are no mentions of IW in the 2016 version,[1] whereas it was used twice in 2000.[2] Instead of using the term *information warfare,* the new doctrine uses *information confrontation.* Another discourse is popular science; in this scope, there is a great amount of cited works, which are rather populist in their origins. Media discourse is closely connected with popular science, thus creating false ideas about the relevance and significance of the Russian practice for internal and external audiences. The perception of IW is also influenced by the conceptual (cognitive) metaphor "argument is war" introduced by George Lakoff and Mark Johnson.[3] Thus, the word *war* used in context of *information war* activates a huge complex of negative associations in the public mind. Such linguistic features indirectly affect the fact that, to determine the phenomenon of IW, a large number of different interpretations are used as opposed to a singular unambiguous definition. The discourse on IW is closely related to the discourse on information-psychological operations and methods exposure. In this chapter, I give a brief overview of the Russian media environment and some classifications of methods; in particular, I demonstrate several media cases of information-psychological operations. In the final part of the chapter, I discuss a controversial tool created by the Russian Institute for Strategic Studies (RISS) for monitoring the level of anti-Russian narratives in the media publications of different countries, and the escalation process from informational peace to informational war.

The Russian View on IW: Background and Origins

The concept of "psychological warfare," which can be designated as a precursor of IW, was studied in the Soviet period amid the Cold War.

Nikolay Zhiveynov wrote one of the most widely quoted works of the time. He analyzed the psychological warfare nature of the example of the US-USSR relations and claimed that it was based on the concept of "cold war," which he defines as "a type of inter-country relations, when they are aggressive and hostile towards each other yet still have no armed conflict."[4] He continues that in human history "peacetime" is just period of "no war"; thereby, "cold war" is a period of "armed truce." This, in turn, explains the continuous use of "war" in peacetime. Usage of such a forceful conceptual metaphor keeps the audience in constant tension, and psychologically prepares them for the beginning of the "armed war." Moreover, Zhiveynov describes different types of audiences by introducing two terms: "internal forefront" and "external forefront." The usage of the word *forefront* instead of *audience* amplifies Lakoff and Johnson's conceptual metaphor that argument is war. Zhiveynov defines the process of "public opinion formation" as "psychological operations" or "psychological actions," which in fact are based on methods of propaganda in wartime that are the responsibility of special forces. In the context of such an approach, there is an amalgamation of the concepts of information warfare and psychological warfare. To some extent, both are reduced to the struggle of ideologies. This idea was further developed by other authors during the last years of the USSR (e.g., Dmitry Volkogonov and Kirill Razlogov). Despite the fact that their works were aimed for different audiences (Volkogonov's book targeted specialists[5] and Razlogov's was intended for a general audience[6]), both considered psychological warfare as a system of subversive ideological influences of imperialism intended to change the social psychology of a foreign (hostile) audience. Over time, the focus of scientific consideration shifted from psychological warfare to IW. Nevertheless, the phenomenon of psychological warfare is still being investigated as an independent phenomenon. Within the psychological paradigm, IW is usually understood as an implicit impact on the audience, its social value orientations and attitudes.

After collapse of the USSR, many works appeared dealing with the phenomenon of IW as a reason for its disintegration. Most were intended for a mass audience and exploited different conspiracy theories. However, some set new research vectors. For example, Vladimir Lisichkin and Leonid Shelepin use a new conceptual metaphor of "Third World War," and describe with it information-psychological warfare.[7] In their opinion, a significant role in this confrontation is given to mass media, as a channel of impact communication; thus, IW is a direct consequence of the information (or postindustrial) society's emergence. Another basis is the consumer society. Lisichkin and Shelepin correlate methods of informational warfare and methods of advertising, stressing that these have a lot in common. Another approach to the definition of IW began to form in the late 1990s. It is based on representations of society as a system; the pioneer of this approach is Sergey Rastorguyev. A key component of his theory is an "information self-learning system" that assumes an object of IW as "man, state, humanity."[8] Every system has its own definite structure and makes decisions guided by its need to evolve, when emotions serve as a criterion of truth. However, Rastorguyev later extends the concept of "information self-learning system," splitting the technological level as "computer systems" and the biological level as "living being" or social space. Though IW involves both, this distinction allows for making an easy explanation of IW: "[IW] is an explicit and implicit interaction through information between different systems in order to obtain a certain benefit in the material sphere. Information impact is carried out using information weapons, i.e., such means that allow carrying out the intended actions with transmitted, processed, generated, destroyed, and perceived information."[9]

Vladimir Tsyganov and Sergey Bukharin use a rather closed notion of "self-organising system" as a key term in their research, and interpret IW as a type of crisis by focusing on different instruments of management, which can help to resolve critical situations in socioeconomical systems.[10] They assert that IW is "a dynamic process that takes place in a complex self-organising system with a large number of elements. The nature of communication between elements of such a system is not deterministic, but probabilistic."[11] IW, they argue, can start if one system component outstrips the development of the rest, leading to the system's transformation or extinction.

The strongest and most vocal approach to IW in Russian discourse is "geopolitical," with its two most prominent authors Igor Panarin and Aleksandr Dugin. Some foreign researchers even write about "geopolitical schools" named after Panarin and Dugin and describe both as "mentors of the young generations of geopoliticians."[12] Such mentions, in fact, seem to show a lack of understanding of the Russian authors' relevance for the Russian discourse. In the early 2000s, Panarin defined "IW" as a "way to create an information flow management system in order to organise the noosphere of the global information and psychological space to one's own interests."[13] He also uses the construct of "geopolitical information confrontation," which is "one of the modern forms of struggle between states, as well as a system of measures carried out by one state with the aim of violating the information security of another, and at the same time protecting itself against similar actions of the opponent."[14] Panarin's geopolitical information confrontation can be divided into "information-technical" and "information-psychological," an argument that resembles Rastorguyev's distinction between technical and biological levels. About ten years later, Panarin focused his research on the so-called color revolutions in the former Soviet republics and countries of North Africa and Middle East as a part of the US global IW strategy against Russia. Importantly, the ideas of color revolutions prove themselves to be quite popular in Russia's public and media spaces, and Panarin supports this tendency by arguing that the Snow Revolution[15] in Russia was a classic example of "information-psychological operation."[16] In his opinion, the protests at Bolotnaya Square in Moscow[17] were just a part of the Western information-psychological operation code-named "Anti-Putin." Panarin argues that "we should note that methods and techniques (falsehood and disinformation) of 'Anti-Putin' were basically the same as those used during operation codenamed 'Anti-Stalin' in Soviet period. The only difference now is the usage of modern mass media (the Internet, global television, social networks, NGO [non-governmental organization] network and financed bloggers)."[18]

Panarin's works are important because he introduces a broad range of complex terms and the establishment of a linkage between IW and different modern media activities. He asserts that successful protection from IW depends on the speed of problem analysis and reaction, thus arguing for the development of some sort of "information special forces" department that can serve as "strategic information intelligence operating in the global information space and building a system of forecasts and modelling of the information noosphere in pursuit of national interests."[19] In the context of color revolutions and mass media activities, Panarin changes the previous definition of "IW" and explains it via metaphors: "Information warfare is a struggle of two swords and two shields. In our country, there must be a strong shield and a sharp information sword, and between them there should be an intelligence space or analysis. These are the three components of an information war: impact, analysis and reaction."[20] The most important task of intelligence space, from Panarin's point of view, is media monitoring. This is necessary due to the growing importance of social networks as a new dimension of IW.

Dugin's views are even more complicated than Panarin's. He promotes the term "network warfare" as a part of IW. Dugin's concept is based on the metaphor of rhizome (a multiple nonhierarchical structure of society) that helps him to conceptualize "network-centric warfare."[21] Regular references to an external enemy (the West) logically leads Dugin to the idea of the immediate introduction of countermeasures; as a result, the "Eurasian netcentric warfare model" arises, the main aim of which is counterbalancing the "Atlantic" one created by the United States and Europe. The influence of conspiracy theories is strongly felt in the works of Dugin. Yet among other things, this makes his metaphor-saturated ideas popular among the general audience.

Another interesting point of view on IW belongs to Andrey Manoylo. He claims that IW is an integral part of postindustrial society, a substitute of armed warfare. The main purpose of IW is economic, military, and political domination. If it operates in the political dimension targeting government, IW becomes "a political struggle with a set of information-psychological operations."[22] Manoylo distinguishes between IW and information confrontation. Therefore, he is closer to the official discourse than many others. He identifies "information confrontation" as:

> the most general category of social relations. . . . [It] can be attributed to any form of social and political competition where achieving a competitive advantage requires using means and methods of information and psychological impact. The concept of "information confrontation" includes a broad range of conflict situations in the information and psychological sphere: from interpersonal conflicts to open confrontation between social systems. Information-psychological warfare is also one of the types of information confrontation.[23]

As demonstrated, there are many approaches to the concept of information warfare in Russian realities; most depend on historical periods and the rising popularity of another phenomena or world agenda. They allow for comprehensive study but, at the same time, create difficulty for the formation of a unified definition. The emergence of a single definition of IW in modern Russia is seemingly impossible because of the close intertwining of media and popular science discourses. Authors who are represented in both discourses often define IW too metaphorically or by means of other terms. In addition, their works, which do not always contain correct definitions, are widely disseminated among the internal audience. This, in turn, creates false ideas about significant bases in Russian practice. It seems that the problem would be partially resolved if the term IW was fixed in the relevant official documents at the state level, but "information warfare" is not even mentioned.

The Russian Media Environment
in the Context of Information Confrontation

Russia has made significant efforts to influence foreign audiences, actively developing its media system by taking into account the experience of the Soviet Union and the United States during the Cold War. The main recognized problem is heterogeneity of the audience as a highly differentiated construct. There are no universal approaches toward influencing both domestic and foreign audiences; each of them have their own, though not entirely isolated, characteristics. Furthermore, there are both foreign and domestic actors that operate within the media space of each country. Among them, it is also possible to identify a number of subcategories (which can be further subdivided into smaller groups by sociodemographic and psychographic parameters). According to the main purposes of an actor's influence, these can be listed as follows:

- Supporters—who have to be strengthened in the opinion that they are on the right side;
- Doubters—who should sympathize with the actor and condemn actions of the actor's enemies;
- Enemies—who must be demoralized and have to feel despair and confusion.

The current media system must take into account the experience of the past and the challenges of the digital age. Thus, the role of old and new media is changing, as are their tasks that are conditioned by the new goals. Old media positions are quite weak: there are many different information sources and every audience's category can easily and quickly access them to reflect or verify news and other information. For example, the domestic audience can access what a foreign audience might consume. Russia understands this problem and tries to challenge it by using a broad system of different media and methods of influence. For example, Russia learned lessons from the devastating defeat in the information space of the Georgia–South Ossetia conflict 2008, the first important confrontation between Russian and Western interests since the collapse of communism. Russia was not ready for the fact that the military and economic potential ceased to be the main argument, and many propaganda techniques of the Soviet period did not work. The key mistakes made by Russia are as follows:

- Underestimating the gravity of the situation and, as a result, an extremely low rate of response to the rapidly developing events;

- Uncoordinated information policy within the country at the initial stage;
- Lack of understanding of the opponents' goals, discourse, and rhetorical strategy;
- Lack of Russian journalists in the conflict area;
- Lack of a Russian media strategy to challenge Western and Georgian media.

These mistakes forced Russia to play by the opponent's rules. Russia's modern campaigns are much more interesting and strong tactically and strategically, which is supported by an increased variety of methods and channels of communication. The country's media system has started to change and become more aggressive, rude, and rapid since that time. The strategy of simply declaring an official point of view during that conflict was powerless and too slow and, as a result, underwent changes. Now, the main strategy is directed toward a comprehensive system of counternarratives that undermine the confidence of the domestic audiences in their own countries' media resources, thus undermining the social institutions in general.

The most notable and controversial cases of Russian foreign broadcasting are the RT (formerly Russia Today) television network and Sputnik International (formerly Voice of Russia) radio.[24] Valeriy Solovey describes the phenomenon of RT in detail. According to Solovey, the channel was tested for strength in 2014: "Unconditional proof of the success of RT on the formation and reporting of an alternative point of view on Ukrainian events was the public irritation of US secretary of state John Kerry, former secretary of state Hillary Clinton and President Barack Obama expressed toward the Russian television company. It was accused of biased coverage of the Ukrainian crisis, spreading conjectures and lies."[25] Some reasons for RT's success include: its aggressive and operational style of information delivery; it broadcasts to the non-Western world (i.e., "disputed territory"); and its social media marketing (YouTube and social networks).

However, a lack of politically neutral media is a problem for Russian foreign broadcasting. In 2009, the Russian Travel Guide (RTG) TV documentary channel was launched, focusing on nature, science, culture, and history of Russia. Currently, the channel is broadcast in twenty EU countries, Asia, and the Middle East. RTG declares "the long-term project of the channel's owners is to produce documentaries about the [Commonwealth of Independent States] and former Soviet Union." The appearance of such politically neutral broadcasting could be interpreted as an intensification of Russia's efforts in the formation of a positive image of the country, yet subtly promoting the official agenda. This refers to two cases: the notification text "This film was created before the inclusion of the Republic of Crimea and Sevastopol with Russia," which appears over video and lasts for about ten seconds and the title sequence "Open the World." "Travel Through Russia" shows a virtual map of Russia's regions, including Crimea. The purpose of the information in both cases can be viewed as a declaration of Moscow's official position. In addition to traditional media, Russia now relies on the Internet and social networks as faster and cheaper communication channels with its desired audience. The boundless nature of the Internet is, in fact, an advantage and a threat. This also complicates the formation of a regulatory framework for the Internet, in light of the government's intensified attempts since 2015 to gain control over the Internet in Russia. Censorship and the filter system, similar to that in China, can become a cornerstone of sovereignty in accordance with the Soviet scenario during the Cold War.

A notable aspect of Russian online information-psychological operations is the usage of "trolls" (managed by humans) and "bots" (managed automatically). This broad system of fake accounts in social networks helps to provide "necessary" points of view in some debates by diverting and shifting public attention or by suppressing unwanted opinions. It is complicated by the trolls' and bots' mimesis, as they accurately simulate the behavior and emotions of ordinary people. As a method of information exposure, they are rather effective for domestic and foreign environments and have become an integral part of the Russian information-psychological operation and information confrontations or warfare. Moreover, trolls and bots allow for ensuring the achievement of the actor's main goals with the active support of the impact's targets and creating a semblance of free democratic choice.[26] Thus, it is possible to assert that, despite significant successful steps made by Russia, it still borrows a lot from Soviet practices and faces a wide range of unsolved problems in the media environment that lack a clear long-term strategy. Nevertheless, some specific methods of information-psychological manipulation and exposure are used successfully in the media.

Methods and Means of the Information-Psychological Operations

An integral part of information confrontation in peacetime is information-psychological operations, based on a complex of methods and means. The greatest effect was made by psychology, communication studies, advertising technologies, and so forth. In this regard, it is possible to define explicit and implicit layers of exposure as well as positive and negative consequences. A large number of different notions and classifications of methods and techniques can be found in the Russian academic field. They mainly refer to the classification proposed by the American Institute of Propaganda Analysis in 1937. Those seven techniques (name-calling, glittering generalities, transfer, testimonial, plain folks, card stacking, and bandwagon) usually are featured as the "ABC of Propaganda."[27] The main methods of information exposure for forming the appropriate public opinion, as well as modification of behavioral practices, during the information-psychological confrontation were conceptualized by Yury Kuleshov and are listed as follows:[28]

- Direct lie for the purpose of domestic and foreign audiences' disinformation;
- Concealment of critically important information;
- Dissolution of valuable information in data smog;[29]
- Simplification, confirmation, and repetition (suggestion);
- Terminological substitution: usage of concepts and terms whose meanings are not clear or have undergone qualitative changes, making it difficult to form an event's real picture;
- Tabooing of certain types of information and news categories;
- Image recognition: famous politicians or celebrities can take part in political events, influencing a certain impact on the worldview of their fans;
- Providing of negative information, the audience response to which is higher than to positive information.

Kuleshov's conception is rather concise; another classification of information-psychological exposure methods is detailed in the research of Nataliya Romashkina and can be summarized as follows:[30]

- Translation of deformed images: distortion of amounts; simplification of the topic; change of cause-effect, timing, and spatial connections; simulated misinformation; focus or concentration of attention and the reduction of significance of the topic; attention focus shift inside the topic; pseudological inferences.
- Use of reference groups: identification with the reference group; method of the reference to the authority.
- Comparison and contrast.
- Reframing information: transfer of inferences and derivations; transfer of the game situation on the real world, forming predestinations.

- Nonviolent conviction: official announcements; communication with a large audience; pressure on particular people; public meetings.
- Linkage: linkage of emotional words; linkage by the similarity in the parameters; linkage by a particular case or generalization; linkage by the instrument of implementation, joint sphere of application; cause-effect linkage; linkage by the third object; linkage by joint demonstration; linkage by attitude and support; linkage by use of polysemantic words, terms, images.
- Problem–solution (threat–rescue): linkage of the object with the problem (threat) with direct appeal to the target audience; linkage of the object with the problem (threat) with indirect appeal to the target audience.
- Preemptive answers and propaganda ("vaccination"): direct preemptive answers and propaganda; indirect preemptive answers and propaganda.

Case Studies

The Case of Lisa

Germany drew attention to Russian media in January 2016, when its mass media intensively discussed a story about a Russian girl living in Germany with her parents. The Russian TV channel Perviy Kanal (One) claimed that Lisa was kidnapped and raped by Arab migrants.[31] Shortly afterward, RT joined the discussion.[32] The next stage involved the support of social networks, where not only were active debates conducted, but also a protest movement was formed with the aim of the girl's defense and relief.[33] It is remarkable that a collective decision was formed and the protest movement began on the Internet, and then moved off-line in the form of demonstrations. Off-line actions launched a new circle of discussions—this time in the German domestic media.[34] During the last stage, the top diplomatic circles began to comment on the story. Russian foreign minister Sergei Lavrov accused the German authorities of hushing up the case.[35] His German colleague, Frank-Walter Steinmeier, warned against using the case "for political propaganda, and to enflame and influence what is already a difficult debate about migration within Germany."[36] Later, the Berlin Police found out that the girl spent that night at her friend's place; thus, the story was fake. Before this was revealed some time later, German-Russian relations were quite strained.

The Case of Lack of Food

In February 2017, the Norwegian media reported that, according to Perviy Kanal, there was a shortage of fresh vegetables in the country. Grocery stores even introduced quotas for buyers that limited the possibility of acquisition.[37] Origins of this information were in the messages of the British supermarket chains Tesco and Morrisons, and not in Norway: "Due to continued weather problems in Spain, there is a shortage in Iceberg lettuce. To protect the availability for all our customers, we are limiting bulk purchases to three per person. We apologise for any inconvenience it may cause."[38] Norway's media report is an example of a short-term information-psychological operation but, at the same time, it is an element of a global strategy whose main purpose is to discredit the governments of European Union (EU) countries in their citizens' eyes. This example includes "change of cause-effect" (violation of cause-effect relationships for the substitution of the topic); "change of spatial connections" (a small crisis in the UK is transformed into a big one in Norway); and "simulation misinformation" (changing part of the facts, except those that determine a particular source of information) methods.

The World Mass Media Hostility Index: A Russian Approach to IW Estimations

To increase the effectiveness of the methods that are used for information-psychological exposure and the creation of counteractions, Russian experts have been focusing on monitoring the foreign media environment. In this regard, a group of scientists at the Russian Institute for Strategic Studies under the direction of Igor Nikolaychuk developed and presented the so-called World Mass Media Hostility Index (HI). The origins of political media metrics can be traced back to the information and analytical system Russia in the World that was founded by the international news agency Russia Today.[39]

Throughout 2015–2016, articles flashed up in various Russian media outlets commenting on the Ukraine-EU agreement. Essentially, the story was that, in exchange for a visa regime with the EU, Ukraine assumed an obligation to adopt refugees from the Middle East in its territory. This information fit perfectly into the main discussion on the problem of refugees in Europe. The effect was supported by vivid headlines; for example, "The EU Will Force Ukraine to Accept Migrants from Africa and the Middle East,"[40] "Ukraine Was Offered to Settle by Migrants in Exchange for a Visa-Free Regime with the EU,"[41] and "Ukraine Began to Build a Camp for Refugees from Syria."[42] This is an example of a long-term information-psychological operation, and reveals the methods of direct lying and transfer of inferences and derivations, which is a particular case of reframing, as well as the method of fact-finding (a mix of fiction and reality). The main purposes of the operation are reconstructing images of a negative future in the audience's imagination and discrediting the government's intentions via extrapolation of the European "problem" on Ukraine.

The most interesting question arising after a consideration of Russian media cases is why such cases generally can appear. The answer is quite ambiguous and complicated, but the main idea is that they are Russia's response to the Western exposure in global IW in the past several years. This is partly confirmed by a number of sources. In his research, Il'ya Sergeyev studied Jennifer Psaki, former US State Department spokesperson, as a new tool of information forgery and the result of successful work by US media technologists.[43] Sergeyev claims that the main goal of "the 'Psaki' project was to test the open (public) usage of concepts' substitution, games with meanings and absurdities as a tool to draw attention to US policy."[44] With Psaki's help, the US government drew time because it was not able to think over the coverage of a different situation in the period of information confrontation. "This technology also helped to avoid answers to uncomfortable questions, which in turn could lead to the discrediting of the United States as an information aggressor, including towards Ukraine," according to Sergeyev. In my view, several methods of information exposure were used during the Psaki project:

- Cognitive dissonance (inconsistency of reality and expectations);
- Effect of information overload (too many topics discussed, with low quality of answers);
- Identification of the external enemy (in most cases, Russia was blamed);
- Implicit misinformation (it is hard not to believe the government's spokesperson, even if he or she is incompetent in most cases).

Thus, it is possible to claim that the Russian cases of information exposure and manipulation can be the result of a counterstrategy toward the Western double standards and partly even a kind of acquired reflex and long life tradition.

The HI system, developed by RISS scientists under Nikolaychuk's direction, helps to rank data on macro and micro levels. The *macro level* can be defined as media activity toward Russia whereas the *micro level* is defined as media activity toward personalities or in some topic framework.

The Russia in the World system allows for monitoring frequency and prevalence of the information on the part of individual countries and assessing the information environment's aggressiveness toward Russia. Moreover, as Nikolaychuk asserts, "We can define some objective characteristics of IW using media metrics. Furthermore, we can pinpoint the moment of its initiation, intensity, applied pressure towards the adversary, or even find out who of journalists is writing most actively in the context of the information war."[45] In addition, Nikolaychuk draws a parallel between IW against a certain country and aggression toward a certain person; he illustrates this relationship with an example of the foreign media's aggressive attitude toward Vladimir Putin during the Ukrainian crisis of 2014.[46] Thus, it was the individual who became the object of the information war, not the country as a whole. Nikolaychuk describes the media system as sensitive to changes in the political and economic environment and, in this regard, fluctuations in HI three times cannot be a coincidence. As an argument, he cites two cases of Russian-US relations:[47]

- US media demonized the Russian authorities in the framework of the Dima Yakovlev case in 2012–2013. There were ten neutral publications per every twenty to twenty-five negative ones about Russia, with a sheer absence of positive articles. Later, the political strategy of the United States changed and the rapprochement between the two countries began. During that period, for several months the negative pressure on Russia in the US media was significantly reduced; the proportion was as follows: for the same ten neutral articles, there were only six negative ones. Suddenly, the rapprochement program was terminated and the proportion of media publications immediately returned to the original level.
- Another case refers to Ukraine. Russia was defined as an axis of evil in the US media again: there were ten neutral publications per every thirty-five negative ones in August 2015. After discussions of Russian-US operation perspectives in Syria began, the modality of Western media content was changed: there were ten neutral publications per every twenty-five negative ones in September and twelve negative publications in October.

The data for HI have been monitored for more than sixty countries since 2014. About 70,000 media pieces published between 1 January and 30 December 2014 were analyzed in that year. Authors of HI excluded blogs and, apparently, social networks from consideration, calling them a "communication phenomenon that has no relation to propaganda, no matter how someone tried to prove otherwise."[48] Ordinary news was also excluded from the analysis. Calculations of HI are based on qualitative-quantitative content analysis of the ratio of negative publications to neutral publications. A unit for analysis is a significant media publication that references Russia. For the convenience of interpretation and visualization, levels of foreign hostility toward Russia are varied in colors:[49] Green—low hostility (< 0.3); Yellow—medium hostility (0.3–0.7); Orange—high hostility (0.7–1.0); Red—extremely high hostility (1.0–5.0); and Black—a full-scale IW (> 5.0).

According to HI, the most media aggressive countries in 2014 were Germany (8.929), the United States (5.771), the United Kingdom (5.209), France (4.810), and Switzerland (4.105). The HI rating of some countries became the object of intense discussions. Thus, journalist Catherine Fitzpatrick was puzzled how Germany, which had strong business and social ties with Russia, could lead the list of countries.[50] The same question arose with Austria, which supported the Russian South Stream pipeline project. When a small discussion was held on one of the most popular social news aggregation websites—Reddit—users expressed doubt about whether criticism of Joseph Stalin was a criticism of Russia.[51] In 2015, the greatest number of questions arose about the Czech Republic. Publicist Karel Svoboda was surprised that the Czech Republic twice topped the list of aggressive countries in May (18.0) and in November (9.0).[52] He questioned the methodology of selecting texts and authors, which did not take into account the basic attitude toward Russia and lack of journalists who studied Russian realities. The methodology's problem in the case of the Czech Republic was confirmed by Nikolaychuk: "Society and media are split into Russophobes and Russophiles. There are almost no centrists. The HI is now off scale—twenty-one. However, the 'index of benevolence' (the ratio of the number of positive materials to the number of neutral ones) is also unusually high, somewhere around seventeen. That is, one neutral publication accounts for seventeen positive."[53] RISS's index can be also strongly criticized from a scientific point of view. The most significant reproaches are along these lines:

- Methodological vulnerability: lack of software-assisted methods of data analysis. RISS relies on an expert assessment of the modality of publications, but this can lead to the expert's personal opinion influencing the interpretation of the text.
- Editorial policy and political orientation: lack of understanding about origins of this phenomenon and foreign media practice. Many different causes can make an impact on certain publications. These causes may represent not only government but also public

opinion, may become the author's personal point of view, or may be formatted in accordance with the editorial board's rules.

- Term base entropy: lack of understanding and lack of articulating the distinction between the concepts of IW, information hostility, criticism, interest, and so forth.

- Elimination of the situation's context: lack of interpretation in the framework's background. An avalanche of condemnation can arise during truly ambiguous events that are not everyday practice for a particular country such as armed conflicts and civilian casualties.

Finally, the phenomenon of mass media hostility is not new, and origins of the research explicitly point to predetermined prejudice in analyses of this kind. The origins of this state can be found in the research of Robert Vallone, Lee Ross, and Mark R. Lepper.[54] They describe the perceptions of pro-Arab and pro-Israeli students about an identical news broadcast about the First Lebanon War of 1982. In that broadcast the Israeli military operation, called Peace for Galilee, was condemned for the mass killing of civilians. Both groups of students took the news as mutually biased. Vallone, Ross, and Lepper found the reasons for this ambiguous perception to be in the students' personal experience, which indicated enemies. An audience will perceive even 100 percent balanced news in accordance with its own position (i.e., rhetoric and arguments in favor of the opposite side will seem stronger and perfect). These results were subsequently confirmed and refined by other researchers.[55] Thus, it is necessary to apply the semio-socio-psychological approach in studies similar to the RISS one.[56] The founder of this paradigm is Tamara Dridze, who applied such methods for the first time in the framework of the Soviet global research project Public Opinion (1969–1974). The key moment revealed by Dridze is that the number of people who adequately perceive nonart media texts remain a constant in society and amount to some 14–16 percent.[57] Consequently, the methodological drawback of HI gets a certain extension, questioning experts' ability to appraise media texts as negative, neutral, and positive, as well as the possibility of extrapolation of their personal opinions to society as a whole.

Conclusion

It should be noted that the Russian confusion in terms of the concept of information warfare is not a temporary phenomenon and has a long history. Most likely, the terminology unification problems will continue due to the fact that the development of topics such as this one is a peculiar political mechanism of the reconstruction of reality. The dynamic nature of the events surrounding Russia and their speed and range affect the nature and interpretation of terms in different discourses, as it was in the Soviet period and the Cold War with antithetic terms of *information war* and *ideology struggle*. This was also the case when the color revolutions gave impulse to a new discussion of the concepts' meanings.

The concept of IW will be controversial until it is popular in different discourses at the same time (e.g., public, academic, political, and target experts). Unfortunately, the most frequently cited ideas and definitions are still evolving, and substitutions of the term *information warfare* for *information confrontation* that happened in official doctrine cannot seriously change the situation for the better. At the same time, one can be sure that the basic principles of information-psychological methods of exposure will remain unchanged while the channel of communication will be improved. Every country is able to learn lessons from the past and fix the mistakes. Progress does not stand still; every country constantly monitors new technologies of communication and broadcasting to develop systems of countermeasures. It would be a mistake to refuse to use old media since both new and old are likely to be used.

Notes

1. Presidential Decree, "The Doctrine of the Information Security of the Russian Federation," Moscow, 5 December 2016 (in Russian).

2. Presidential Decree, "The Doctrine of the Information Security of the Russian Federation," Moscow, 9 September 2000 (in Russian).

3. The conceptual metaphor "argument is war" was suggested by George Lakoff and Mark Johnson in 1987. Conceptual metaphors are an integral part of our life and are necessary for the explication of an object's properties and its image's formation. For further details of the conceptual metaphors model, see George Lakoff and Mark Johnson, *Metaphors We Live By* (Chicago: University of Chicago Press, 2011).

4. Nikolay Zhiveynov, *Operatsiya "PW": "Psikhologicheskaya voyna" amerikanskikh imperialistov* [Operation "PW": "Psychological War" of the US Imperialists] (Moscow: Politicheskaya literatura, 1966).

5. Dmitry Volkogonov, *Psikhologicheskaya voyna: Podryvnyye deystviya imperializma v oblasti obshchestvennogo soznaniya* [Psychological War: Subversive Actions of Imperialism in the Field of Public Consciousness] (Moscow: Voinizdat, 1983).

6. Kirill Razlogov, *Konveyyer grez i psikhologicheskaya voyna: Kino i obshchestvenno-politicheskaya bor'ba na Zapade. 70-80-ye gody* [The Dream Conveyor and the Psychological War: Cinema and Socio-Political Struggle in the West, 1970s to 1980s] (Moscow: Politizdat, 1986).

7. Vladimir Lisichkin and Leonid Shelepin, *Tret'ya mirovaya (informatsionno-psikhologicheskaya) voyna* [The Third World (Information-Psychological) War] (Moscow: Eksmo, Algoritm, 2003).

8. Sergey Rastorguyev, *Formula informatsionnoy voyny* [The Information Warfare Formula] (Moscow: Radio i svyaz', 1999).

9. Ibid.

10. Vladimir Tsyganov and Sergey Bukharin, *Informatsionnyye voyny v biznese i politike* [Information Warfare in Business and Politics] (Moscow: Akademicheskiy proyekt, 2007).

11. Ibid.

12. Jolanta Darczewska, "The Anatomy of Russian Information Warfare: The Crimean Operation, A Case Study," Point of View No. 42 (Warsaw: Centre for Eastern Studies, 2014).

13. Igor Panarin, *Informatsionnaya voyna i tretiy Rim* [The Information Warfare and the Third Rome] (Moscow: NOU ShO "Bayard," 2003).

14. Ibid.

15. The name "Snow Revolution" was given by foreign media to the number of protests against the 2011 Russian legislative election results. For example, Andrew Osborn, "Bloggers Who Are Changing the Face of Russia as the Snow Revolution Takes Hold," *The Telegraph,* 10 December 2011; Julia Ioffe, "Snow Revolution," *New Yorker,* 10 December 2011.

16. Igor Panarin, *SMI, propaganda i informatsionnyye voyny* [Mass Media, Propaganda and Information Warfare] (Moscow: Pokolenie, 2012).

17. The protest movement on Bolotnaya Square was a stage of the Snow Revolution in Russia.

18. Igor Panarin, *Informatsionnaya voyna i kommunikatsii* [Information Warfare and Communications] (Moscow: Goryachaya liniya—Telekom, 2016).

19. Panarin, *SMI, propaganda.*

20. Ibid.

21. See for example, Gilles Deleuze and Félix Guattari, *A Thousand Plateaus: Capitalism and Schizophrenia* (New York: Viking Press, 1977); Aleksandr Dugin, *Setevyye voyny: Ugroza novogo pokoleniya* [Network Wars: The Threat of a New Generation] (Moscow: Yevraziyskoye dvizheniye, 2009). Aleksandr Dugin's concept of network-centric warfare has little in common with the concept of network-centric warfare proposed by the US military. For further discussion on network-centric warfare, see Chapters 3 and 4 of this book.

22. Andrey Manoylo, "Informatsionno-psikhologicheskaya voyna: Faktory, opredelyayushchiye format sovremennogo vooruzhennogo konflikta" [Information-Psychological Warfare: Factors that Determine the Format of a Modern Armed Conflict], paper presented at the fifth International Scientific and Practical Conference "Information Technologies and Security," Kiev, November 2005, http://psyfactor .org/lib/psywar35.htm.

23. Ibid.

24. For example, Jasper Jackson, "RT Sanctioned by Ofcom over Series of Misleading and Biased Articles," *The Guardian,* 21 September 2015.

25. Valeriy Solovey, *Absolyutnoye oruzhiye: Osnovy psikhologicheskoy voyny i mediamanipulirovaniya* [Absolute Weapon: Fundamentals of Psychological Warfare and Media Manipulation] (Moscow: Eksmo, 2015).

26. Yuriy Kuleshov, Boris Azhutdeev, and Dmitrii Fedotov, "Informatsionno-psikhologicheskoye protivoborstvo v sovremennykh usloviyakh: Teoriya i praktika" [Information-Psychological Warfare in Modern Conditions: Theory and Practice], *Vestnik Akademii voyennykh nauk,* no. 1 (2014): 104–110.

27. For example, Solovey, *Absolyutnoye oruzhiye.*

28. Kuleshov, Azhutdeev, and Fedotov, "Informatsionno-psikhologicheskoye protivoborstvo."

29. The term *data smog* was first used by journalist David Shenk, *Data Smog: Surviving the Information Glut* (San Francisco: Harper, 1997). *Data smog* means an overwhelming amount of data and information, which confuses the audience and obstructs separation of truth from fake.

30. Andrey Zagorskiy and Nataliya Romashkina, eds., *Information Security Threats During Crisis and Conflicts of the XXI Century* (Moscow: IMEMO, 2016).

31. "Avstriya vremenno priostanavlivayet deystviye Shengenskogo soglasheniya iz-za sluchayev nasiliya v Germanii" [Austria Temporarily Suspends the Schengen Agreement Due to the Cases of Violence in Germany], TV channel One, 16 January 2016, www.1tv.ru/news/2016-01-16/3330-avstriya_vremenno_priostanavlivaet_deystvie _shengenskogo_soglasheniya_iz_za_sluchaev_nasiliya_v_germanii.

32. For example, "Delo Lizy: MID RF prizval k obyektivnomu rassledovaniyu intsidenta s russkoy devochkoy v Germanii" [Lisa Case: Russian Ministry of Foreign Affairs Called for an Objective Investigation of the Incident with a Russian Girl in Germany], RT, 26 January 2016, https://russian.rt.com/article/144393.

33. Unfortunately, the content of social networks is rather fickle; groups and communities and their content can be closed or deleted quickly. Now, there are a lot of mentions of girls' support and relief groups in social networks in mass media publications. They mostly refer to the Russian community on Facebook, Der Russen Treff, www.facebook.com/DasIstDerRussenTreffOriginal, that actively supported Lisa and discussed the possibility of organizing protests against refugees and violence on their part. For example, "Aufgestachelt zum Protest" [Incitement of Protest], *Schwäbische,* 25 January 2016, www.schwaebische.de/politik/inland_artikel,-Aufgestachelt-zum -Protest-_arid,10381768.html. The other notable statement was made by the Berlin Police on its official page on Facebook, www.facebook.com/PolizeiBerlin. It contained some facts on this case and a request to users of social networks to calm down. For further details, see "Information zum Vermisstenfall einer 13-Jährigen" [Information on the Case of a Missing Person of a 13-Year-Old], Berlin Police official Facebook page, 18 January 2016, www.facebook.com/PolizeiBerlin/posts /473314102852699:0.

34. For example, "Das missbrauchte Mädchen" [The Abused Girl], *Zeit Online,* 21 January 2016, www.zeit.de/politik/ausland/2016-01/russland-propaganda-entfuehrung -maedchen-berlin; "Der Fall Lisa F. und russische Medien" [The Lisa F. Case and the Russian Media], *Sächsische Zeitung,* 27 January 2016, www.sz-online.de/nachrichten /der-fall-lisa-f-und-russische-medien-3307759.html.

35. For example, Andreas Rinke and Paul Carrel, "German-Russian Ties Feel Cold War–Style Chill over Rape Case," Reuters, 1 February 2016, www.reuters.com /article/us-germany-russia/german-russian-ties-feel-cold-war-style-chill-over-rape -case-idUSKCN0VA31O.

36. "Germany Warns Russia over Teen 'Rape' Case," BBC News Services, 27 January 2016, www.bbc.com/news/world-europe-35424648.

37. Lisa S. Hadland, "Russian TV: Vegetable Crisis in Norway," *Norway Today,* 8 February 2017, http://norwaytoday.info/news/russian-tv-vegetable-crisis-norway.

38. "Iceberg Lettuces and Broccoli Rationed as Vegetable Crisis Hits Supermarkets," BBC News Services, 3 February 2017, www.bbc.com/news/uk-38851097.

39. Mariya Druzhinina, ed., "Politicheskaya mediametriya" [Political Media-Metrics], Russian Institute for Strategic Studies (RISS), 30 March 2015, https:// riss.ru/smi/11189.

40. "ES zastavit Ukrainu prinyat' migrantov iz Afriki i Blizhnego Vostoka" [EU Will Force Ukraine to Accept Migrants from Africa and the Middle East], Zvezda, 18 August 2015, http://tvzvezda.ru/news/vstrane_i_mire/content/201508181828-47mr .htm.

41. "Ukrainu predlozhili zaselit' migrantami v obmen na bezvizovyy rezhim s ES" [Ukraine Was Offered to Settle By Migrants in Exchange for a Visa-Free Regime with the EU], Lenta.ru, 28 November 2016, https://lenta.ru/news/2016/11/28/petukhov.

42. Oleg Bazak and Igor Subbotin, "Na Ukraine nachali stroit' lager' dlya bezhentsev iz Sirii" [Ukraine Began to Build a Camp for Refugees from Syria], *Moskovskiy Komsomolets,* 29 February 2016, www.mk.ru/politics/2016/02/29/na-ukraine-nachali-stroit-lager-dlya-bezhencev-iz-sirii.html.

43. Il'ya Sergeyev, "Dzhennifer Psaki—Instrument informatsionnogo protivoborstva" [Jennifer Psaki Is an Instrument of Information Confrontation], *Yevraziyskiy soyuz uchenykh* 27, no. 6 (2016): 92–93.

44. Ibid.

45. Druzhinina, "Politicheskaya mediametriya."

46. Igor Nikolaychuk, *Politicheskaya mediametriya: Zarubezhnyye SMI i bezopasnost' Rossii* [Political Media-Metrics: Foreign Media and Security of Russia] (Moscow: RISS, 2015).

47. Igor Nikolaychuk, Tamara Yakova, and Marina Yanglyaeva, "Media kak sistema-trend: Novyye podkhody v medialogii" [Media as a System-Trend: New Approaches in Medialogy], *Mediaal'manakh,* no. 1 (2016): 12–24.

48. Druzhinina, "Politicheskaya mediametriya."

49. Nikolaychuk, *Politicheskaya mediametriya.*

50. Catherine Fitzpatrick, "Russian Think-Tank RISI Issues 'World Media Hostility Index'—With Germany First, US Second," *The Interpreter,* 26 February 2015, www.interpretermag.com/russia-update-february-26-2015.

51. "Russian Think Tank RISS Releases 'World Mass Media Hostility Index,'" Reddit's discussion, 26 February 2015, www.reddit.com/r/russia/comments/2x9kt2/russian_think_tank_riss_releases_world_mass_media.

52. Karel Svoboda, "USA prý vedou mediální válku proti Putinovi, Česko je hlavní loutkou a bojištěm" [USA Are [*sic*] Allegedly Conducting Media War Against Putin, the Czech Republic Is Main Puppet and Battlefield], *Reflex,* 5 April 2016 (in Czech), www.reflex.cz/clanek/komentare/70516/usa-pry-vedou-medialni-valku-proti-putinovi-cesko-je-hlavni-loutkou-a-bojistem.html%20.

53. Igor Nikolaychuk, "Rossiya v zerkale mirovykh SMI: Rossiysko-germanskiy razdray" [Russia in the Mirror of the World's Media: Russian-German Discontent], *RIA Novosti,* 27 November 2014, https://ria.ru/analytics/20141127/1035454703.html.

54. Robert Vallone, Lee Ross, and Mark R. Lepper, "The Hostile Media Phenomenon: Biased Perception and Perceptions of Media Bias in Coverage of the Beirut Massacre," *Journal of Personality and Social Psychology,* no. 3 (1985): 577–585.

55. For example, Roger Giner-Sorolla and Shelly Chaiken, "The Causes of Hostile Media Judgements," *Journal of Experimental Social Psychology,* no. 2 (1994): 165–180; Richard Perloff, "Ego-Involvement and the Third Person Effect of Televised News Coverage," *Communication Research,* no. 2 (1989): 236–262.

56. For example, Tamara Dridze, *Tekstovaya deyatel'nost' v strukture sotsial'noy kommunikatsii: Problemy semiosotsiopsikhologii* [Text Activity in the Structure of Social Communication: The Problems of Semio-Socio-Psychology] (Moscow: Nauka, 1984).

57. For example, Boris Grushin and Leon Onikov, ed., *Massovaya informatsiya v sovetskom promyshlennom gorode: Opyt kompleksnogo sotsiologicheskogo issledovaniya* [Mass Information in the Soviet Industrial City: Experience of Complex Sociological Research] (Moscow: Politizdat, 1980).

PART 3

Information Warfare:
The Case of the Islamic State

10

The Battle for Mosul: An Analysis of Islamic State Propaganda

Charlie Winter

On 16 October 2016, Prime Minister Haydar al-Abadi of Iraq announced the launch of a military campaign to liberate Mosul from the Islamic State.[1] After controlling the city for twenty-eight months, Abu Bakr al-Baghdadi's organization suddenly faced a serious impending challenge to its rule.[2] In the weeks that followed, the group slowly lost its grip on the city's eastern bank. The Iraqi Security Forces (ISF) penetrated Mosul's limits, capturing the outermost district of Kawkjali within thirty days.[3] Two weeks later, no fewer than nineteen neighborhoods had been secured—about 30 percent of Mosul proper.[4] In December, the campaign's prospects appeared to sour when an entire tank division was routed by the Islamic State at Salam Hospital, resulting in heavy losses.[5] In the wake of the ambush, the campaign stuttered on, before eventually coming to a full standstill or—to borrow a coalition euphemism—an "operational refit."[6] When things picked up again, "85 to 90 percent" of the Islamic State's territory in the eastern bank was recaptured.[7] And on 24 January—exactly 100 days into the campaign—the Iraqi prime minister returned to the pulpit, this time to declare victory.[8]

The first phase of the battle for Mosul received ample attention from international media. Journalists aimed to be present at every juncture: *BBC News* correspondents traveled alongside counterterrorism service units as they penetrated the city limits,[9] *New York Times* writers sent dispatches from newly liberated neighborhoods,[10] and some news channels even set up live video feeds for observers to stream footage of the fighting in real time.[11]

Coalition-backed forces were not alone in encouraging battlefield reporting, as the Islamic State media cabal communicated the campaign with equal, if not greater, enthusiasm, depicting its defense of the city in vivid detail. Each suicide operation was celebrated individually,[12] the destruction of every enemy vehicle prompted "Breaking News" notices,[13] and front-line video clips were disseminated on average twice a day.[14] As the battle for Mosul continued, the Islamic State, already infamous for the scale and scope of its strategic communication operations, went into information overdrive.

While this strategy surprised neither the US-led coalition, nor its Iraqi partners, nor the journalists covering the battle, the mainstream understanding of the Islamic State information campaign was hampered by a myopic focus on propaganda deliberately geared toward receiving global publicity, which amounted to only a small proportion of the full corpus.[15] Consequently, my main purpose in this chapter is to correct this imbalance.

In the following analysis, which is based on an exhaustive database of official Islamic State propaganda published between 16 October 2016 (when the campaign to recapture east Mosul first began) and 24 January 2017 (when the campaign was declared completed), I evaluate the Islamic State's information operations from two different analytical perspectives. After outlining the data collection methodology I present the first perspective, which is based on a structural examination of the data itself through mapping the media nexus charged with delivering the propaganda messages and outlining the various forms of output. The second perspective is based on the work of French propaganda theoretician Jacques Ellul; in it, I thematically dissect the story that Islamic State propagandists told during this information campaign.[16] I introduce and discuss the three foundations of the Islamic State brand in Mosul—warfare, victimhood, and utopia—and track the evolution of each. I conclude this two-stage analysis by discussing the unprecedented nature of the Islamic State's information response to the battle in general, and the notable absence of execution propaganda across the 100-day period in particular.

Data Collection Methodology

In September 2015, the Islamic State's official media cadre began using Telegram, a Russian-owned and Berlin-based encrypted communications platform, as its rear-operating base for propaganda dissemination.[17] Telegram offered an efficient and resilient way for the group to market itself online, as it was more difficult to navigate, infiltrate, and, therefore, censor than similar platforms such as Twitter or Facebook.[18]

In the context of official Islamic State strategic communication operations during the analyzed period, there were two most-dominant Telegram channels operated by the Islamic State: (1) Nashir and (2) the A'maq News Agency. While the former was an official clearinghouse for all propaganda produced and curated by the Islamic State's central and provincial media offices, the latter, which runs its own channel on Telegram, was the principal point of issuance for media products attributed to its newswire—the A'maq News Agency. Operating autonomously, an Islamic State–administered disseminator bot network calling itself "the Nashir News Agency" aggregated output from both sources and published its content.

The database, on which this chapter is based, consists of archived media products disseminated by the Nashir News Agency bot network during the 100-day data collection period on a daily basis, and regularly cross-referenced with the official Nashir and A'maq News Agency Telegram channels to ensure that nothing was missed. After all data unrelated to the Mosul campaign items were weeded out, the rest were individually translated and coded.

The Media Nexus

Between 16 October 2016 and 24 January 2017, the Islamic State's official media houses published over 1,000 propaganda products that addressed the campaign to retake east Mosul. Most were short operational briefs—claims that were disseminated shortly after individual attacks or incursions. The rest were photo-essays, radio bulletins, video clips, written supplements, and feature films. In analyzing this vast of amount of data, it is possible to point to just five of the Islamic State's fifty-four official propaganda outlets that were responsible for all Mosul-related information operations.[19]

The A'maq News Agency

The A'maq News Agency was the most productive outlet by far, publishing a steady stream of Mosul-related propaganda in four forms during the data collection period. First, it circulated brief operational digests, usually Arabic-language statements ranging from ten to thirty words in length. They tended to be delivered as image files, something that facilitated their rapid dissemination across different social media platforms.

The second-most-prominent form in the agency's repertoire was video clips, with one to five clips being circulated from Mosul each day. These videos tended to be staged but received little editing, which meant they could be disseminated on a highly tactical basis. Most of the videos depicted one of three events: military clashes (*muwajihat, ishtibakat, isti'ada, ma'raka,* and *hujum* videos); suicide operatives driving off into the distance before detonating their vehicle-borne improvised explosive devices (*'amaliyyat istishhadiyya* videos); and the aftermath of coalition artillery or air strikes, principally in the form of destroyed infrastructure and dead or dying civilians (*athar* or *qusf* footage). On a less regular basis, the agency circulated video clips showing civilian life in Mosul, including carefully choreographed recruitment fairs[20] and tours of vegetable markets.[21]

The third form of the agency's propaganda was infographics disseminated on a weekly and monthly basis, providing detailed statistical updates on the state of the battle.[22] The propaganda campaign did not feature maps, presumably because documenting the Islamic State's territorial loss could prove itself to be counterproductive. Therefore, infographics were a useful way to distract from defeat and reframe the Islamic State's gradual loss of land as an economic weapon with which it was draining its enemies.

The final A'maq News Agency product—the detailed news articles—appeared on only a handful of occasions.[23] Since they uniquely focused on conveying news of successful counteroffensive operations, that might explain their relative scarcity in the Mosul context.

The Nineveh Province Media Office

The Nineveh Province Media Office produced the second-largest number of Mosul-related propaganda products between October 2016 and January 2017. According to the group's own documents, as one of the Islamic State's forty-four centrally coordinated regional units, it is "affiliated with the provincial governor himself and [operated] in coordination with the [top] military and security official. [It] covers military operations and their results, as well as [the work of] services facilities, the implementation of shari'a rulings, and the course of life in the province."[24] During the campaign, the Nineveh Province Media Office was more active than it had ever been before, even compared to June 2014 when the Islamic State first captured the city of Mosul.

The office circulated propaganda in three main forms: detailed operation claims, photoreports, and feature-length videos. Unlike the

A'maq News Agency equivalents, the Nineveh Province Media Office operation claims provided a high degree of granularity. Its coverage of the Islamic State's resistance in Mosul was less frequent, but more nuanced. And because it consolidated many tactical events into one comprehensive product, it was ultimately easier to digest.

Besides operation claims, which appeared between one and eight times a day, the office published formal and informal photoreports. Formal photoreports, usually shot on single-lens reflex cameras by proficient photographers, depicted civilian and military activities in the city[25] while informal reports, typically published under the tagline "Breaking News," presented collections of images hastily captured on the front lines.[26]

The additional Nineveh Province Media Office product was the feature-length video documentary. Only five were published between October 2016 and January 2017, but they were of fundamental importance to the Islamic State's information operations in Mosul.[27] Unlike most other media products disseminated by the group, these videos were technically impressive and weaved together multiple narrative strands.

Bayan Radio

During the battle for Mosul, the Islamic State published its daily Bayan Radio news bulletin on Telegram, shortly after broadcasting it in Iraq and Syria at about noon Mosul time.[28] Offering an operational digest for the previous twenty-four hours in Arabic, English, French, and Turkish, Bayan Radio's FM and digital broadcasts were an important pillar of the group's Mosul information operations.[29]

These operational digests were of relatively low impact individually—for instance, many mentioned Mosul only in passing. However, they served an important purpose by allowing the Islamic State to steadily and strategically relay a certain narrative to its supporters. When refracted through Bayan Radio's microphones, the campaign looked very different from the mainstream version of events. Indeed, according to the Islamic State's carefully crafted story line, what happened in the east of the city between October 2016 and January 2017 was a calculated and deliberate tactical retreat, not the strategic defeat that objective observers perceived.[30]

The Naba' Newspaper

The Islamic State circulated an electronic copy of its newspaper *Naba'* every Thursday during the battle for east Mosul. Sixteen pages in length—about 12,000 words in total—*Naba'* reiterated the line conveyed by the rest of the group's propaganda.[31] The newspaper's aggregated form made it an approachable source for Arabic-speaking supporters, perhaps even more than the group's radio broadcasts or operation claims; simply put, it was easy to keep track of. Moreover, the battle for Mosul featured heavily across the data collection period, as it was front-page news every week bar one.[32]

The Furqan Foundation

The final media production unit to participate in the Islamic State's information campaign during the battle for Mosul was the Furqan Foundation, the central propaganda office that was in charge of publishing audio statements from the group's leader, Abu Bakr al-Baghdadi, and its spokesman, Abul-Hassan al-Muhajir. While it was dormant for most of the campaign, two statements, one from al-Baghdadi and the other from al-Muhajir, were published in November and December 2016, respectively.[33] In each, the Islamic State's Mosul resistance figured prominently, though it was referenced only indirectly.

Content Analysis

This thematic analysis of the Mosul propaganda database benefits from prior reference to the work of Jacques Ellul, which provides a useful lens allowing us to evaluate the structure of the Islamic State's information operations, both in general and in the specific context of this campaign.[34]

Using Ellul's classifications, most of the group's media output was "strategic"—that is to say, individually indistinct and relatively low impact, but cumulatively effective and far-reaching.[35] The remainder was "tactical"—that is, irregular, agitative, and proactive.[36] Generally speaking, strategic propaganda was intended to maintain and curate the information atmosphere, keeping the Islamic State brand relevant and credible, even in the face of inexorable territorial loss. Through strategic propaganda, al-Baghdadi's media cabal sought to engender a long-term psychological shift in the minds of sympathetic audiences by altering the entire worldview of the consumers, rather than just their understanding of a particular event or series of events.[37] Conversely, it also used tactical propaganda to work toward more obvious objectives such as recruiting supporters, intimidating enemies, and countering the messaging operations of adversaries.[38]

The information campaign on Mosul offered a paradigmatic example of this bifurcated approach toward communication. Most of the time, the propaganda that emerged was simply strategic filler, a component part of the broader caliphate narrative that accumulated with time. Along with the incidental "regulars" (e.g., the radio bulletins and weekly news roundups), these products were fundamental to the perpetuation of the caliphate myth, no matter how unremarkable they appeared at first sight. Throughout the battle for the city, they served as supporting evidence for the Islamic State's narrative of defiance and—whether they depicted civilian governance or collateral damage, individual skirmishes or distant suicide attacks—offered a continuation of an ideological line that was established years ago. In this sense, the strategic propaganda products were more or less business as usual for the propagandists, and the fact that Mosul was their subject was largely incidental.

At the other end of the Ellulian spectrum was the high-impact tactical campaign propaganda, which the Islamic State disseminated in an effort to aggressively redirect the information agenda around Mosul. During the 100 days of the battle, tactical propaganda took two forms: provincial feature films and leadership statements. Some called for action and others merely reiterated what had previously been said but, in any case, each was distinct from the general flood of strategic propaganda. There was nothing automatic about these products, which demanded active conscientious consumption. Fusing together incitement and entertainment, they were meant to be watched, read, or listened to in full, perhaps even multiple times. They were an event of their own, a disruptive moment at which supporters online and fighters off-line were meant to stop and think, to take stock of their position, and to suppress any personal doubts or concerns.

It would be wrong to think that propaganda at one end of Ellul's spectrum was more important than propaganda at another. While each one had a very different role, one in isolation of another would have been a fraction as effective than a combination of them. In any case, it is important to reiterate that, during the Mosul campaign, propaganda not only was used by the Islamic State to intimidate, repudiate, recruit, or radicalize, as is commonly conceived.[39] But it also was geared toward maintaining a strategic atmosphere of resilience for the benefit of those who were already active supporters, perpetuating a sense that things remained in motion and that the divine winds were continuing to blow in the direction of the caliphate.

Thematic Analysis

In response to the battle for east Mosul, the Islamic State propagandists focused on three overlapping elements operating within rigid strategic narrative parameters that rarely shifted. The first element was the military dimension of the campaign. Comprising the vast majority of the database, this dimension consisted of suicide mythicism, foot soldier heroism, and strategic denialism. The second and third elements were civilian victimization and propaganda that focused on depicting the Islamic State as utopia.

The Military Dimension

Suicide mythicism. From the outset of the Mosul campaign, it was clear that suicide operations would come to characterize the Islamic State's defense of the city. Indeed, in the first week alone, the group claimed that its fighters perpetrated no fewer than fifty-eight vehicle-borne attacks.[40] Although information regarding the particularities of these operations was initially scarce, the Islamic State's reporting changed tactically three weeks after the beginning of the campaign, at which point it began to release detailed claims through the A'maq News Agency, along with special martyrdom reports from the Nineveh Province Media Office, Bayan Radio, and *Naba'* newspaper.[41]

It is important to note that the propagandistic communication of suicide attacks was nothing particularly new for the organization. Many years prior to this campaign, its media team had developed a relatively convoluted system for martyrdom reporting, whereby it would issue announcements on password-protected forums, followed by sporadic photographs, and, on some occasions, video wills.[42] For a long time, it seemed that this formula was deemed sufficient, even after the Islamic State caliphate was declared in 2014 and its use of the tactic ballooned.[43] However, in the context of Mosul, the Islamic State suicide attacks were so regular that the group needed to enhance these tributes—if nothing else, just to keep up a steady flow of suicidal volunteers. To this end, the propagandists were hyperactive in their efforts to simultaneously humanize and deify the perpetrators, seemingly attempting to turn them into demigods, inspirational "big brothers" that were bearing the brunt of the Islamic State's defensive operations.[44] Would-be suicide operatives were repeatedly cast as selfless sons of Islam, just as excited to be defending the Islamic State as they were at the prospect of certain paradise. This was at its most extreme in *The Knights of the*

Ministries, a video in which would-be bombers were shown praying, eating, and joking around together, before drawing lots in a competition to see who would embark on the first mission.[45] For the one who "won," his seemingly uncoerced happiness at the prospect of impending death—and the apparent envy of his associates—was almost palpable.

In this sense, the campaign was a game-changer for jihadist martyr-dom media. The propagandists devoted more attention than ever to telling the stories of individual attackers, not only sharing their names and nationalities but also interviewing them about their broader life. Teenage bombers were quizzed about their time as youth cadets,[46] and adult men were filmed describing happiness at the prospect of leaving behind their friends.[47] On occasion, family members were even asked to discuss on camera the pain—or pride—they felt at the prospect of los-ing a loved one to an Islamic State suicide operation.[48]

As well as lionizing the operatives involved, the group experi-mented with different techniques for depicting the attacks themselves. Between 2014 and 2016, the norm for martyrdom propaganda had been carside chats with soon-to-be bombers followed by zoomed-in footage of distant mushroom clouds.[49] But this format downplayed the sheer scale of urban suicide bombings in Mosul and failed to show the level of damage a single human sacrifice could cause. To work around this problem, the propagandists turned to drone technology; and, in early January 2017, they reached a milestone when they released a single forty-minute-long video of high-definition aerial footage that depicted thirty-eight separate suicide attacks.[50] Each operation was expertly gam-ified: they were shown in quick succession from start to finish, the tar-gets highlighted with computer-generated graphics, and the resultant explosions delivered in slow motion. In Mosul, the Islamic State revo-lutionized its marketing of suicide tactics, framing them as an unparal-leled tool—the caliphate's decisive asymmetric weapon.

Foot soldier heroism. In conjunction with the first narrative, Islamic State foot soldiers were portrayed as stoic and fearless. The propagandists evidently wanted to demonstrate that the organization was not going to crumble without a fight and, even if they felt that defeat would ultimately be unavoidable, it was vital that they communicated this with grace and enthusiasm. Hence, they worked to idealize those who were fighting, con-stantly emphasizing their masculinity, altruism, and strength of faith.

At the beginning of the battle, Islamic State media operatives pri-oritized depictions of personal defiance over anything else. Soldiers were shown declaring that, if the Iraqi Security Forces penetrated the city, they would be there, personally prepared to fight until the death.[51] One month after the beginning of the campaign, when it had become clear that the ISF and its allies were making progress, this idea of provocative defiance was supplanted with something else: depictions of joy. Whether the foot soldiers were filmed firing SPG-9 recoilless rifles,[52] laying down covering fire with heavy machine guns,[53] or lobbing homemade grenades over walls,[54] they were shown to be enjoying themselves. Skirmish footage often concluded with images of tired but smiling soldiers,[55] and elated shouts of "Allahu akbar" were routine in front-line video clips.[56] This footage typically ended with a favorite trope of the Islamic State propagandists: photographs of carefully arranged *ghana'im* (war booty) alongside *juthuth* (the charred corpses of enemy soldiers).[57]

In its tactical propaganda, the media team was even more intensely emotive. Videos like *The Promise of Allah* and *Hunters of the Tanks* framed those fighting on the front lines as almost mythic characters: stalwart, courageous, and, most importantly, fully committed to the protection of their "state" and religion.[58]

While at first the propagandists focused on the need for individual forbearance, as the situation became more desperate in Mosul they recalibrated, portraying the campaign as socially intense and emotionally satisfying—an epic collective battle of wills. By framing the resistance like this, they were, paradoxically, able to lace the prospect of defeat with a potent sense of triumphalism.

Strategic denialism. The third pillar of the Islamic State's Mosul-related war propaganda was denialism. It mainly focused on three aspects of the campaign: first, the loss of territory; second, the depletion of recruits; and third, the strategic defeat.

After the first few weeks of the battle, once it was clear that significant loss of land inside the city of Mosul was inevitable, the Islamic State attempted to deflect attention away from the ISF's advances. Instead of using cartographic propaganda, which had been a powerful communicator for the group when it was expanding in 2014 and 2015, they set about challenging enemy claims through infographics jam-packed with military data,[59] photoreports depicting "normal life" in areas that were said to be contested,[60] and video clips showing fighters staking claims in districts that had allegedly already fallen.[61]

The Islamic State's media operatives were also compelled to repudiate rumors about leadership rifts and a dwindling supply of recruits.[62] Whether they were based on sound intelligence or carefully targeted coalition psychological operations, such rumors had the potential to severely damage morale. So—seemingly in response—the propagandists released several videos showing fighters pledging to fight to the death,[63] and civilians signing up in droves.[64]

However, in January 2017, after it became clear that the Islamic State defense of Mosul was down to its last few hundred men, the propagandists did eventually accept that the flow of new recruits had dried up. Reflecting this in a set-piece video, they told stories of doctors, road workers, police officers, and propagandists who had put themselves forward for suicide operations in the city, seemingly wanting to make it appear that the group was, ideologically speaking, just as powerful and popular as it had ever been.[65] The narrative indicated that, even though the caliphate was contracting and no longer able to govern because of the global campaign against it, it was still able to inspire the same level of fervor.

Perhaps the most important aspect of the Islamic State's Mosul denialism was the claim that, against all odds, such as significant loss of territory, depleted ranks, and dead leaders, the organization was continued to make strategic headway in its war against the rest of the world.[66] This idea was manifested in two ways. First, the propagandists reframed the prospect of defeat as evidence that the apocalypse was nearer than ever. In conveying this, the lengthy Furqan Foundation statements from al-Baghdadi[67] and al-Muhajir[68] were crucial, as they were infused with eschatological references and linear comparisons between 2017 and the time of the Prophet Muhammad. The same reverential exaggerated tones dominated the videos produced by the narrators at the Nineveh Province Media Office.

Second, the propagandists also worked to cultivate a sense that this battle had long been anticipated by the Islamic State, and that the city of Mosul was in fact a lure intended to exhaust the ISF and its allies, thereby setting the stage for a future offensive that would ultimately bring Iraq and the rest of the world to its knees.[69] Through this lens of attrition, the eventual loss of Mosul did not matter, as long as the group was able to make it as expensive and painful to the adversary as possible.

By consistently subverting mainstream claims about the Islamic State resistance in Mosul, the group mitigated the damage caused by its incremental loss of the information agenda. Engaging obliquely with the opposing narrative, they deflected and detracted by implication, denying its credibility and reframing what seemed to be impending defeat as a step toward cosmic victory.

The Civilian Victimization Dimension

The constant torrent of warfare propaganda about the east Mosul campaign was interspersed with graphic, but infrequent, allusions to the victimization of Sunni Muslims in and around the city. This narrative—particularly as it pertained to children, women, and elderly people that had been killed or injured by the coalition air campaign—had been an integral part of the Salafi-jihadist ideology long before the rise of the Islamic State, let alone the battle for Mosul.[70] This is intuitive: if the enemies of Islam are said to be deliberately targeting Sunni Muslims, then Sunni Muslims require protection. Therefore, Salafi-jihadists have historically exaggerated this sense of shared victimhood because doing so allows them to legitimize and justify their very existence.

With that in mind, the Islamic State propagandists covering the battle for east Mosul created content that emphasized the civilian costs of war. Broadly speaking, it took two forms: (1) footage of human casualties caused by artillery and air strikes;[71] and (2) occasional videos specifically geared toward showcasing damage to civilian infrastructure.[72]

Somewhat surprisingly, these products were not a regular feature of the information campaign. Indeed, instead of emphasizing and amplifying civilian collateral damage as they had done in other similar circumstances in previous years, the propagandists were notably restrained. Perhaps they had determined that it was not appropriate to emphasize the notion of victimization at that particular juncture. Although victimization had played a much more prominent role in its propaganda in 2014 and 2015,[73] the Islamic State's prospects and priorities had since changed. During those early years, the group's provincial media offices frequently released set-piece videos and photo-essays that iterated and reiterated the "crimes" being committed against Sunni Muslims in Iraq and Syria.[74] This idea was championed as an international call to arms; that is, a way to incite supporters to act, and to foment global credibility.

However, as the Islamic State's territorial outlook diminished over the course of 2016, so did its use of victimization in propaganda. Indeed, it was largely ignored aside from occasional references by the A'maq News Agency. This was probably a result of the fact that the propagandists wanted to control audience perceptions. After all, given that the Islamic State was the defending party, an illustration of the costs being borne by the civilian population could be counterproductive; it could be interpreted as a sign of the Islamic State's impotence—evidence that the group was inadequate as a protector.

The Mosul Utopia Dimension

In the summer of 2014, the Islamic State, which had long aspired to be more than just an insurgent group, redoubled its efforts to brand itself as a divinely guided Islamic utopia, eventually announcing that it had established a global caliphate.[75] In the months and years that followed its caliphate declaration in June 2014, this idea became a unique selling point for the group, and depictions of civilian life in its "state" were soon placed at the forefront of its branding operations.[76] The organization called on supporters to join—not just to fight and, ultimately, die—but to live within it, too, and become one of its founding fathers or mothers. It is difficult to overstate the importance of this ideological promise; indeed, foreign members of the group consistently pointed toward its pseudostatehood as the principal reason they chose it over other Salafi-jihadist organizations such as al-Qaeda.[77]

The city of Mosul—the Islamic State's largest population center for more than two years—figured highly in the propagandists' efforts to market the utopia. Whether it was through images of orphanages,[78] fairgrounds,[79] markets,[80] mosques,[81] or hotels,[82] media operatives milked the city for all it was worth, even using captive British photojournalist John Cantlie to advertise the advantages of living there.[83] Over the course of 2016, as the Islamic State began to lose territory in Iraq, the Mosul utopia theme became markedly less prominent. Indeed, in the period that preceded the battle for Mosul, it had almost entirely vanished from the propaganda roster.

From 16 October 2016 onward, though, this downward trend momentarily reversed; in the early days of the battle, the group began to circulate an unusually high number of propaganda products looking at the continuation of "normal" life in the city: humming markets,[84] blossoming crops,[85] social welfare distribution,[86] and gay men being thrown from tall buildings.[87] On one occasion, the Nineveh Province Media Office even released a photo-essay exhorting the state of dental care in the city.[88] Here, the Islamic State appeared to be using reports of normal life to mark territory and repudiate rumors of discontent. Through depictions of the still fertile economy and, by default, the still buoyant citizenry, they seemed to be hoping to subvert the rumors that civilians in the city were rushing to welcome the encroaching ISF. In a sense, the message of utopia was weaponized and used to directly counteract one of the mainstays of the coalition's information operations strategy in Mosul—namely, the external exacerbation of internal dissent.

As the campaign progressed and the Islamic State's resistance crumbled, the appearance of the Mosul utopia theme declined almost exponentially. Although it was initially used to illustrate that the campaign was ineffectual, and that Islamic State governance would persevere despite immense pressure, this narrative eventually became impossible to sustain and the propagandists dropped it.

Conclusion

The Islamic State's communications from east Mosul between 16 October 2016 and 24 January 2017 were extraordinary. The organization expertly used propaganda to repudiate enemy information operations and, more importantly, to establish a strategic narrative that would ultimately enable it to emerge from the battle conceptually unscathed. While both supporters and adversaries will not forget its defeat in the eastern bank of the city, aside from the obvious material implications its loss did not result in the end of the Islamic State caliphate.

This may seem surprising. After all, the city had been a prized possession for the organization for over two years; its most populous and strategically significant stronghold in Iraq, and the centerpiece of its insurgency.[89] Losing it could easily have spelled the end of the Islamic State brand—which was built on foundations of triumphalism[90]—but due to effective propaganda, it did not. Indeed, through this carefully orchestrated information campaign, al-Baghdadi's caliphate was able to weather the worst of the ideological storm presented by the battle.

It is worth noting that the Islamic State's propagandists developed a new approach during the fight for Mosul. Unlike in previous defensive operations—such as that of Fallujah in May and June 2016—they embraced the Mosul challenge from start to finish. Recognizing that their default approach—to just look the other way—would not work given the city's unparalleled symbolic clout, they flooded the information battlefield with propaganda. Supplementing their torrent of military misinformation with twin streams of victimization- and utopia-themed media, the propagandists were able to spin the defeat in a manner that maintained morale among supporters inside and outside of the caliphate borders. Indeed, despite the battle's outcome, the Islamic State insurgency in Iraq and Syria struggled on—at times even escalating. Moreover, outside of its heartlands, international supporters continued to launch terrorist attacks in its name. Given that the result of the Mosul campaign could easily be predicted, as over 100,000 coalition-backed troops were pitted against less than 6,000 ill-equipped Islamic State fighters—this was probably the best outcome that the organization could have hoped for.[91]

Whatever the case, it is worth ruminating on one notable absence from the Mosul information war: the ultraviolent propaganda for which the Islamic State had become notorious in earlier years. Given that it had made its name through the publication of high-definition videos depicting extreme brutality in 2014 and early 2015, it was striking that throughout the battle for east Mosul, the group did not release a single execution video from the city. Indeed, there were just two instances of execution media during the 100-day period, and both were tacked on to other propaganda products as though an afterthought.[92] The relative absence was even more confounding in light of the fact that, in the months running up to the campaign, the Nineveh Province Media Office's output from Mosul had been more sadistic than ever before, with a series of videos emerging in the autumn months that depicted dozens of alleged spies being executed en masse.[93]

This absence was significant, as it demonstrated that the group's previous videographed ultraviolence was anything but mindless. Rather, it was used selectively, adopted according to the specific situational exigencies of the time. When those exigencies changed, so did the propagandists' communication priorities. This seemingly small anomaly thus dispels the notion that the Islamic State has been a death cult, irrational in its approach toward meting out and communicating violence. Instead, it indicates that al-Baghdadi's media cabal has used brutality tactically, only when it made "sense." The fact that its ultraviolence appears to have been a means to an end and not an end in itself has profound implications. Moreover, it upends the mainstream misconception that violence is instrumental to the organization and, therefore, requires that political and military leaders adjust the framework through which they are challenging it.

Notes

1. Adam Schreck, "Iraqi PM Signals Start of Operations to Drive IS from Mosul," Associated Press, 16 October 2016, http://bigstory.ap.org/article/48dc6eada 72f456fa58d9d78cd93fcb3/iraqi-pm-signals-start-operations-drive-mosul.

2. Moni Basu, "As Iraqi City of Mosul Braces for Battle with ISIS, Its People Recall Gentler Times," CNN, 14 October 2016, http://edition.cnn.com/2016/10/13 /world/iraq-mosul-after-isis.

3. Tim Arango, "Mosul Neighbors Wake Up to a Day Without ISIS," *New York Times,* 2 November 2016.

4. "Iraqi Special Forces Retake 19 Mosul Neighbourhoods," *New Arab,* 1 December 2016, www.alaraby.co.uk/english/news/2016/11/30/iraqi-special-forces -retake-19-mosul-neighbourhoods.

5. Ahmed Rasheed and Dominic Evans, "Iraqi Police Say Ready to Join Assault on East Mosul," Reuters, 12 December 2016, www.reuters.com/article/us -mideast-crisis-iraq-idUSKBN1411FE.

6. Stephen Kalin, "Iraqi Forces in Mosul Mostly in Refit Mode: U.S. General," Reuters, 21 December 2016, www.reuters.com/article/us-mideast-crisis-iraq-mosul -idUSKBN14A197.

7. "US Military Official: 85–90 percent of Eastern Mosul Cleared of ISIS Militants," *Fox News*, 17 January 2017, www.foxnews.com/world/2017/01/17/iraqi -troops-capture-historic-site-in-mosul-destroyed-by-is.html.

8. "Haider al-Abadi: East Mosul Fully Liberated from ISIL," Al Jazeera, 24 January 2017, www.aljazeera.com/news/2017/01/haider-al-abadi-east-mosul-fully -liberated-isil-170124181328309.html.

9. Ian Pannell, "Mosul Battle: BBC Team's Tweets from Front Line," *BBC News*, 1 November 2016, www.bbc.co.uk/news/world-middle-east-37833661.

10. Tim Arango, Eric Schmitt, and Rukmini Callimachi, "Hungry, Thirsty and Bloodied in Battle to Retake Mosul from ISIS," *New York Times*, 18 December 2016.

11. "Live from the Outskirts of Mosul," feed via Rudaw/Associated Press, Al Jazeera English, 17 October 2016, www.facebook.com/aljazeera/videos/10154763661373690.

12. For example, "The Brother Abu Bakr al-Muslawi—May God Accept Him—One of the Operatives of the Martyrdom-Seeking Operations on the Gathering of the Rafidah Army and Its Militias in the Outskirts of Shaqqaq al-Hadaba' in North East Mosul," photoreport, The Islamic State: Nineveh Province Media Office, 8 January 2017.

13. For example, "Three Humvee Vehicles Were Destroyed, Two More Disabled and 14 Members of the ISF Killed During a Martyrdom-Seeking Operation in the Outskirts of al-Ta'mim in Mosul," operation claim, The Islamic State: A'maq News Agency, 15 December 2016.

14. For example, *The Destruction of a Humvee Vehicle Belonging to the Hashd Militias in Talal al-'Adhba South of Mosul*, video, The Islamic State: A'maq News Agency, 4 December 2016.

15. For example, Hannah Al-Othman, "'It's Complete Destruction, Absolute Carnage. Like Something from a Spielberg Film': Worryingly Gaunt ISIS Hostage John Cantlie Appears in New Propaganda Video from Mosul," *Daily Mail*, 15 December 2016; Indra Warnes, "ISIS' Drone Strike: Sick ISIS Jihadis Release 'Teaser Trailer' Showing Extremists in Mosul Dropping Bombs from DRONES and Carrying Out Suicide Bombings," *The Sun*, 23 January 2017.

16. Jacques Ellul, *Propaganda: The Formation of Men's Attitudes*, translated by Konrad Kellen and Jean Lerner (New York: Random House Vintage Books, 1973).

17. Steven Stalinsky and R. Sosnow, "Germany-Based Encrypted Messaging App Telegram Emerges as Jihadis' Preferred Communications Platform," Middle East Media Research Institute, 23 December 2016, www.memri.org/reports/germany -based-encrypted-messaging-app-telegram-emerges-jihadis-preferred-communications.

18. Christopher Stewart and Mark Maremont, "Twitter and Islamic State Deadlock on Social Media Battlefield," *Wall Street Journal*, 13 April 2016.

19. See Charlie Winter, "Map of the Islamic State Media Nexus," Twitter, 18 December 2016, https://twitter.com/charliewinter/status/810467872199872517.

20. For example, "Men from the People of Mosul Flock to Sign Up to the Islamic State," video clip, The Islamic State: A'maq News Agency, 15 January 2017.

21. For example, "A Snapshot of Life in the City of Tal'afar to the West of Mosul," video clip, The Islamic State: A'maq News Agency, 20 November 2016.

22. For example, "One Week into the Battle for Mosul," infographic, The Islamic State: A'maq News Agency, 24 October 2016.

23. For example, "12 Martyrdom-Seeking Operations and Fierce Battles During the First Few Days of the Battle for Mosul," detailed news, The Islamic State: A'maq News Agency, 17 October 2016.

24. Abu Abdullah al-Masri, "The Isis Papers: A Masterplan for Consolidating Power," translated by Aymenn Jawad al-Tamimi, *The Guardian,* 7 December 2016.

25. For example, *The Ignition of War,* video, The Islamic State: Nineveh Province Media Office, 29 October 2016; *The Promise of Allah,* video, The Islamic State: Nineveh Province Media Office, 14 November 2016; *The Impact of the Bullets,* video, The Islamic State: Nineveh Province Media Office, 28 November 2016; *The Hunters of the Tanks,* video, The Islamic State: Nineveh Province Media Office, 13 December 2016; *The Procession of Light,* video, The Islamic State: Nineveh Province Media Office, 3 January 2017; *The Knights of the Ministries,* video, The Islamic State: Nineveh Province Media Office, 24 January 2017.

26. For example, "Breaking News: Aspect of the Ongoing Battles with the Rafidi Army and Its Militias in the East of Mosul," photoreport, The Islamic State: Nineveh Province Media Office, 9 November 2016.

27. *The Promise of Allah; The Impact of the Bullets; The Hunters of the Tanks; The Procession of Light; The Knights of the Ministries.*

28. Asma Ajroudi, "'It Sounded Like BBC': ISIS Seeks Legitimacy Via 'Caliphate' Radio Service," Al Arabiya, 12 June 2015, http://english.alarabiya .net/en/media/television-and-radio/2015/06/12/-It-sounds-like-BBC-ISIS-seeks -legitimacy-via-caliphate-radio-service-.html.

29. For example, "Thursday 29th Rabi'a al-Awwal 1438," news bulletin, The Islamic State: Bayan Radio, 28 December 2016.

30. "The Apostates Will See What the Mujahideen Have Prepared for Them After Their Campaign on Mosul Has Been Broken," interview with military amir, The Islamic State: *Naba',* 17 November 2016.

31. For example, "Naba' Newspaper, the 61st Edition," The Islamic State: *Naba',* 28 December 2016.

32. The exception was: "Issue 61," The Islamic State: *Naba',* 22 December 2016.

33. For example, "This Is What Allah and His Messenger Promised Us," audio statement by Abu Bakr al-Baghdadi, The Islamic State: Furqan Foundation, 2 November 2016.

34. Charlie Winter, "The Virtual 'Caliphate': Understanding Islamic State's Propaganda Strategy," Quilliam Foundation, July 2015, www.stratcomcoe.org/charlie -winter-virtual-caliphate-understanding-islamic-states-propaganda-strategy.

35. Ellul, *Propaganda,* p. 62.

36. Ibid.

37. Ibid., p. 24.

38. Ibid., p. 32.

39. Pamela Engel, "ISIS Has Mastered a Crucial Recruiting Tactic No Terrorist Group Has Ever Conquered," *Business Insider,* 9 May 2015, http://uk.businessinsider .com/isis-is-revolutionizing-international-terrorism-2015-5.

40. "One Week into the Battle for Mosul."

41. See, for example, the case of Khattab al-Imarati in Charlie Winter, "War by Suicide: A Statistical Analysis of the Islamic State's Martyrdom Industry," No. 10 (The Hague: International Centre for Counter-Terrorism, February 2017), https:// icct.nl/wp-content/uploads/2017/02/ICCT-Winter-War-by-Suicide-Feb2017.pdf.

42. For an early example, see Mohammed Hafez, *Suicide Bombers in Iraq: The Strategy and Ideology of Martyrdom* (Washington, DC: United States Institute of Peace, 2007).

43. Margaret Coker, "How Islamic State's Win in Ramadi Reveals New Weapons, Tactical Sophistication and Prowess," *Wall Street Journal,* 25 May 2015.

44. *The Procession of Light.*

45. *The Knights of the Ministries.*

46. Ibid.

47. Ibid.

48. *The Procession of Light.*

49. For example, "Snapshot of the Clashes Which Took Place Last Night Between the Fighters of the Islamic State and the Iraqi Security Forces in the al-Qadisiyya al-Thaniyya District of Mosul," video clip, The Islamic State: A'maq News Agency, 30 November 2016.

50. *The Procession of Light.*

51. For example, "Deployment of Islamic State Fighters on the Streets of Mosul," video clip, The Islamic State: A'maq News Agency, 18 October 2016.

52. For example, "Targeting One of the Rafidi Army and Militia Positions in Ba'uiza with an SPG-9 in Northern Mosul," photoreport, The Islamic State: Nineveh Province Media Office, 11 December 2016.

53. For example, "Snapshot of the Clashes Between Islamic State Fighters and Iraqi Security Forces in al-Zarqawi District," video clip, The Islamic State: A'maq News Agency, 9 November 2016.

54. For example, "Aspect of the Clashes with the Rafidi Army and Its Militias with Light and Medium Weapons in al-Hadaba' District in Northern Mosul," photoreport, The Islamic State: Nineveh Province Media Office, 13 January 2017.

55. For example, "Glimpses of the Clashes in al-Hamdaniyya to the South East of Mosul," video clip, The Islamic State: A'maq News Agency, 23 October 2016.

56. For example, "Disabling an Abrams Tank of the Iraqi Army Near Qayyara, to the South of Mosul," video clip, The Islamic State: A'maq News Agency, 17 October 2017.

57. For example, "Aspect of the Destroyed Vehicles and Booty of the Mujahideen Near Salam in South Mosul," photoreport, The Islamic State: Nineveh Province Media Office, 30 December 2016.

58. *The Hunters of the Tanks.*

59. For example, "Month One of the Battle for Mosul," infographic, The Islamic State: A'maq News Agency, 18 November 2016.

60. For example, "Glimpses from al-Karama District in the East of Mosul," video clip, The Islamic State: A'maq News Agency, 31 October 2016.

61. For example, "Glimpses of Life in al-Intisar District After the Expulsion of the Iraqi Security Forces," video clip, The Islamic State: A'maq News Agency, 8 November 2016.

62. "Report: ISIL Crushes Rebellion Plot in Mosul," Al Jazeera, 14 October 2016, www.aljazeera.com/news/2016/10/report-isil-crushes-rebellion-plot-mosul-161014142437833.html; Kim Sengupta, "ISIS Leaders 'Accepting Defeat in Mosul and Raqqa and Encouraging Recruits to Commit Terror in Europe,'" *The Independent,* 20 October 2016.

63. For example, "Fighters of the Islamic State Pledge to the Death in Tal'afar to the West of Mosul," video clip, The Islamic State: A'maq News Agency, 19 October 2016.

64. For example, "Men from the People of Mosul Flock to Sign Up to the Islamic State."

65. *The Knights of the Ministries.*

66. "The Apostates Will See What the Mujahideen Have Prepared for Them After Their Campaign on Mosul Has Been Broken."

67. "This Is What Allah and His Messenger Promised Us."

68. "And You Will Remember What I Say to You," audio statement by Abul-Hassan al-Muhajir, The Islamic State: Furqan Foundation, 5 December 2016.

69. "The Apostates Will See What the Mujahideen Have Prepared for Them After Their Campaign on Mosul Has Been Broken."

70. Mohammed Hafez, "Martyrdom Mythology in Iraq: How Jihadists Frame Suicide Terrorism in Videos and Biographies," *Terrorism and Political Violence* 19, no. 1 (2007): 99–103.

71. For example, "Remnants of America Bombing on the al-Quds District of Mosul," video clip, The Islamic State: A'maq News Agency, 2 November 2016.

72. For example, "John Cantlie Discusses the Bombing of the Bridges and Water and Electricity Infrastructure in the City of Mosul," video clip, The Islamic State, A'maq News Agency, 7 December 2016.

73. Charlie Winter, "Documenting the Virtual 'Caliphate,'" Quilliam Foundation, October 2015, http://truevisiontv.com/uploads/websites/39/wysiwyg/doctors/jihad/FINAL-documenting-the-virtual-caliphate.pdf.

74. Ibid.

75. "Isis Rebels Declare 'Islamic State' in Iraq and Syria," *BBC News,* 30 June 2014, www.bbc.co.uk/news/world-middle-east-28082962.

76. Winter, "Documenting the Virtual 'Caliphate.'"

77. For example, Jacob Sheikh, "'I Just Said It. The State': Examining the Motivations for Danish Foreign Fighting in Syria," *Perspectives on Terrorism* 10, no. 5 (2016): 59–67.

78. For example, "An Orphanage in Nineveh Province," photoreport, The Islamic State: Nineveh Province Media Office, 3 September 2014.

79. For example, *A Day Out for Those Living in the Shade of the Caliphate,* video, The Islamic State: Nineveh Province Media Office, 10 March 2015.

80. For example, "A Tour of Najafi Street in the City of Mosul," photoreport, The Islamic State: Nineveh Province Media Office, 3 March 2015.

81. For example, "Special Coverage of the Khutba and Prayers in Mosul's Great Mosque," video, The Islamic State: Furqan Foundation, 5 July 2014.

82. For example, "Refurbishment and Opening of the al-Warithin Hotel in the City of Mosul," photoreport, The Islamic State: Nineveh Province Media Office, 15 May 2015.

83. *Inside Mosul,* video, The Islamic State: Al Hayat Media Center, 3 January 2015.

84. For example, "Photographs from the City of Mosul: The Market in the Nabi Yunus (Peace Be upon Him) District," photoreport, The Islamic State: Nineveh Province Media Office, 21 November 2016.

85. For example, "Agricultural Activity in the City of Mosul," photoreport, The Islamic State: Nineveh Province Media Office, 14 November 2016.

86. For example, "Aspect of the Work of the Zakat Office in Mosul: The Distribution of Flour to the Needy," photoreport, The Islamic State: Nineveh Province Media Office, 28 December 2016.

87. For example, "Implementing the Hadd of Allah upon One Who Has Acted the Action of the People of Lut," photoreport, The Islamic State: Nineveh Province Media Office, 11 November 2016.

88. "Photo Report: A Tour in One of the Dental Care Centres in the City of Mosul," photoreport, The Islamic State: Nineveh Province Media Office, 9 October 2016.

89. Jared Malsin, "The Next War for Iraq," *Time,* 22 June 2016.

90. See Winter, "Documenting the Virtual 'Caliphate.'"

91. "Islamic State's Myriad Enemies Make for Awkward Alliance," Reuters, 2 November 2016, www.reuters.com/article/us-mideast-crisis-iraq-military-idUSKBN 12X1UR; "Islamic State Has 5,000 to 6,000 Fighters in Mosul: Iraqi Army," Reuters, 19 October 2016, www.reuters.com/article/us-mideast-crisis-iraq-mosul -idUSKCN12J0XG.

92. Those instances were during the final minutes of: *The Impact of the Bullets,* video, The Islamic State: Nineveh Province Media Office, 28 November 2016; *The Procession of Light.*

93. For example, *But If You Return, We Will Return III,* video, The Islamic State: Nineveh Province Media Office, 19 September 2016.

11

Islamic State Propaganda as a Strategic Challenge

Vladimir Sotnikov

The Islamic State is one of the most complex, closed, and relatively effective military and political phenomena in contemporary international relations. Although in Russia, as well as in many Western countries, it is classified as a "terrorist organization," in the Middle East the attitude toward DAESh (which is the Arabic abbreviation of the Islamic State)[1] is not so unambiguous. In the Greater Middle East and among many pro-Western elites, there is a firm opinion that the Islamic State is an artificially created political structure literally stuffed with agents of the most diverse secret services in the world. In response to the question, "How can such a confrontational attitude from the US and Western countries to DAESh be explained by Washington and its allies?" usually, after some pause, a strange answer follows: no one knows what alliances emerge at this level, who is against whom, and who is a "friend" of whom.[2]

It is possible to argue that, in an increasingly complicated and complex picture of the Greater Middle East (where systemic intricacies are constantly becoming more and more confusing), the Islamic State occupies one of the most mysterious places. One of the main reasons for this is the involvement of various secret services in its emergence and formation. As a certain prototype organization, the Islamic State was created by experienced officers from Saddam Hussein's (hereafter, Saddam) secret services, including representatives of the powerful intelligence services of the Ba'ath Party.[3] Therefore, the Islamic State is distinguished by a rather high professional level of officer corps, management personnel, propaganda mechanisms, and management of the sphere of internal security.[4] The internal structure of the organization, in accordance with the traditional rules of functioning of the Mukhabarat (special services) combines open, semiofficial, and fully closed organizational components.[5] In fact the special services of Syria and Turkey to some extent, as well as the US and British military intelligence services (to a lesser extent), along with Saddam's Mukhabarat, have participated in the creation and formation of the Islamic State since 2003.[6] This is because Iraqi special services have accumulated significant experiences developing close ties with their colleagues from other countries during the Iran-Iraq War. Thus, the best way in which we may describe the origins of the Islamic State can be found in a good account by Yezid Sayigh, senior associate and professor at the Carnegie Middle East Center in Beirut. His provocative thesis is that the Islamic State—whether it is called the Islamic State in Iraq and Syria (ISIS), the Islamic State of Iraq and Levant (ISIL), or DAESh—is, in organizational and strategic terms, a clone of Saddam's Iraqi Mukhabarat state. The heart of ISIS, he contends, is Iraqi. Abu Bakr al-Baghdadi mimics Saddam through his deliberately brutal behavior and his ruthless consolidation of power. But being Iraqi is also a drawback as it seeks to extend its domination in Syria, where it is challenged by the al-Qaeda-linked Jabhat al-Nusra Front, which has a stronger Syrian base.[7]

At the highest strategic level, albeit temporarily, US and former Ba'athist interests coincided.[8] The US military intelligence community, which seeks to create a new system of power balance in the Greater Middle East, makes a strategic bet on the pressure toward the Islamic Republic of Iran, which they have long sought after since the Iranian revolution. Waiting for a convenient moment in Iranian internal politics, the US military intelligence services simultaneously need a significant regional counterweight to Tehran so that it does not have to become dependent on it as a regional superpower.[9] For various reasons, neither Turkey, Saudi Arabia, nor Israel can become such an effective regional counterweight to Iran, and it is here that DAESh represents an important factor in involving the Iranian security forces in a series of flaring regional power conflicts. In 2014 some US intelligence agencies used the Islamic State effectively against the Nouri al-Maliki government in Iraq, which was actively supported by the leadership of the Iranian Islamic Revolutionary Guard Corps (IRGC).[10] In addition, the Islamic State weakened the IRGC in another realm by taking control of territories in Syria and Iraq, which are Iran's allies. At the same time, the current conspiracy intrigue with the use of the Islamic State objectively plays into the hands of the political grouping of Iranian president Hassan Rouhani. Strengthening the position of the Islamic State in the region facilitates a more rapid establishment of the entire complex of relations between Tehran and Washington.[11]

The current confrontation between the West and the Islamic State is consistent, and serves the long-term strategic interests of the organization because it can be exhibited as the only military-political vanguard of the entire Islamic world in confrontation with the "Western Crusaders."[12] However, the Islamic State is the brainchild of the metaphysical energy of the most implacable fundamentalist jihadism, based on the eschatological credo, the deepest faith in the early incarnation of ancient prophecies about the "end of the times," and the special fate of those Muslims who will participate in the realization of these prophecies.

Historical Background

Initially, an ordinary and almost unremarkable unit of al-Qaeda in Iraq, the Islamic State originally called Jamaat at-Tawhid al-Jihad (the Organization of Monotheism and Jihad), led a classic insurgency war committing terror attacks against the Shiite population of Iraq, pro-US government forces, and their facilities. Such tactics pursued no long-term goals; the stake was placed on the process itself but not on the final result.[13] However, even in this initial period among the fighters and the leadership of this organization (which later was renamed the Islamic State of Iraq), there were representatives of Saddam's former security agencies and special services who were deeply disillusioned with Ba'athist ideology.[14] A major organizational transformation took place in 2010, when former high-ranking officers of the army and secret services of Saddam, who were released from US prisons in Iraq, headed to lead the organization. At that time, all of the original top leadership of the Islamic State had been killed. Of the forty leaders, financiers, senior liaison officers, and moderators of the Iraqi underground network, only eight remained alive. Two key leaders had also been killed: Abu Omar al-Baghdadi and Abu Ayyub al-Masri.[15] Military professionals of Saddam managed to take places in the higher and middle hierarchy of the organization.

At the same time, the main impetus was given to two strategic directions. First, the leader of military experts, Haji Bakr, quickly and rigidly regrouped and reformed the disparate regional groups operating in the Sunni territories, creating a flexible umbrella structure of governance with a single headquarters center whose role was performed by the *shura* (council) of commanders. It is quite natural that most of the *shura* were occupied by the former military, and Bakr managed to press the election of Abu Bakr al-Baghdadi, who at that time was just one of the group's territorial leaders, to head the practically new organization. The second strategic direction was the special attention given to the formation or recreation of the agent network, cells of the organization in various state bodies and institutions of Iraq and in the law enforcement agencies in particular.[16] Thus, the main components of the structure of the Islamic State were largely based on the templates of the Ba'athist organization by experienced army officers and special services of Saddam, including representatives of the key party intelligence of the Ba'ath Party.[17] Since this system of special services was one of the most effective in the Middle East, the systemic experience that special services executives brought into the Islamic State largely explains its surprising success. Unlike numerous other radical jihadist organizations, the Islamic State radically differed by the high professional level and discipline of the officer corps, management cadres, the propaganda mechanism, and the management of the sphere of internal security. The special psychological character of the Islamic State in many respects resembles the echeloned underground specifics of the Iraqi Ba'ath Party.[18]

Organizational Structure

The Islamic State is based on a flexible combination of a network-centric model and the classical principles of hierarchical structure. This makes it possible for the organization's leadership to efficiently use open, semiclosed, and covert organizational components.[19] The highest level of command as discussed above is the military-political *shura* and specialized headquarters centers. The second level is a certain amorphous community of field commanders. These field commanders have a decisive influence on the everyday execution of power in controlled territories. Taking into consideration the combination of hierarchical and network principles of the organization, the decisionmaking processes in the Islamic State go simultaneously from top to bottom and vice versa. The third level in the organization's structure is the public and its growing social support. This support comes not only from Syria and Iraq, but also from throughout the Middle East and Islamic world.

To understand the specific characteristics of this three-level structure, it is important to focus on some of the outcomes of combining radical jihadism and the specific experience of Saddam's Mukhabarat. Since the Islamic State represents a creative use of hybrid warfare methods in the framework of network-centric wars, even the physical elimination of a leader or his deputy does not seriously affect the effectiveness of its combat operations.[20] An important place in the model of hybrid wars of the Islamic State takes the techniques of forming and deploying agent networks, primarily based on ideology. The Islamic State has (with a high probability) the most extensive intelligence network in the Middle East, with a tendency to expand into other geopolitical zones such as Afghanistan and Pakistan, Central Asia, and Southeast Asia. Gradually, a network of volunteer sympathizers and informers was formed that only gather the necessary information, primarily about the representatives of the enemy's power structures, military and security services, representatives of social strata, clans and tribes hostile to the DAESh, mass enemy agents, and so on. This information makes it possible to strike a decisive blow to the enemy's intelligence network almost immediately, such as in spring of 2015 in Ramadi and Palmyra (Syria), and prevent the deployment of subversive and guerrilla actions in the rear of DAESh.[21] At the next stage, working deep underground in the territories of Saudi Arabia and Jordan and based on a network of ideologically motivated informers, it becomes possible to start the formation of separate cells (often called "sleeper cells") and groups capable of individual subversive and guerrilla-style actions for the purpose of critical sociopolitical destabilization. This is currently happening in Baghdad. Third, such cells gradually begin to reunite into some common subregional or national networks.

In spring of 2015, the Qatar TV channel Al Jazeera conducted a survey of its television audience and found that almost 70 percent of viewers (likely only in Arabic) endorse the goals of the Islamic State. For some Arab countries, this figure can sometimes reach 90–95 percent.[22] In a closed mode, the Islamic State supports a significant number of Sunni elites, primarily Arab elites. In any case, it is the financial cash flows of these elite groups that make up one of the main articles, perhaps even the main article, of the revenue for the Islamic State's hefty budget. In a number of Islamic countries, the Islamic State already was perceived as the leading political entity of the Sunni majority. By August 2015, the Islamic State controlled almost 45 percent of Syria and about 35 percent of Iraq, with a total population of 8–10 million.[23] In the occupied territories, the bodies of territorial administration were forcibly created or recreated, uniformed sharia norms of conduct were introduced, and representatives of all hostile or disloyal groups of the population were severely exterminated. The relevant information was provided by the agent network, criminal gangs were also destroyed, and competing extremist groups were either brought to submission or liquidated. In Syria, the primary goal of the Islamic State was not to overthrow the

Bashar al-Assad regime, but to form its own unique Islamic State. The realization of the idea of Pan-Arab unity, as it was formulated in the party documents of the Iraqi Ba'ath Party, was intended to begin by the unification of Iraq and Syria, including by the consolidation of the Ba'athist parties of both countries.

In this entire captured space, ISIS monitors and manages numerous oil and gas facilities, electric power plants, banks and other existing economic enterprises, and continues to receive huge subsidies from different external supporters. The economies of these territories are gradually starting to work for the new caliphate state entities, providing goods for commodity markets and filing tax revenues. Although the US dollar and existing national currencies are still the legal tender in the territory of the caliphate, the Islamic State had planned to issue its own currency in 2016 (dinars and dirhams); however, as of spring of 2017, it had not been issued.[24] The focus on current state building is given to the restoration and development of traditional Muslim social infrastructures: advocating for equitable distribution of resources, the Islamic State is building hospitals, new roads, schools, and improved transportation links. Where possible, DAESh seeks to restore the administrative infrastructure for all state institutions responsible for social livelihoods to smoothly function and for disciplined officials to obediently work. Social life in the Islamic State–controlled territories has been restored in accordance with the laws and rules of sharia, which essentially represent the main Islamic laws and customs of day-to-day life of Muslims. Outfits of the religious police Hizb drive around the settlements and carefully monitor the preservation of fair prices and compliance with the rules of sharia. Everywhere, there are sharia judicial and executive authorities. The internal policies of the Islamic State are based on the principles and norms of social justice, social solidarity with the underpaid and poor, and the need to develop a self-organizing society based on traditional Islamic principles. The Islamic State's leadership conducts policies to encourage social support in different directions at the same time. These include direct-targeted support for the disadvantaged sections of the population; for example, the mass distribution of food and medicines and provision of medical care, as was the case immediately after the capture of Palmyra. This is widely branched, large-scale religious and ideological work. It involves the reconstruction of the state structures aimed for the support of life, and also includes substantial measures to ensure social justice in the territories under control of the Islamic State. In January 2015, the leadership of the organization officially stated that the Islamic State's budget for the current year would amount to more than $2 billion.[25] The main purpose of this disclosure, at the time of a sharp drop in oil prices, was a public demonstration to the world that the long-term megaproject of the Islamic State with its influential and wealthy allies in the Islamic world could not fail.

Ideology and Political Strategy of the Islamic State

Since mid-2014, the Islamic State has proved to be a powerful strong-willed ideological force, which has transferred the ideas of a caliphate from the historical sphere into the most practical domain. DAESh is an effective political and ideological phenomenon, not only in the Greater Middle East but also arguably in the world. A key criterion for success in the area of political ideology in any part of the globe is a large-scale deployment of the "common cause" project, constantly negotiated with the majority of society. It is not solely (or so much) the historical and propagandistic support for the common cause for the widest strata of the population, but the promotion and support of practical mechanisms and technologies where hundreds of thousands, even millions of people, can personally and directly participate in the implementation.[26] Such, for example, is the ideological meaning behind the call of ISIS leader Abu Bakr al-Baghdadi for Muslims from other countries to travel to Iraq and Syria and jointly build a caliphate. However, he particularly emphasizes that immigration to the the Islamic State presents a religious duty of all Muslims in the world. By mid-2015, citizens from more than 100 countries had moved to the Islamic State.[27]

As part of the ideology of the Islamic State, its caliphate is not a "nation" ideology in the Western sense. The caliphate is a political embodiment of the Islamic *ummah* as a fundamentally new social reality. On one hand, this ideology gives a real sense of meaning to the Muslim identity and will continue to have a growing influence on millions of predominantly young people across the Islamic world. The concept of a caliphate created by all Muslims, and unifying in practice the sacred, social, and political meanings of the *ummah,* becomes a natural pole of attraction to the system. Yet on the other hand, such an ideology firmly sets the Muslim world against the rest of civilization.[28] The proclamation of the caliphate is a deeply symbolic action of ISIS against the Sykes-Picot Agreement of 1916 as well as the division of the Arab region, which had been recognized 100 years ago by the West.[29] As is well known, the Sykes-Picot Agreement was contrary to the then

unwritten agreement with the Arab leaders, to whom Europe had promised an independent Arab state with its capital in Damascus in exchange
for their support in fighting against the Ottomans. For the Islamic State,
the public rejection in words and practice of the Sykes-Picot Agreement
is advantageous since it provides motivation for its fighters who consider themselves the avengers of historical injustice as well as the rightful heirs of the caliphate after the fall of the Ottoman Empire.

The unexpected forced conversion of ISIL into the Islamic State suggests (in practice) a declaration of jihad to all secular elements of the
West in the Muslim world. This means that the reality of a civilizational
conflict between Islam and the West goes into a specific sphere of political and military confrontation, at least in the Greater Middle East. On the
other hand, the appearance of the actual Islamic State, the caliphate,
means that an underlying hatred of hundreds of millions of Muslims in
the West is capable of being channeled with unpredictable political implications in the medium term. The proclamation of the caliphate in the
global ideological context presumes a strategic challenge to the very existence of senseless Western materialistic civilization, and refers to Islam
thought and the Islamic world. The issue is that the caliphate for many
Muslims refers to a clear expression of a fundamentally new social community in the history of humankind, the *ummah*. Within this occurs a
mystical process of universal, group, and personal life sense of being.

Why are millions of people, and not just those in the Islamic world,
supportive of the radical and ultraradical ideological views of DAESh
despite strong global counterpropaganda? This influence is not only manifested on the "Muslim street" or "Muslim bazaar" level, but among the
elites.[30] For example, ministers of the Republic of Chad came to listen to
the preaching of Mohammed al-Yusuf, the leader of Boko Haram, an ally
of DAESh in the region.[31] Another notable example is that many influential political elite groups and clans of the Gulf are rendering financial aid
to DAESh, and also are establishing confidential communication with its
senior leadership. The reason for the political and ideological influence of
the Islamic State is that the organization is consciously or unconsciously
perceived in the Islamic world as (perhaps) the only alternative to
impending global and regional chaos. Therefore, the operational commander of US forces in the Middle East, Major General Michael Nagata,
and General John Allen, who in 2014 led an international coalition
against DAESh, note that in the West the Islamic State's ideology is not
perceived as an extremely dangerous strategic threat. However, according
to these generals, it is the ideological delegitimization of DAESh that
becomes critical in all attempts to inflict serious damage.[32]

The advocacy of the Islamic State, which serves this ideology, is dominated by a strategic scientific approach: DAESh has a special administration that is systematically engaged in such activities. The Islamic State has its own already substantially hyped magazine *Dabiq*, a film studio, webmasters, a marketing group, a group of hackers, and the experience of effective use of mass media as well as other means of mass communication such as social networks. Moreover, the Islamic State has the potential of experienced professional cadres in this area. In this regard, they are ahead of the Ba'athists. These talented propagandist cadres produce clear and simple promotional products, refraining from abstract, complex, and incomprehensible ideas for large social groups and using the effective impact on the collective unconscious of the masses of the simplest ideas—methods of the repetition of binary and mimetic principles. Such propaganda techniques and technologies can effectively act on the collective and individual consciousness of the majority. For example, the corresponding ideological department of the Islamic State publishes annual reports about its actions, military victories, murders, and financial cash flows. These reports have been massively "propagandized" in the international media and countering this, incidentally, has been one of the main reflective propaganda purposes of the Islamic State. The hidden task of these documents has been to promote expansion of the global unconscious panic among Westerners, to recruit new staff, to intimidate enemies, and to encourage potential new donors to continue funding the jihad against the crusaders, Shiites, and other enemies of the Islamic State. A long-term military and political strategy of DAESh can be labeled as "a big boost to the common Islamic revolution."[33] This is similar to the strategy of the Prophet Muhammad, aimed at stimulating the social revolutionary sentiment among the tribes and nations that oppose the so-called initial Islam.

Therefore, it should be said that the long-term military and political strategy of the Islamic State includes several important components. First, this is systemic propaganda of the special promotion of a new sociopolitical community based on the principles of social justice, social solidarity, and social responsibility. Second, the main attention is not so much given to capturing and retaining territories, but to the total long-term demoralization of the enemy and its armed forces by leaders and groups who support these terror acts. It is worth highlighting here that the system is to essentially impel the most urgent social, political, and ideological contradictions smoldering in many Arab countries, and make them publicly manifest on the surface of the political confrontation. In other words, this is a "purposeful pushing [of] the pan-Arab revolution."[34] As part of this strategy under the existing political and psychological conditions, the Islamic State believes it necessary to promote and further advance the constant active offensive operations undertaken by the combat units of the Islamic State, which involve the application of rapid and unexpected counterattacks with a flexible maneuvering by the available combat forces. In other words, conducting such combined military operations in the absence of the advantage of having heavy military assets and combat aircraft requires that the Islamic State's military commanders perform precise staff coordination and have available proven and reliable communication systems. In addition, such demonstrations of the offensive will, in turn, provide a constant flow of new experienced personnel into the ranks of the group, especially trained military.[35]

Development of Military Capability and Military Tactics

The Islamic State has actually formed a specific regular army to conduct a "hybrid war," the overall strength of which, according to most experts, is 70,000 to 90,000 troops, although other estimates range from 200,000 to 300,000 troops. To the best estimates, five critical factors have led to notable military successes by the Islamic State during the 2014–2015 military campaigns:

- The Islamic State leadership formed its own effective specialized military council, a sort of general chiefs of staff, which consists of eight to thirteen senior officers. The Islamic State has some of the best foreign intelligence and counterintelligence in the Middle East.
- There is a clear presence of high morale and initiative among the officers and soldiers of the Islamic State. This greatly contributes to the decentralization of the military command structure, when the decisions in close combat situations are made by mobile battle groups themselves.
- The Islamic State has already gained a lot of military experience. Many of the commanders of the Islamic State combat units have been progressively in a state of continuous warfighting for several years.
- The military command of the Islamic State effectively leverages and combines in a single tactical model the three interrelated techniques: background information and psychological demoralization of the enemy, the use of unconventional methods of warfare with pressure on the internal weaknesses of the enemy, and conventional military operations after gaining the military advantage.

- Thus, in the 2014–2015 military campaigns, the Islamic State often combined strategic restraint and the ability to plan complex integrated combat operations simultaneously in Syria and Iraq, which involved essentially a kind of multilayered hybrid war, including the use of branched methods of terrorism, urban guerrilla warfare, subversive information-psychological warfare, and traditional methods of conventional war. Thereby, the Islamic State achieved systemic consistency in strategic, operational, and tactical levels of conducting warfare and military force operations.

Among other techniques developed, especially at the tactical level, were weakening the enemy's line of defense by sheltering with massed artillery fire and the formation of "holes" in the defense by using suicide bombers, followed by a large-scale attack on SUV armored cars, equipped with large-caliber antiaircraft guns. A characteristic feature of the Islamic State's attacking tactics is the use of heavy machine guns and RPG fire, with unprecedented use of snipers to whose mass training the Islamic State paid special attention during 2015. The main combat units of DAESh are mobile groups of eight to twelve people mounted on two to five cars. Using Facebook or Twitter, members of a group are picked up at an appointed place at an appointed time. An hour and a half is then spent providing the group with an explanation or the specifications of the combat mission, after which the group rapidly pushes to the point of operation. A significant number of offensive operations are carried out in the morning, after the morning *namaz* (prayer), usually at 5 A.M.[36]

Yet one of the most effective tactical achievements of the Islamic State has been conducting night attacks using armored vehicles and battle tanks equipped with night vision devices. The Islamic State's strategy that focused on provoking panic directly among enemy battle orders, and indirectly by supporting its own people, has repeatedly proved its effectiveness in military history, among the Chinese, the Huns, the Mongols, and during the first Muslim conquests.[37] This strategy, which is widely used by the Islamic State's military leadership, combines tactics of military operations, ambushes, distributed terrorist attacks, hostage taking, and sophisticated psychological warfare relying on hype, frightening rumors, and ostentatious brutality that are designed to induce both horror and admiration through visual and emotional shock.[38] This shock is intended to deprive the enemy soldier or officer of any will and any desire to fight and resist.[39] The tactics of preliminary psychological propaganda and intimidation must lead the enemy into a state of paralysis and stupor. And it is for this purpose that the

Islamic State uses footage (usually staged) of men, women, children, and the elderly, who have been decapitated, buried alive, hung on a meat hook, castrated, or sold like cattle in the markets of Mosul.[40] The induced feelings are inseparable from the underlying traditional marketing of a subconscious identification principle. In its videos Islamic State radicals could just show faceless mountains of corpses, but that would be far less effective than live broadcasts of beheading Western citizens who can easily be identified by a regular viewer. After all, the automatic imitation and basic need for self-identification is an elementary principle of functioning of the human psyche, the use of which is the basis of the work of public relations and marketing. Therefore, the Islamic State is using the elements of the hybrid wars[41] in its military operations and combat warfare against its enemies that presumes the overall strategy tasks of propaganda and psychological numbing and intimidation are as follows:

- Intimidate potential dissidents and dissenters in the Islamic State's own camp. The fear of suspicion of betrayal of the group strengthens the loyalty of its members.
- Create admiration and attraction among people with potential sadistic and psychopathic deviations and inclinations. As psychologists say, in any society of a hundred people at least two or three persons have these tendencies.
- Inflict a psychological and potentially demoralizing blow to the "neighbor" (local population) and "far" enemy (the West), by placing the blame on the executed hostages who, before their deaths, are forced to make the government of their country be responsible for the coming massacre.
- Cause the enemy to experience the so-called Stockholm syndrome;[42] that is, to achieve voluntary submission through fear and expectation. The enemy must be intimidated and bewildered by the dangerous fusion of visual terror and demonization.

In sum, it may be that "ISIL fits the definition of a hybrid threat, effectively using tactics and techniques in a manner similar to other threat actors. It is better funded than many groups the US has faced recently and has attracted a large number of recruits to its cause. ISIL's success so far is due to its ability to control large numbers of fighters, many of whom are recruited foreigners, against ineffective opponents."[43]

When a representative of Western society sees a hostage holding the imperialist West and Western crusaders responsible for the murder of infidels, he or she becomes a potential ideological accomplice, who out of fear spreads DAESh claims. One of the major leitmotifs of the Islamic State's propaganda is substantiated allegations of Western crusaders' "invasion of Muslim lands" (Afghanistan and Iraq) and "oppression" of Muslims. According to this logic, the Islamic State's cruelty is valid because it undertakes this cruelty as a just countermeasure with respect to Western policies toward the Islamic world. One example of the effectiveness of these strategic tactics, such as propaganda influences on the public, is Spain's election results after the Madrid attacks in 2004. The Socialist Party was victorious, even though polling before the tragedy predicted a Popular Party win. The radical Islamist attacks were blamed on the right-wing government of José María Aznar.[44]

Today, the Islamic State actively and widely cultivates its barbaric reputation, which creates an atmosphere of panic not only among real opponents but also among potential ones. Such propaganda terror by the Islamic State's mujahideen leads to a screeching halt and demoralizing of the enemy before the fight and has allowed it to capture whole cities without any resistance after mid-2014. According to most Russian and international experts on terrorism, the Islamic State recruits only those with military training and relevant military experience for their combat units. The most preferred recruits are former officers of any professional army. In the Islamic State ranks are former officers from the armies of Tunisia, the United Kingdom, France, Germany, Kazakhstan, Russia, and Tajikistan, to name a few.[45] Until recently, basic training of new recruits and volunteers was carried out in twenty-five training camps. By August 2015, that number had at least doubled since the Islamic State's losses in human strength had increased substantially. The main training course usually lasts from two weeks to a year. During this period, the recruits receive military, political, and religious education and undergo an intensive course of study of Arabic. Certain components of combat tactics, used by DAESh, have quickly spread throughout the region. For example, in Nigeria the militants of Boko Haram have already adopted Islamic State tactics during the capture and holding of territories.

The Coalition Potential of Radical Islamists in the Middle East

Religious and ideological leadership of DAESh tried to create common dogmatic interpretation of Islam and, on this basis, to gradually consolidate the various groups and organizations of the radical mujahideen (despite the presence of the traditional competition in their ranks). The leaders of the Islamic State demonstrate political and ideological flexibility with the aim of forging alliances with representatives of other Sunni groups. It not only is an active interaction with the Ba'athists. A number of former senior army and security forces officers of Saddam, the prominent functionaries of the Ba'ath Party, are among the senior advisers to DAESh's leadership. In addition to strong ties with the Ba'athists, the representatives of the Islamic State's leadership are actively, and with some success, trying to build relationships with Sufi tribal leaders and Sufi military formations. These relationships bring political benefits. In less than a year, DAESh became the largest radical Sunni Muslim center on Earth where various extremist groups gradually become Islamic State branches.

However, the situation in terms of building relations between larger regional jihadist groups, such as between DAESh and al-Qaeda-Maghreb (AQIM), is more challenging. For example, in Iraq and Syria, their representatives periodically fight with each other. It would seem that their enmity or struggle is also reinforced by the theological and ideological differences; in particular, the contradictions in the interpretation of sharia law. For example, AQIM does not adopt many "innovations" that the Islamic State had imposed on the regulation of social and family life.[46] Nevertheless, despite the theological and ideological discussions, specific evidence suggests a development in their practical cooperation. For example, after the Islamic State captured the gold and foreign currency reserves of the Central Bank of Syria in the city of Raqqa, it transferred a significant portion of the seized amount to AQIM "to fund its operations in the northern part of Mali."[47] Something similar happened after the capture of the city of Mosul in Iraq.[48] Thus, the old enmity between groups of radical Islamists usually (but not always) gives way to collaboration and cooperation in the fight against the common enemy. This particularly applies to the junior enlisted persons of these organizations. It is, above all, cooperation in the fight against the secular regimes in the region. However, even many fighters of the pro-Saudi Islamist groups that seemingly conflict with the Islamic State, especially the rank and file militants, share ideas on the need to overthrow "corrupt pro-Western regimes."

Recognized as one of the spiritual leaders of modern Salafism, Abu Muhammad al-Maqdisi, as well as another jihadist authority, Abu Qatada, both support Jabhat al-Nusra and the traditional al-Qaeda in their religious disputes with DAESh. The spiritual mentor of Abu Musab al-Zarqawi, al-Maqdisi entered into fierce theological debates with alims (religious teachers) of the Islamic State and sharply opposed the proclamation of the caliphate and Abu Bakr al-Baghdadi as its caliph. In response, he was accused of heresy and blasphemy.[49] Nevertheless, al-Maqdisi said publicly, for example, that if he were faced with a choice (to support US intervention or DAESh), then he would certainly support the Islamic State. The same is likely true of most traditional Salafi shaikhs and imams. This kind of radical Islamist coalition maneuver enabled the Islamic State to achieve at least three important tactical objectives: to divert attention from Damascus and Palmyra, as the situation in Idlib demanded that the Syrian army command transfer all their elite units (Tigers, Desert Hawks, and part of the 106th Brigade of the Republican Guard) in this area; to strengthen the confidential communication between the Islamic State secret services and Jaish al-Fatah; and, finally, to demonstrate to its allies in Damascus political and military capabilities of the Islamic State.

The Islamic State as a Strategic Challenge and Existential Threat to Civilization

As the Islamic State rapidly gained strength, its cause presented a serious strategic challenge to our civilization in both Russia and the West. In the latter case, there was a serious deterioration of relations within the senior Western political establishment. Part of the elite believes the Islamic State is a serious long-term threat to the West, which must be destroyed quickly by using all possible means. In line with this trend, the Western media actively demonstrate and emphasize the "barbaric, savage face" of the Islamic State, its brutal and bloody attitude toward non-Muslims, its vandalism and intolerance, and its inability to negotiate. Representatives on this side insist on conducting the harshest maximum power politics against DAESh. This reflects the typical recommendations by Max Boot, representative of the US Council on Foreign Relations (an important component of the US foreign policy elite) in 2014. Boot believes that it was necessary to send 30,000 US troops and establish no-fly zone in Syria, involving Turkey as much as possible in carrying out large-scale ground operations. This is occurring today, as Turkish army combat units are fighting against the Islamic State in Iraq near Mosul and in Syria near Raqqa. There is a good probability of their continuing military involvement in the civil conflicts, and a high rate of certainty that they will be fighting against Iraqi and Syrian Kurds as well, to prevent the creation of an independent Kurdish state on Turkish borders. Another trend represented, mainly by the US military and intelligence community, is based on the fact that the Islamic State is a long-term factor that could not be eliminated in the near future. Therefore, it is necessary to allow for it to work jointly, including for the strategic deterrence of Tehran, based on the vital US interests in the Greater Middle East. Overall, we could already postulate rather than predict and foresee that in the medium term, the Islamic State will be perceived and interpreted by the US elite as a major global and strategic threat. In fact, this trend is already evident. President Donald Trump in his inaugural address stated that a vital national interest includes the most serious threat: the terror activities of the Islamic State.[50] The Islamic State is a threat to the United States, despite the nuclear potential of Russia. As for Russia, President Vladimir Putin also has stated that the threat of the Islamic State is a major threat to Russian national security and the greatest challenge to our civilization. Therefore, we must unite our efforts to eliminate the Islamic State. The terrorist attacks in Saint Petersburg confirmed this statement.[51] There are nine factors that account for the special importance of this existential danger to civilization, including the Western world headed by the United States as well as Russia and all humankind:

1. The Islamic State is a long-term, civilizational, and ideological threat, and it is not possible, in principle, to find a compromise with it. That is a direct and immediate standoff with the world based on the principle of either-or. After all, the Islamic State, in contrast to al-Qaeda, not only declares the superiority of Islamic civilization in comparison with the West, but also demonstrates it constantly and in every way. Islamic State ideologists emphasize that the United States is the leader of the atheistic materialism of modern civilization, and Russia after its military intervention in Syria is an archenemy of the "true Islam."

2. The Islamic State, potentially by virtue of its anti-Americanism, has huge social support for its goals and ideology not only among Sunnis, but also in the West where anti-American sentiment has strengthened in various strata of society.

3. DAESh is the only structure in the Islamic world that has a systemic long-term political megaproject, which is attractive and understandable for millions of people. China is trying to formulate such a long-term project, but even among the top Chinese leadership sharp contradictions are growing on this issue.

4. The United States, with all its political, advocacy, and intellectual power, is losing the ideological and information war with the

Islamic State. This is openly admitted by leading analysts and strategists from the US military-intelligence community.

5. The Islamic State, according to Washington officials, is the main force that undermines the existing Western world order. In this respect, DAESh is much more dangerous than Russia and China. They see the Islamic State as an uncompromising enemy of world order in the West.

6. Europe and the United States have sleeper cells of the Islamic State and there are no effective secret service agents who are tracing Islamic State terrorist activities in these countries. Accordingly, the United States and most of Western Europe have shaky primary information about the ongoing and future terrorist activities of the Islamic State. The recent terrorist acts in Paris and London have demonstrated this.[52] These further reinforce the strategic concerns of US and Western European military-intelligence elites, leaving room for untargeted speculations and predictions, which could be the next target for the Islamic State.

7. DAESh is headed by thousands of leaders and field commanders, the employees of the former Mukhabarat of Saddam and, above all, high-ranking representatives of the Ba'ath Party intelligence who are convinced and principal enemies of the United States. The officer corps of the Mukhabarat never participated in the cooperation or collaboration with US occupation authorities.

8. The United States is not ready for a long-term large-scale military confrontation with DAESh using their ground forces for a variety of strategic, political, social, geopolitical, ideological, and other reasons. The aerial bombardments of the Islamic State positions in Syria and Iraq, in which the United States has already spent billions of dollars, cannot fundamentally change the military situation in any way. As is recognized by senior analysts, the United States has no military option to control the Islamic State. Neither antiterrorist operations, nor counterinsurgency strategy, nor full-scale military action will provide the possibility of a decisive victory over the Islamic State.

9. Those highest ranked in the US establishment do not even know intellectually what to do with the Islamic State in the long run. Washington is forced to use the so-called strategy of offensive deterrence.[53] As a well-known analyst in the US military-intelligence community puts it: "At least, for some time, the most effective policy for meeting our goals and means, and having the best chance to protect our interests, will be 'offensive deterrence.'

That is a combination of a limited military campaign with serious diplomatic and economic efforts to weaken IS, and the coordination of different countries' interests who are threatened by the offense of this group."

Conclusion

The problems of a rapidly emerging and growing power of the structure, ideology, strategy, and military tactics of the Islamic State that I considered in this chapter have demonstrated that the Islamic State is a unique phenomenon in the dark world of international and domestic radical Islamist groups and terrorist organizations. The Islamic State grew from al-Qaeda as its small regional branch in 2006 and showed its amazing resilience to any kind of fight against it. So far, it has demonstrated its stubborn will and striking iron discipline with the ultimate purpose of establishing a new caliphate. Justifying this cause is its strong desire to return to the times of "purified Islam" existing in the contemporary globalized world inhabited, according to the leaders of the Islamic State, by the Western as well as the Eastern crusaders and infidels. This terrorist group, which is unheard of in the modern history of our civilization with regard to its cunning, intricate, and cruel manner of conducting a contemporary kind of hybrid war, has managed so far to attract huge funding, to recruit thousands of followers from over 100 countries, to make a successful business enterprise or megaproject called a "state," and to be so hard to resist that even the only superpower (the United States) with all its military might and superiority is not able to find an effective remedy for ridding the planet and our civilization of this "incarnation of evil." No other global powers even united in coalitions, such as Russia, the United Kingdom, France, and Germany, could put an end to this terrorist organization. In fact, this proved the only credible truth about the Islamic State: it is essentially a systemic megaproject that poses a systemic threat to mankind, and the fact that it is Islamic in nature does not make the goal of eliminating it any more reasonable in the foreseeable future. This does not mean that the world should sit still and simply wait for the moment when this organization would dissipate due to internal strife and rivalry factions inside its structure. Neither does it mean that we should simply rely on the future alliance of the world powers, which would unite to fight it off. It is in this real world that there are real day-to-day terrorist acts and suicide bombings that could take place in any capital city of the world, or even any part of our small and vulnerable planet, when it comes to cruelty and human victims of the global jihadist war against humankind. Action should occur now and a remedy to cure "our succeeding generations from the scourge of war" regardless of the nature of this war (in this case, the global terror war) must be found. The first part of the previous sentence partly repeats a sentence in the Preamble of the UN Charter, and this is a symbolic coincidence. The entire world wants to live in peace and be free from the fear of being the next target of an act of terrorism, be it conventional, nuclear, or any other, regardless of what terrorist organization (Islamic or non-Islamic by its nature) committed it and then claimed responsibility. This requires a credible scenario plan. With the Islamic State in mind, this task is not at all easy. Nevertheless, one future scenario that seems to be credible for the coming years is that, after its final defeat in Syria and Iraq, DAESh will promptly rush to the Central Asian region via the territories of highly unstable and conflict-prone countries such as Afghanistan and Pakistan, as well as Iran, thus trying to realize its goal of the world caliphate by enlarging its so-called *vilayet* (province). This scenario needs separate and thorough research.

Notes

1. For further details about the different names and abbreviations, see Luna Shamieh and Zoltán Szenes, "The Rise of Islamic State of Iraq and Syria (ISIS)," *AARMS Journal* 14, no. 4 (2015): 363–378.

2. For example, Shamil' Sultanov, "DAESh—Strategicheskiy vyzov zapadnoy tsivilizatsii" [DAESh—A Strategic Challenge to Western Civilization], *Politicheskoye obozreniye,* 24 December 2015, http://politobzor.net/show-75846-sultanov-daish-strategiskiy-vyzov-zapadnoy=civilizacii.html.

3. Ibid.

4. For example, Jacques Neriah, "The Structure of the Islamic State ISIS," Jerusalem Center for Public Affairs, 8 September 2014, http://jcpa.org/structure-of-the-islamic-state.

5. For further details about the origins of Mukhabarat, see Jessica Stern and J. M. Berger, *ISIS: The State of Terror* (London: HarperCollins, 2015), pp. 10–15; Ibrahim al-Marashi, "Iraq's Security and Intelligence Network: A Guide and Analysis," *Middle East Review of International Affairs* 6, no. 3 (2002), http://blisty.cz/files/2002/al-marashi.pdf.

6. Stern and Berger, *ISIS,* pp. 21–24.

7. Yezid Sayigh, oral presentation at the study group "The Crisis of the Arab State," Berlfer Center for Science and International Affairs, 31 March 2015, http://ow.ly/Q0iIN (audio).

8. For a detailed account of the relationship between the US intelligence agencies and former Ba'ath Party members or Iraqi officers, see Stern and Berger, *ISIS,* pp. 30–32.

9. Sultanov, "DAESh,"

10. Ibid.

11. Stern and Berger, *ISIS,* p. 28.

12. Sultanov, "DAESh."

13. Ibid.

14. Ibid.

15. Stern and Berger, *ISIS,* p. 35.

16. Ibid.

17. Efraim Karsh and Inari Rautsi, *Saddam Hussein: A Political Biography* (New York: Grove Press, 1992), p. 45.

18. Sultanov, "DAESh."

19. See Stern and Berger, *ISIS,* p. 34.

20. Sultanov, "DAESh."

21. Ibid.

22. Ibid.

23. Ibid.

24. Stern and Berger, *ISIS,* p. 105.

25. Sultanov, "DAESh."

26. Stern and Berger, *ISIS,* p. 266.

27. Ibid., p. 270.

28. Ibid., p. 288.

29. Sykes-Picot Agreement, World War I Document Archive, Official Papers, www.saylor.org/site/wp-content/uploads/2011/08/HIST351-9.2.4-Sykes-Picot -Agreement.pdf (accessed 3 June 2017).

30. For example, Matthew Levitt, ed., *The Rise of ISIL: Counterterrorism Lectures 2015* (Washington, DC: Washington Institute for Near East Policy, 2015), www.washingtoninstitute.org/uploads/Documents/pubs/PolicyFocus148_CT7.pdf.

31. For further details about Islamic State provinces outside of Syria and Iraq, see Daveed Gartenstein-Ross, et al., "Islamic State vs. Al-Qaeda," *International Security,* December 2015, p. 25, https://static.newamerica.org/attachments/12103 -islamic-state-vs-al-qaeda/ISISvAQ_Final.e68fdd22a90e49c4af1d4cd0dc9e3651.pdf; Joshua Koontz, "Desknote: The Growing Threat of ISIS in Yemen," American Enterprise Institute, 6 May 2015, www.criticalthreats.org/yemen/koontz-desknote-growing -threat-isis-inyemen-may-6-2015; "Will ISIS Find Fertile Ground in Egypt's Sinai," *AlMonitor,* 23 June 2014.

32. Stern and Berger, *ISIS,* p. 289

33. Ibid., p. 290.

34. Ibid., p. 292.

35. Sultanov, "DAESh."

36. Ibid.

37. For detailed account of war tactics of great Asian warriors, see Kallie Szczepanski, "Asia's Great Conquerors," *ThoughtCo,* 9 February 2017, www.thoughtco.com /asias-great-conquerors-195682.

38. Compare with the tenets of fourth-generation warfare. See Thomas Hammes, *The Sling and the Stone: On War in the 21st Century* (Saint Paul: Zenith Press, 2006).

39. For the comparison of the war tactics described, see Evgeny Messner, *Vsemirnaya Myatezhvoyna* [Worldwide Subversion-War] (Moscow: Zhukovskoye Pole, 2004).

40. Stern and Berger, *ISIS,* p. 296.

41. There is no accepted definition of a *hybrid war* either in Russia or in the West. For further discussion of term usage, see Chapter 5 of this book.

42. *Stockholm syndrome* is a paradoxical psychological phenomenon of victims' empathy and sympathy toward their captors, discovered by Swedish criminologist and psychiatrist Nils Bejerot. For a detailed account of this phenomena, see also James Turner, "Factors Influencing the Development of the Hostage Identification Syndrome," *Political Psychology* 6, no. 4 (1985): 705–711.

43. US Army Training and Doctrine Command, "Islamic State of Iraq and the Levant, Threat Tactics Report," November 2014, https://info.publicintelligence.net /USArmy-TRISA_ISIL.pdf.

44. Sultanov, "DAESh."

45. Ibid.

46. Ibid.

47. Juan Zarate and Thomas Sanderson, "How the Terrorists Got Rich," *New York Times,* 28 June 2014.

48. Ibid.

49. Stern and Berger, *ISIS,* p. 311.

50. "Donald Trump Inauguration Speech Full Transcript," *Belfast Telegraph,* 21 January 2017.

51. Andrew Griffin, "St Petersburg Metro Explosions: Vladimir Putin Says Blasts Could Be Terror Attacks," *Independent,* 3 April 2017, www.independent.co .uk/news/world/europe/st-petersburg-metro-terror-attack-vladimir-putin-explosion -bomb-attack-russia-city-casualties-train-a7664331.html.

52. Chuck Goudie, Christine Tressel, and Ross Weidner, "Terror Trend: London and Paris Latest in Vehicle Attacks," *ABC7 Eyewitness News,* 19 June 2017, http:// abc7chicago.com/news/terror-trend-london-paris-latest-in-vehicle-attacks/2120043.

53. James Thomson, *Strategic Defense and Deterrence,* Statement Before the Defense Appropriations Subcommittee of the House Appropriations Committee, 9 May 1984, www.rand.org/content/dam/rand/pubs/papers/2006/P6985.pdf (accessed 3 June 2017).

12

Islamic State Propaganda in the North Caucasus

Akhmet Yarlykapov

The North Caucasus is a historical and geographical region of Russia, located in the mountains and northern slopes of the Caucasian ridge, with adjoining foothills and plains. This is a unique region of Russia: more than two dozen peoples live here with more than four dozen languages among them. The population density in the North Caucasus is high: about 1.5 percent of its territory is home to more than 10 percent of its population (more than 14 million people).[1] The North Caucasus includes the seven regions of the North Caucasus Federal District (NCFD)—the Stavropol Krai, the Republic of Dagestan, the Chechen Republic, the Republic of Ingushetia, the Republic of North Ossetia-Alania, the Kabardino-Balkarian Republic, and the Karachay-Cherkess Republic—as well as two regions of the Southern Federal District, Krasnodar Krai and the Republic of Adygea.

This chapter is based on my field anthropological research studies, which I have regularly conducted since the late 1990s in Adygea, Karachay-Cherkessia, Kabardino-Balkaria, Stavropol Krai, and Dagestan; in the North Caucasian communities in Moscow and the Moscow region; and in the North Caucasian communities in the oil- and gas-producing Russian North (Tyumen region: Surgut and Khanty-Mansiysk). I analyzed the results of these sociological surveys (mainly focus groups) conducted with students and working youths in the Republic of Dagestan (2011—students and working youths; 2015—students and young businesspeople), Karachaevo-Cherkessia (2014, 2015—young ethnic and religious leaders), and Moscow (2015—young ethnic leaders). I also utilized the results of interesting sociological studies that were conducted in the Republic of Dagestan at the initiative of the

republic's Ministry for Youth Affairs in 2015–2016. Monitoring sentiments among Dagestan's youth is funded by the ministry and covers up
to 3,000 people in all cities and districts. The results of the survey are
used by the ministry for internal work and are not officially published;
however, they are not classified.[2] For comparison, I used the results of
similar studies of Dagestani sociologists from the local branch of the
Russian Academy of Sciences under the leadership of Zaid Abdulagatov. These studies were conducted in 2016, and covered Muslim youth
throughout the republic. The results of these studies have not yet been
published in scholarly articles, but have been partially disclosed in a
series of interviews and presentations.[3]

The majority of Muslims in Russia live in the territory of the North
Caucasus Federal District. There is a high rate of population growth,
despite the fact that there have been several major conflicts and a restive
background. From 1990 to 2010, the population increased by almost 1.7
million to 13.4 million people. Accordingly, in the structure of the population, the proportion of persons younger than the able-bodied age is
high. The North Caucasus can without exaggeration be called one of the
most youthful regions of Russia, and the share of the young among the
able-bodied population is also high. Traditionally, a large proportion of
the three predominantly Muslim republics in the northeastern Caucasus
are young people: the Chechen Republic, 32.9 percent; the Republic of
Ingushetia, 28.9 percent; and the Republic of Dagestan, 25.4 percent.[4]
Islam itself in the North Caucasus has a long and rich history. The first
Muslims appeared within the first century of Islam's establishment,
with the conquest by the Arabs of Derbent and its environs.[5] Traditionally, Islam has come to the North Caucasus from two directions. First,
from the south (Mesopotamia and Iran), there was a penetration of
Sunni Shafiite Madhab and Shiai Imamit (or Jafarit) Madhab. The second came from the north (Central Asia through the Golden Horde), and
then from its splinters penetrated Sunni Hanafi Madhab. Once arrived,
the Hanafi Madhab of Sunni Islam was propagated in the area by the
Crimean Khanate and the Ottoman Empire.[6] Sufi influence also
appeared in the Caucasus and the practice of various Sufi orders spread
to Naqshbandiyya, Qadiriyya, and Shadhiliyya.[7]

The Islamic State and the North Caucasus

After collapse of the USSR, destructive tendencies, based on long-standing
problems and contradictions that were not solved under the regime,

spread rather quickly in the North Caucasus. Yet the region did not fall into chaos after a series of crises. The apparent collapse of extremist political projects in the North Caucasus is due to the fact that none of them have ever been able to gain broad support among Muslims in the region. In general, from the late 1990s to early 2000s, the level of support for extremist movements seriously fell amid the general disillusionment of the local population with the ideas of separatism. Since this time, no nationalist movement has spoken about the possibility of armed separatism, which clearly indicates the extreme unpopularity of such methods. Even more surprising is the enthusiasm of young Caucasians, who after 2011 began to leave the region to join the war in Syria. This movement to join various sides of the conflict saw an ever increasing share of them flock to the Islamic State in Iraq and Syria (ISIS). Despite the fact that thousands of young Muslims from all over Russia participated in this movement, the majority was indeed North Caucasians. The peak of resettlement with the aim of joining various warring factions in Syria (with the ever growing component of the Islamic State) came during 2013–2014. Several factors came into play here. On the one hand, aggressive online propaganda was conducted purposefully in the North Caucasus on behalf of both the Islamic State and al-Qaeda, which is why many of the "Caucasus Emirate" combatants traveled to the Middle East and joined the structures of al-Qaeda such as Jabhat al-Nusra. In the Middle East, young Muslims from the North Caucasus saw a controlled territory and a chance to realize their dreams of living in a society regulated by sharia law. On the other hand, it also affected the authorities' policy of squeezing Salafis beyond the boundaries of the North Caucasus and Russia as a whole on the eve of the Sochi Olympic Games in 2014, which continued for a while after their completion.

In 2014, along with the encouragement of joining the militants in Syria, ISIS began to pursue a policy of enlisting commanders and militants of the Caucasus Emirate affiliated with al-Qaeda. By the end of 2014 to early 2015, this policy started to gain traction: one by one, the commanders of the main units swore an oath to the self-proclaimed caliph Abu Bakr al-Baghdadi. Success in 2015 was confirmed by the announcement of the creation of the Vilayat Kavkaz in the North Caucasus as part of ISIS.[8] During late 2015 to early 2016, terrorists from this association conducted four terrorist attacks in Dagestan, mainly in the southern part of the republic. At the same time, it should be noted that the activation of the insurgents who changed the terrorist "brand" in the North Caucasus came almost immediately after the receipt of information on the establishment of their funding from the Middle East. It is also a characteristic feature that in the arsenal of militants, such methods as the attacks on the army and police columns, almost forgotten in the North Caucasus, have returned.[9] In other words, successfully getting rid of the Caucasus Emirate did not lead to a solution of the radicalization problem, and the apparent lack of mass support for extremist Islamist movements is nevertheless accompanied by their stable replenishment of young Muslims in the region. The emergence of the Islamic State networks in the Northern Caucasus is a bad sign, indicating that the potential for radicalization is still present and unlikely to be exhausted in the near future.

Why Is the Islamic State Propaganda Successful in the North Caucasus?

When discussing the causes of radicalization, one often asserts that they are limited by only external causes. But with the undoubted influence of the external factor on the processes of radicalization, the internal causes are still the main ones. In addition, external factors did play a significant role in the beginning of the 1990s, when the ongoing processes of re-Islamization led to the inevitable penetration of various ideas from abroad, including radical ones. The process of undergoing training in the foreign centers of Muslims, mostly by the young, was accompanied by an active perception of radical ideas. Today, in connection with the large penetration of modern means of communication and the virtualization of Muslim youth communities, the process of the exchange of radical ideas occurs across national borders and has a multidirectional character, from abroad to the North Caucasus and vice versa. That is why it is important to understand that the internal factor in radicalization is the main one.

First, it is necessary to name the systemic crisis that swept the region. The components of this crisis play a big role in spreading protest sentiments among Muslims, which then are channeled toward radical interpretations of Islam.[10] Among the components of this crisis are economic problems associated not only with recurring crisis phenomena in the Russian economy, but also with the absence of structural transformations in the region. Grandiose tourist projects were ineffective and unable to solve the problem of unemployment and reduce the dependence of the North Caucasian subjects of the federation on the subsidies from the Russian center. This dependence on subsidies from the budget makes it (the budget) in the North Caucasus one of the serious resources, access to which is perceived as an opportunity to receive a stable income. Hence, an unprecedentedly high level of corruption exists at all levels, where a person is forced to pay bribes almost every time they appeal to budget institutions and not only to the authorities. This is particularly noticeable for the young people, who are faced with this system quite early such as in their admission to higher education institutions or for undergoing professional training.[11] A serious radicalizing factor is the absence of social elevators, though in many cases this lack is not very obvious. This is evident from the example of young people who outwardly appear well-off, but increasingly are becoming radicalized: they have good jobs, good prospects for personal professional growth, and so forth. As a whole they feel the injustice of the established rules in the local communities, which causes their protests.[12] Closely associated with the lack of social elevators is the factor of the so-called glass ceiling. This ceiling exists due to the actions of various components of the sociopolitical system—such as ruling clans, corruption, and ethnic quotas in the sociopolitical establishment. That is why the lack of social justice is one of the first issues raised in focus groups that I conduct. The request for social justice is one of the most urgent, and this request covers not only young people, but also the economically active population in general.[13]

The failure of the post-Soviet construction of a democratic society and state structures in the North Caucasus should also be added to the systemic crisis. Instead, the importance of clannishness and nepotism, born in the late Soviet period, grew substantially. The lack of fair and transparent elections, the impossibility of changing those in power through democratic procedures, strongly discredits the established political system. The appeal of young people to alternative political systems is also provoked by the fact that, under the present conditions where political institutions are practically privatized by clan groups, they do not have the legal means to display opposition sentiments.[14] Young people cannot do this through legally acting political parties or elections. In particular, formal opposition parties are sometimes ethnically engaged and are used to express the interests of certain ethnic groups and the same clans, which sharply narrows the possibility of expressing oppositional sentiments and approaches by politically active youths in general. Accordingly, one finds alternatives in radical Islamist teachings that declare Islam to be the only possible political solution to contemporary problems. Extremists just have to push young people to the idea that existing political channels are practically closed or unacceptable and therefore Islam can be used to solve the problem by armed struggle.

Despite the fact that there are quite influential groups and structures of so-called traditional Islam in the North Caucasus, they have not become attractive to disappointed and angry young people. This also applies to Sufi Islam, which in Chechnya and Dagestan has always been a representation of protest moods. However, in post-Soviet Russia, Sufism was able to integrate into the existing sociopolitical system, as well as find a common language with the authorities, which discredits it in the eyes of many young Muslims. Sufism sees them as a part of a corrupted system, unable to express their protest and offer a fair alternative. In their search for social justice, young people are forced to seek it outside the limits of the sociopolitical system that has developed in the North Caucasus. They believe that it is unreachable within the existing political and legal system. One of the main arguments of these young Muslims is that invented and imposed human laws cannot be justified at all since they stand guard over the interests of only those groups of people who are behind their adoption—as a rule, the rich and powerful people who constitute a privileged minority in the society. However, Muslims believe that they have the source of the Divine Law, which is the Quran. It is the Quran as well as the Sunnah, the example of the Prophet Muhammad, that are the sources of the sharia law, which can be called a law that is pleasing to Allah. The Divine Law cannot be unjust a priori because it was not created by man and was revealed in the Divine Revelation. Accordingly, radical preachers convince young Muslims that the solution to the problems of modern society is the sharia law and the Islamic political system. After the Islamization of legal and political systems, social justice will be established automatically, they say.

Success of Islamic State Propaganda: Sociological View

If before 2011 the extremists joined the militant ranks of the Caucasus Emirate, affiliated with al-Qaeda, the successful takeoff of the Islamic State 2013–2014 left the emirate in a practically depopulated state. Hundreds of militants left the emirate for the sake of joining the Islamic State. In Syria and Iraq, young Muslims saw a controlled land, where Islamic rule was announced with supposedly successful workings of Islamic laws. The analysis of the recruiting efforts of the Islamic State in the territory of Russia suggests that this was not a chaotic, but a quite ordered, activity that had its own strategy. Recruiters of the organization likely had instructions as to who should be recruited first. Much attention was paid, for example, to information technology specialists, oil workers, and doctors (primarily surgeons). The network of recruiters in Russia, unfortunately, is becoming more and more ramified. Contrary to the widespread view of the Internet's exceptional role in recruiting supporters for the Islamic State, it is real recruiters who often complete what began as agitation from the Internet. They supply the ripened young people with instructions on how to drive to the territory of the Islamic State, who to contact, how to cross the border, and so forth. This recruitment network, which in itself violates the security of North Caucasus, can be regarded as the germ of the future terrorist network of the organization in Russia. In 2017, the stream of young Muslims from Russia to Syria to join the Islamic State practically ceased. However, this does not mean that the problem of violence associated with religious symbols and based on religious beliefs has been resolved. On the contrary, the willingness to commit violent acts among Muslim youth in the North Caucasus remains high. In this sense, the data of sociological studies conducted in Dagestan becomes especially interesting. In particular, the Ministry of Youth Affairs of the Republic of Dagestan initiated a large-scale sociological monitoring of the Muslim youth in the region, and the results for 2015 are available. According to those results, 8.1 percent of the interviewed young people said that they were ready to join ISIS whereas another 30.8 percent were hesitating. At the same time, the Islamic State was considered a real true caliphate by 15.0 percent, and the same number had fluctuating views. The overall level of discontent among young people was high, which rested on the glass ceiling and seeing no prospects for themselves: 43.0 percent said that they could not be successful in the current situation in Dagestan. Accordingly, 11.5 percent of the respondents considered Salafism to be the religion most suitable for Dagestan.

Quite clearly, young people also expressed their attitude about the policy of local authorities: 24 percent of respondents believed that their policy was stimulating the growth of Salafi moods among Muslim youth. To the question "Why is the situation in Dagestan getting worse?": 15 percent of the respondents answered "Because of the corruption," 23 percent "Because of social injustice," another 13 percent "Because of the lack of youth support programs." At the same time, it should be noted that 60 percent of the young people surveyed supported the actions of the Russian Federation in Syria.[15] No less impressive figures were obtained in the course of the 2016 surveys by Dagestani sociologists under the leadership of Abdulagatov. According to this research, 3.8 percent of the surveyed young people said they supported the Dagestanis fighting in Syria for the Islamic State, another 8.7 percent said that they hadn't made up their mind yet, 3.5 percent said they were ready to join the Islamic State, and 7.2 percent said that they were thinking about it. It is curious that 19.8 percent of young Muslims said that they could not be patriots of a non-sharia state.[16]

Success of Islamic State Propaganda:
Anthropological View

Anthropological studies conducted in the North Caucasus, overall confirm the findings of sociological research. Observations show that the resettlement to Syria to join the Islamic State and the al-Qaeda-related Jabhat al-Nusra began in 2012 and reached its peak in 2013. However, after 2013, the number of people leaving for the Middle East has decreased every year and practically ceased in 2017. Initially, the militants from the Caucasus Emirate, who started to move to the Middle East, joined not the Islamic State, but Jabhat al-Nusra. However, the movement for resettlement then began to affect those who were not connected with the underground in the North Caucasus; these were people who responded to the gaining power of propaganda on the Internet. Young people actively watched propaganda materials on the Internet; the practice of accessing the Internet for this purpose from so-called one-time SIM cards, which were purchased for only one day and were not registered to a particular subscriber, was widespread. After that, real recruiters joined the activities via the Internet, personally recruiting young people and helping them move to Syria. This "shuttle" mode of recruiters, who preferred to be based in safe places (usually in large cities of Russia and the Russian North) and came to the North Caucasus for only a short time to conduct recruiting work, helped recruiters build highly sophisticated networks throughout the country.

Field studies showed that all of those who left for the Middle East have kept their ties with relatives and friends. In each village, people know who left, where they went (to the Islamic State or Jabhat al-Nusra), who is still alive, and who died. The preservation of the ties with relatives in the organization was encouraged since it is considered one of the channels through which it is possible to carry out recruitment. At least those who were in the Islamic State purposefully created a picture of paradise life under Islamic law, so that the hijra would become attractive to even more people.[17] In 2014, it became clear that the North Caucasus was an important region in terms of supplying militants for war. That is why the Islamic State expanded its propaganda on the Internet, aimed at the Russian-speaking audience. The Russian language by the number of issued propaganda materials, although not equal to Arabic and English, is ranked third. Since the beginning of 2015, ISIS has even launched a networked Russian-language magazine *Istok* (Source) containing materials interesting for immigrants from Russia and from the countries of Central Asia.[18]

The propaganda of the Islamic State proved to be successful in the North Caucasus. However, it should be kept in mind that not all of the region responded equally to the propaganda. The number of those who joined ISIS is growing more in the west of the region compared to the east: for example, just over two dozen people from Adygea; hundreds from Karachaevo-Cherkessia, Kabardino-Balkaria, and Ingushetia; up to 3,000 people from Chechnya; and, according to some estimates, up to 5,000 from Dagestan.[19] Naturally, questions may arise as to how much these figures correspond to reality, but examples from field studies indicate that these figures are quite reliable. In particular, the example of the small Dagestani village Oguzer from the Kizlyar District (incidentally, not the most religious one) is indicative. This is a village of 250 households, 150 of which, as a result of labor migration within Russia, were in Surgut, in the Russian North. As of the end 2014, four young Muslims from this village left for the Islamic State.[20] Anthropological studies have also shown that the composition of those who joined the Islamic State differs from the usual stereotypes about poor and disadvantaged people. It turned out that among those who left for the Middle East was an unexpectedly large number of formally successful young people.[21] A case in point is the example of a successful surgeon from the city of Astrakhan who went to Syria with his wife and child. Although his relatives managed to get his wife out of Syria afterward, he did not allow his son to be taken. Analysis of those leaving for the Islamic State from Dagestan in 2015 showed that about 80 percent were from well-off families, including those of officials and police officers.

Conclusion

The sudden rise of the Islamic State in the Middle East has already had a huge impact on the regions that are hundreds of kilometers away from it. One of these regions is the North Caucasus, from which thousands of young people went to the ghostly caliphate. The tremendous effectiveness of the propaganda of ISIS has revealed the serious vulnerability of modern society, the problems of which can become an advantage for its enemies. Today, the Islamic State is losing its territories in the Middle East, but the reasons why it has attracted thousands of young people from around the world remain. In addition to military efforts, it is necessary to address socio-political problems that nourish anti-establishment extremist ideology in order to defeat the organization. After all, we cannot be sure that another, more bloodthirsty, terrorist organization will not come to replace the Islamic State tomorrow, one that also will want to take advantage of the difficulties of modern society for its own purposes.

Notes

1. "Severnyy Kavkaz," Encyclopedia *Vokrug sveta,* www.vokrugsveta.ru/ (accessed 1 April 2017).

2. "Itogovyy informatsionno-analiticheskiy otchet Ministerstva po delam molodezhi Respubliki Dagestan po osushchestvleniyu postoyannogo sotsiologicheskogo i statisticheskogo monitoringa i analiza situatsii v Respublike Dagestan s tsel'yu vyyavleniya prichin vozniknoveniya ekstremistskikh proyavleniy sredi molodezhi v 2015 godu" [The Final Information and Analytical Report of the Ministry of Youth Affairs of the Republic of Dagestan on the Implementation of Ongoing Sociological and Statistical Monitoring and Analysis of the Situation in the Republic of Dagestan in Order to Identify the Causes of the Emergence of Extremist Manifestations Among Young People in 2015], author's archive.

3. See, for instance, Zaur Gaziyev, "Statisticheskiy shok" [The Shock of Statistics], *Svobodnaya respublika,* 2 September 2016; Suleyman Frantsev, "Kak dagestantsy otnosyatsya k ekstremizmu" [How Dagestan People Respond to Extremism], *Svobodnaya respublika,* 25 August 2016.

4. For more information on the demographic situation in the North Caucasus, see "Demograficheskaya situatsiya na Severnom Kavkaze" [Demographic Situation in the North Caucasus], Russian Government, http://government.ru/media/2010 /10/4/35578/file/1485.doc (accessed 1 April 2017).

5. Vladimir Bobrovnikov, "Dagestan," in *Islam na territorii byvshey Rossiyskoy imperii: Entsiklopedicheskiy slovar* [Islam on the Territory of the Former Russian Empire: Encyclopedic Dictionary], ed. Stanislav Prozorov (Moscow: Lexicon, 2006), p. 120.

6. Alikber Alikberov, "Severnyy Kavkaz" [North Caucasus], in *Islam na territorii byvshey Rossiyskoy imperii: Entsiklopedicheskiy slovar* [Islam on the Territory of the Former Russian Empire: Encyclopedic Dictionary], ed. Stanislav Prozorov (Moscow: Lexicon, 2006), pp. 353–357.

7. Kachivek Aliyev, Zagir Arukhov, and Kaflan Khanbabayev, *Religiozno-politicheskiy ekstremizm i etnokonfessional'naya tolerantnost' na Severnom Kavkaze* [Religious-Political Extremism and Ethno-Confessional Tolerance in the North Caucasus] (Moscow: Nauka, 2007), p. 112.

8. Akhmet Yarlykapov, "'Islamskoye gosudarstvo' i Severnyy Kavkaz v blizhnevostochnoy perspektive: Vyzovy i uroki dlya Rossii" ["The Islamic State" and North Caucasus from the Perspective of the Middle East: Challenges and Lessons for Russia], *Mezhdunarodnaya analitika* 17 (2016): 118.

9. For example, "Yacheyka IG vzyala na sebya otvetstvennost' za podryv kolonny MVD v Dagestan" [An IGIL Unit Takes the Responsibility for the Attack on the MVD Convoy in Dagestan], *Lenta.ru,* 30 March 2016, https://lenta.ru/news /2016/03/30/is/; Akhmet Yarlykapov, "Terrorism in the North Caucasus," *Experts*

Comments, DOC Research Institute, 23 March 2017, http://doc-research.org/en
/terrorism-north-caucasus/.

10. On the systemic nature of the crisis in the North Caucasus, leading to
increased conflict in the region, see Irina Starodubrovskaya and Denis Sokolov,
Istoki konfliktov na Severnom Kavkaze [The Sources of Conflicts in the Northern
Caucasus] (Moscow: Delo, 2013], pp. 13–15.

11. Anna Matveeva, "Golosa, kotoryye dolzhny byt' uslyshany: Analiz vzglyadov
na sushchestvuyushchiye problem" [Voices that Must Be Heard: An Analysis of
Views on Existing Problems], in Anna Matveeva, Alexander Skakov, and Igor Savin,
eds., *Severnyy Kavkaz: Vzglyad iznutri: Vyzovy i problemy sotsial'no-politicheskogo
razvitiya* [The Northern Caucasus: A View from Inside Out: Challenges and Problems of Social and Political Development] (Moscow: Institut Vostokovedeniya RAN,
2012), p. 33; focus group with students from the universities, conducted by the
author, Makhachkala, 20 September 2011.

12. Focus group with Dagestani youth, conducted by the author, Makhachkala,
24 July 2015.

13. Focus group with Dagestani young businesspeople, conducted by the author,
Makhachkala, 24 July 2015.

14. Matveeva, "Golosa, kotoryye dolzhny byt' uslyshany," pp. 14–15.

15. "Itogovyy informatsionno-analiticheskiy otchet Ministerstva po delam
molodezhi Respubliki Dagestan."

16. Gaziyev, "Statisticheskiy shok."

17. A parent of an ISIS fighter, interviewed by the author, Dagestan, 26 September 2016.

18. Alexander Orlov, A. Vavilov, Y. Zinin, A. Kazantzev, A. Krylov, A.
Fedorchenko, A. Chechevishnikov, A. Yarlykarpov, "'Islamskoye gosudarstvo':
Fenomen, evolyutsiya, perspektivy" ["The Islamic State": The Phenomenon, the
Evolution and the Perspectives], *Analiticheskiye doklady* 46, no. 1 (2016): 32.

19. Naima Neflyasheva, "Adygeya: Protsessy reislamizatsii i vyzovy islamskogo
radikalizma (1990-ye–2015 g.)" [Adygea: The Processes of Re-Islamisation and the
Challenges of the Islamic Radicalism (1990–2015)], *Vestnik Volgogradskogo gosu-
darstvennogo universiteta, Seriya 4, istoricheskaya* 21, no. 2 (2016): 112.

20. A relative of an ISIS fighter, interviewed by the author, village of Oguzer in
Kizlyar District, Dagestan, 26 September 2014.

21. Orlov et al., "'Islamskoye gosudarstvo,'" p. 31.

13

A New Paradigm
of Hybrid Warfare

Craig Whiteside

[It will be] the new beacon that will light the path of the monotheists, and
revive the negligent minds so that they may join the caravan of jihad.
—al-Furqan establishment,
Ministry of Information of the Islamic State of Iraq,
20 October 2009

Proponents of the concept of hybrid warfare often use the democratization and proliferation of information technologies to buttress their case for a rapidly changing character of war, with successful combatants waging campaigns using disparate types of forces executing synchronized campaigns in different domains of conflict. The expansion of the information domain, and the increased use of propaganda and psychological warfare by nonstate actors, figures highly in the field's literature. In this chapter, I attempt to add to the ongoing discussion by using the case study method to explore the self-proclaimed Islamic State's media enterprise—the history and the ideas behind it, the people that ran it, and the infrastructure that by 2015 could produce over 200 unique propaganda products a week.[1] There is little question that this effort is far-reaching and effective, as demonstrated by its influence on the second-largest foreign fighter migration in history.

The Islamic State movement started precariously with a few stateless individuals operating far from their homelands and grew into one of the most successful and far-reaching insurgent groups in history; its media department has no peer in the past or present. While there has been excellent research into the content, quantity, and quality of the products that the Islamic State produces, little has been written about the history and evolution of the enterprise itself. While its operations are no doubt complex today, their formula for success has always been relatively straightforward: start with carefully constructed narratives, add some righteous people, and invest heavily in infrastructure to produce a superior product—a formula that helped recreate an "Islamic State" in the heart of the Middle East.

Influence operations are a key component for insurgencies, particularly revolutionary movements like the Islamic State that are attempting to alter all elements of the political order in addition to the social, legal, religious, and economic systems in the polity to which it belongs. Throughout history, insurgents have used media to recruit, raise funds, justify, claim credit, and transmit psychological warfare and terror.[2] The importance of this effort is indisputable to actors large and small, and yet the results of strategic communications campaigns are quite varied.

How did the Islamic State movement distinguish itself in this field, and grow from a cast of dozens to hundreds of contributors, scriptwriters, photojournalists, online moderators, videographers, and managers? What was the process of innovation, what inspired it, and what can we learn from this evolution? This case study is divided into three parts that mirror the stages of development of the Islamic State movement: early growth (2002–2006), defeat and adjustment (2006–2010), and its expansion to caliphate (2011–2014).[3] Each part outlines the general situation of the movement during each particular period and the role that the ideas, people, and enterprise played in the development of the phenomenon we see today.

Early Growth, 2002–2006

The Islamic State movement began as a small group under the leadership of Abu Musab al-Zarqawi, a Jordanian jihadist who had established a camp in Afghanistan that collected displaced fighters and families from the Levant in the late 1990s. Al-Zarqawi led the group into northern Iraq after being ejected from Afghanistan by US forces in 2002, and the group made its first strikes in the late summer of 2003, striking at the United Nations, the Jordanian embassy, and the Imam Ali Mosque in Najaf with large car or truck bombs.[4] The group neglected to claim the attacks—leaving mystery and confusion in their wake.[5] Al-Zarqawi did not claim these attacks because his group's ability to produce effective media operations was nonexistent. To succeed, al-Zarqawi needed to increase visibility nationally and internationally to gain people, funding, and legitimacy in an environment that was seeing a tremendous growth of Sunni resistance groups. Although the group had existed since 1999, it now had to create a local media organization from scratch to accomplish these objectives.[6]

Early Inspiration

Al-Zarqawi's leadership was able to draw on ideas from recent jihadi experiences in the development of the new media office. One inspiration was Abdullah Azzam's exhortation to the global Muslim community to "join the caravan of martyrs" and travel to Afghanistan to fight against the atheist Soviets. The recreation of the global jihadi community witnessed during this period resonated with al-Zarqawi's group, many of whom had experienced jihad in the South Asian country.[7] The contemporary jihadi efforts in Chechnya and Hezbollah's fight against Israel witnessed an increased use of graphic battlefield video footage for broadcast to friend and foe alike, a more modern update of the concept "propaganda of the deed."[8] Al-Zarqawi's cohort quickly saw the potential of replicating this effort in the developing Internet medium, which would be a slight update from the way hand-copied audiotapes were used in the decade before.[9]

The growth of the Internet allowed jihadists to greatly expand their prospective audience at low cost. Jihadist theorist Abu Musab al-Suri commented on the dynamics of the new media and its paradigm change in his epic tome *Call to Global Islamic Resistance:* it changed the audience from the elite to the masses, communicated a popular purpose (the call to jihad to protect Muslim communities), injected passion and emotion into what had been an academic discussion, and moved from clandestine distribution to an open system.[10]

The opportunity to tap into an expansive worldwide audience angered by the US-led occupation of Iraq allowed al-Zarqawi's group to move to the center stage, where the unique ideology of the future Islamic State could be marketed more effectively than ever to the global Salafi trend. Certainly, al-Zarqawi's vision for his movement was not a dominant or popular version in the greater jihadi community and was highly contested, reflecting the deep ideological differences exposed during the post-Soviet Afghan era.[11] Al-Zarqawi's media department would become the instrument of change for the norms of the Salafi jihadi movement, especially concerning the use of violence and the principle of *takfir* (excommunication). What al-Zarqawi was intuitively attempting is known as "shifting the Overton window," a political concept that refers to how ideas that lie beyond the range of acceptable beliefs can be popularized and normalized through repetitive discourse to the point of eventual inclusion by audiences outside the fringe.[12]

From Imitation to Innovation

Al-Zarqawi's first media interaction as leader of the group, named Tawhid wal Jihad (TwJ), was an audiotape released in January 2004 called "Join the Line."[13] The speech poignantly eulogized one of his closest comrades during the US-led invasion and called for Muslims to join the jihad in Iraq—a blatant imitation of Azzam's call during the jihad against the Soviets in Afghanistan for Muslim men to join the caravan of martyrs.[14] The file was released on a popular jihadist website attributed to al-Zarqawi with no mention of the group.[15] By April, he announced the "formation" of his group on an audio file released to jihadist websites that also retroactively claimed the very first attacks from 2003, along with the horrific attacks on Shia pilgrims in early 2004 that killed and wounded hundreds of civilians.[16] The group's "information department" began releasing regular messages and strategic leadership statements while the "military wing" made its own releases regarding military operations.

TwJ's subsequent release of a series of execution videos is one example of the use of the Overton shift to normalize the killings of civilians and other enemies of the group.[17] These first decapitations were strongly criticized and censored outside of jihadi circles and inside them as well. The shock effect of killing on camera, an act that earned al-Zarqawi the nickname "Sheikh of the Slaughterers," sparked rebukes from the al-Qaeda Central (AQC) leadership who thought that this type of violence poisoned the al-Qaeda brand for the average Muslim. While this opinion seemed to capture conventional wisdom, one researcher tied these videos to a surge in recruits to the movement after the two battles of Fallujah in 2004.[18] Another more localized example of shifting the Overton window was the media department's use of cameramen that trailed slightly behind suicide bombers to capture gory footage of dead civilians in Shia areas, which was then marketed to Iraqi Sunnis angry about the ethnic cleansing of their own areas by Shia militias and rogue police units.[19] While the name Tawhid wal Jihad accurately expressed the values of the organization, its natural marketing appeal was limited in an environment crowded with diverse resistance groups to the US-led occupation. In January 2004, al-Zarqawi applied to his former sponsors in Afghanistan for acceptance as an official branch of al-Qaeda, which would help him with external funding for attacks and boost his brand. Initially hesitant to accept al-Zarqawi, al-Qaeda relented by October and al-Zarqawi fought the second battle of Fallujah under a new banner called al-Qaeda in the Land of Two Rivers (although they were better known as AQI).[20]

For most of 2004 and all of 2005, the "media wing" posted strategic leadership statements by al-Zarqawi, defenses from external critiques, verbal attacks against rival groups or individuals, and denials and counteraccusations onto friendly jihadist forums or hacked Internet sites. The military wing of TwJ posted a majority of the statements, which were celebrations of the attacks by the "knights of monotheism" on a host of "cowardly" enemies.[21] This line of messaging served to affirm al-Zarqawi's wisdom in taking on a powerful array of foes and ingrained this political worldview into the movement's DNA for good.[22] To keep the new and hot brand authentic, TwJ and later AQI regularly reminded their growing audience to look for only authentic statements posted by its official spokesman, a man named Abu Maysara al-Iraqi (hereafter Maysara).[23]

A Face Behind the Screen

This first spokesman for the movement was a young Iraqi from Baghdad and an active member of the underground Salafist networks during the late Saddam Hussein period, which resulted in his imprisonment by the regime's intelligence services. Born into a Shia family in Kazimiyah, Baghdad, Maysara was a convert to Salafism and sought out an extensive education in this trend, including memorization of the Quran, study of the Hadiths and Islamic jurisprudence, and rhetoric and debate. Among his instructors was the famous Subhi al-Badri—a relative and teacher of Abu Bakr al-Baghdadi and a noted anti-Shia polemicist[24]—as well as Muharib al-Jabouri, who would eventually succeed Maysara in the same position.[25] Maysara was one of the earliest Iraqi recruits into TwJ, and al-Zarqawi selected him for the spokesman position because of his ability to accurately communicate the doctrinal elements of the movement's ideology in the highly critical environment of the Salafi-jihadi trend. As a young student (younger than twenty-four years old) with recent university experience, he was uniquely computer savvy with connections that helped connect the movement to an international audience on the Internet, something greatly enhanced by the fall of the Saddam regime and the introduction of Internet service providers in Baghdad. This effort was assisted by the preexisting network of jihadist sympathizers outside of Iraq who would help publicize and spread the statements on multiple hosts.[26]

The tremendous effectiveness of the young spokesman did not go unnoticed by US authorities, and a vigorous effort was made to suppress his connection to the rest of the world. These efforts were largely fruitless, as the TwJ spokesman was always one step ahead, using the latest Silicon Valley file-sharing technology to spread video links on anonymous or hacked websites.[27] In a little over a year's time, US officials went from laughing at Saddam's information minister "Baghdad Bob" to being bested by a millennial Iraqi with part-time Internet access in a café. Maysara served as the official spokesman and deputy emir of the media department for over two years before he was finally killed in a US raid, making him an early casualty of cyber warfare. The coalition's failure to combat al-Zarqawi's online messaging in the cyber domain forced a change in strategy, and the United States moved to prioritize the kinetic targeting of a media wing it could not impact in cyberspace. It is highly probable that US electronic surveillance of the Internet cafés of Baghdad led to Maysara's death,[28] which neither the United States nor al-Zarqawi's group commented on in late spring of 2006.[29] The famous, but faceless, Internet spokesman simply vanished as mysteriously as he had appeared.

Heralding the Proto-Caliphate

After a year and a half of absorbing smaller groups into the fold, al-Zarqawi's AQI orchestrated a merger with some other similar Salafi-styled groups into a political front known as the Mujahideen Shura Council (MSC), in preparation for the establishment of a future caliphate.[30] As impressive a splash as the early media department made on the jihadi community and the rest of the world, the actual infrastructure was rudimentary and lacked depth. As late as summer of 2006 the media group was a small highly centralized cell that maintained close ties to al-Zarqawi. The evolution of the Coalition Special Operations Forces into an efficient manhunting machine chasing al-Zarqawi meant that the media became a target simply due to its close proximity to the leadership.[31] The task force hunting the AQI leader captured a group of five men in April 2006 in Yousifiyah, who later described themselves as high-level leaders in the MSC, including the minister of information, and their interrogations led to the death of al-Zarqawi in an air strike.[32] The killing coincided with a significant disruption of MSC media output, and exposed an urgent and existential need for additional layering and bureaucracy if the department was to survive future strikes.[33]

During this period, a man called Abu Ammar al-Dulaimi (hereafter Abu Ammar) released several statements under the title of spokesman of the MSC.[34] While brief in appearances, Abu Ammar is notable for his role in protecting the identity of the newly announced emir of the MSC, Abu Abdallah al-Baghdadi (hereafter Abu Abdallah), by reading the leader's speech for him in an audio release posted on the Internet in July 2006. As a result, Abu Abdallah's identity was concealed from voice identification for years and when Abu Omar al-Baghdadi (hereafter Abu Omar) was named the first emir of the Islamic State of Iraq (ISI) in October of that year, Abu Abdallah seemed to disappear as suddenly as he had appeared. This mystery lasted until 2016, when a coalition air strike killed Islamic State deputy Abu Ali al-Anbari (hereafter Abu Ali). The Islamic State's newsletter *al-Naba* subsequently revealed that Abu Ali was in fact the mysterious Abu Abdallah, and his disposition was concealed because he had been detained by the coalition around the time of the death of al-Zarqawi, leaving the movement leaderless. This important fact was unknown to the United States, thanks to the role spokesman Abu Ammar had in protecting Abu Abdallah/Abu Ali's identity.[35] The media department had access to important secrets, and the loss of al-Zarqawi caused the department to think deeply and become more involved in efforts to protect the identity of al-Zarqawi's replacements.

The Struggle to Realize an Islamic State, 2006–2010

On 15 October 2006, a man by the name of Muharib al-Jabouri—on behalf of the media department of the Mujahideen Shura Council—announced the formation of the Islamic State of Iraq, an event deliberately timed to coincide with the Ramadan period.[36] The announcement of the long-planned "state" was facilitated by the timely death of an increasingly polarizing al-Zarqawi and meant as a political gambit—along the lines of a fait accompli—to pressure rival insurgent groups to join an Islamic State that was peaking in popularity and territorial control in Sunni areas.[37] The transition was heralded by a video that symbolized the union of Sunni Iraqi tribes with the jihadist groups under the MSC. Al-Zarqawi's movement was now being transformed into a state-like structure.[38] The proposed state, led by an Iraqi named Abu Omar al-Baghdadi as political leader, and al-Zarqawi's former Egyptian deputy Abu Hamza al-Muhajir (hereafter Abu Hamza) as military leader, signaled the transformation from an insurgent group with regional cells to a shadow government with *wilayats* (regional provinces) that contained identical functional bureaus matching those at the national level.

The leaders of the Islamic State created this structure to enforce leader preferences and priorities within the movement such as the application of violence and the management of resources.[39] Known as an "M-form" hierarchy, the emirs at the *wilayat* level had significant autonomy to execute policy and guidance developed at the central level while the central level controlled shared resources such as foreign fighters and excess revenue collected from its subordinate units. According to a RAND research report using captured AQI/MSC documents, the list of functional bureaus in the 2006 structure included: administration, "movement and maintenance," "legal," "military," "security," "medical," "spoils," and "media."[40] The impact of this bureaucratization on the centralized media department was to formalize the relationship between local media units and the central or state level.

The physical disruption of the Islamic State media office increased in 2007, coinciding with the organization's reduced public support and military setbacks. The man tapped to replace Maysara as the group's official spokesman in mid-2006 was a familiar figure to those in the media department: Maysara's former religion teacher, Muharib al-Jabouri.[41] The MSC's deliberative body selected al-Jabouri to announce the formation of the new Islamic State and serve as its new spokesman for several reasons.[42] Al-Jabouri was a member of the same Salafi circuit that produced Maysara and Abu Bakr al-Baghdadi, and he had a legal and religious education including a doctorate from Saddam University. From 2003 to 2006, al-Jabouri led his own insurgent group called Saraya al-Ghareeb (battalion of strangers)[43] and, hence, was not an al-Zarqawi protégé, but instead a key representative of the conservative Sunni groups that Abu Omar and the Mujahideen Shura Council were trying to court so assiduously.[44] His new position was reflective of the division of spoils from the merger.

The continuity of highly educated spokesmen with impeccable Salafi pedigrees had proved to be a constant with this movement, a characteristic that remains to this day. However, along with the appointment of an influential spokesman was the corresponding announcement of a new media emir, a man of tremendous influence and reputation to match the responsibilities of a growing media establishment under the new state-like structure developing during 2006.[45] The new emir, Abu Zayd al-Mashadani, would be a memorable choice for many reasons. Al-Mashadani[46] had originally been a leading Iraqi jihadi in Ansar al Sunna who left to join al-Zarqawi in 2005, along with notables Abu Talha al-Ansari (first Wali of Mosul), Omar Bayizani, and Abu Ali al-Anbari. Al-Mashadani's stature was such that he was one of the three candidates short-listed to replace al-Zarqawi after his death in 2006, and

his appointment as media emir demonstrated the importance the department had in the new proto-state.[47]

The new leadership appointments in the media department were desperately needed in a busy environment of political mergers and the frenzied activities of the military units in 2007 that relied on local media
offices to produce more products that were vetted and edited at the central level. To add to this pressure, a series of coalition raids in summer of
2007 took its toll on the central media office. One of these operations
discovered a media center near Samarra belonging to the newly established video production company al-Furqan, which contained 65 hard
drives with 18 terabytes of data, 500 compact discs of material, and 12
computers. The facility had the capability to mass-produce 156 CDs in
eight hours and had a fully functioning film studio with first-class equipment.[48] In all, over eight separate media offices were destroyed all over
Iraq in mid-2007.[49] While this disruption caused substantial gaps in
video releases, the Islamic State's planned decentralization of media
offices allowed it to continue to produce operational summaries and
leader statements without fail, demonstrating the resiliency that would
bring it through the tough times in the coming years.[50]

The Serious Spokesman and the Serial Liar

The transition to statehood, while aspirational (if not fantastical) from a
territorial control measurement as the fortunes of the movement waned,
was much more concrete from an institutional perspective. Al-Jabouri
introduced the concept of the "institutional spokesman" of the Islamic
State in the video in which he announced the birth of "the State," an
attempt to create the image of a true competitor to the Iraqi government
in Sunni areas. Gone were the martial props of an insurgent group; al-
Jabouri replaced these with a desk, laptop, microphone, and the formal
Arabic dress of a shaikh. These details were meant to convey for the
first time the public routinization of the Islamic State movement.[51] Al-
Jabouri also recruited quality people to work on the editing of Islamic
State propaganda, including the future caliph Abu Bakr al-Baghdadi.[52]

One study of Iraqi insurgent media during this time period found
that compared to other groups, the Islamic State media projected a
more comprehensive operational picture of its activities around the
country through the publication of composite statements of attacks by
wilayat instead of singular attacks, and that it was the only group that
consistently produced strategic communication from the leadership. A
snapshot of insurgent statements for March 2007 highlights the way in
which the Islamic State was diverging from common practice due to

its increasing centralization and expanded structure (see Table 13.1).[53] Examples of the strategic communications included denials of false media reports, criticism of the Nouri al-Maliki administration, an announcement of a new military campaign, a description of Islamic State "programs" and fundamentals, and one clarification of its own messaging. The important point here is that the differences in the use of media between the Islamic State and its Sunni rivals were becoming clear at this critical juncture.

The relentless pursuit of the media as a target by Coalition Special Operations Forces led to the death of al-Jabouri in spring of 2007, but the efforts to create functioning local media outlets continued to be fruitful. By May 2008, the Ministry of Information of the Islamic State of Iraq released a video featuring the spokesman of Ninawa Province speaking in front of two cameras in the formalized setting of a cable news anchor—the first video to give a voice to a province via the state.[54] Provinces had been reporting their own monthly rollups of military operations since the announcement of the Islamic State and its official provinces, but that was a basic evolution of standard procedures in place since the MSC media office grew tired of reporting an ever increasing number of events scattered all over the country and began organizing the reports by geographic region.[55] Nonetheless, as the Islamic State lost its grip on key sanctuaries in Anbar, Diyala, and Babil Provinces, the more the media office was relied on to create the impression of a functioning state.

Al-Jabouri's death roughly coincided with the capture of his boss, media emir Abu Zayd al-Mashadani, and they were the first two cabinet members of the newly proclaimed Islamic State of Iraq to be killed or captured.[56] Al-Jabouri's impact was such that he was later eulogized by Abu Omar al-Baghdadi as one of the founders of the Islamic State.[57] Al-Mashadani's interrogation was also impactful, producing intelligence about the organization that has influenced analysts to this day, albeit in

Table 13.1   Insurgent Statements for March 2007

Group	Statements of Operations	Geographical Composite Statements	Strategic Communications
Islamic Army of Iraq	241	6	1
Mujahideen Army	136	2	1
1920s Brigade	0	0	3
Ansar al Sunnah	180	2	4
Islamic State of Iraq	71	74	15

a detrimental fashion. According to the chief US military spokesman, al-Mashadani revealed deep divisions among the Islamic State between foreigners and local fighters, and attested to the fact that Abu Omar— the newly declared emir of the Islamic State—did not exist; in fact, a US press release claimed that the Islamic State was a "virtual" Internet creation.[58] Instead, Abu Hamza al-Muhajir, al-Zarqawi's longtime deputy and a figure well known to the coalition, was the real leader of the group and hiding behind a fake Iraqi creation named Abu Omar, according to al-Mashadani's confession.[59] Al-Mashadani told his adversaries what they wanted to hear while protecting the identity of his new emir in what can only be described as one of the most successful deception operations in recent times.[60] Once the liability used to endanger the leadership of the organization, the media office was now protecting it by using the best tools at its disposal: information.

Once the font of stability for the Islamic State movement, the media office had now been through three spokesmen in a year and possibly as many emirs by the end of 2007, and some of its major media facilities had been found and destroyed. To impart some stability in the unit, Abu Omar chose a former adviser to al-Zarqawi, Abu Zahra Ali al-'Isawi. Al-'Isawi was a Fallujah native recruited by the legendary TwJ recruiters Abu Anas al-Shami and Abu Muhammad al-Lubnani in the earliest days of the movement. Captured during the coalition manhunt for al-Zarqawi, he escaped from prison and joined up with his old comrades in the new Islamic State in 2007. His biography stresses the immense responsibilities of managing the department during the decline of the state after 2008. This workload no doubt took the form of editing material from the central and provincial media offices. By 2009, he too had been killed by Coalition Special Operations, although without fanfare by either side.[61]

The Third Wave

The Islamic State announced its second cabinet in September 2009, including a new minister of information named Professor Ahmed al-Tai,[62] but the position of spokesman to replace al-Jabouri was not mentioned. Instead, the Islamic State recycled quotes from past emirs and spokesmen, especially the recently deceased al-Jabouri.[63] Part of the rationale for this was undoubtedly security related, but also probably part of an effort not to overshadow their emir Abu Omar, whose prestige while presiding over a declining insurgent group was lower than his charismatic predecessor, al-Zarqawi. As such, Abu Omar delivered the majority of the organizational strategic communications.

While occasionally used as the punch line for rivals poking fun at a translucent Islamic State, Abu Omar deserves some credit for selecting the future leadership of the current movement, including Abu Bakr al-Baghdadi and many others. His choice to send a new release from Camp Bucca to the media department would shape it for the next seven years. Abu Mohammad al-Adnani was a Syrian who swore allegiance to al-Zarqawi in 2002 and fought in the second battle of Fallujah before being captured and jailed. His release five years later and return to the organization was an example of the cyclical flow of the different generations of fighters in the movement, and al-Adnani belonged to the prestigious group of early adopters.[64] Al-Adnani was not just an original "plank owner" in the movement; his reputation for religious zeal and integrity, and his memorization of the Quran had impressed both al-Zarqawi and Abu Omar, according to his biographer.[65] Furthermore, he was a Syrian who had stuck with the Iraqi-based movement into what al-Adnani called "their time in the desert," and there is no doubt that the leadership watched for any future opportunity to expand beyond their logistical activities in Syria—a Sunni majority country with its own sectarian cleavage that bordered Iraq.[66] This knowledge base and reputation as a lifelong Salafi adherent fit the pattern of Maysara, al-Jabouri, al-Mashadani, and al-'Isawi.

Just months after Abu Omar's assignment, al-Adnani's distinctive voice appeared in a series of long and ambitious al-Furqan videos, starting with one against the Kurds released in January 2010,[67] another released in March,[68] and a third released in September.[69] These videos were important elements of Abu Omar's vision of promoting the idea that the Islamic State "remains,"[70] especially during a period when the leadership worked to reenergize its former fighters—who were largely staying home and refraining from operations for a variety of reasons.[71] The year 2010 marked the nadir of the Islamic State movement, which had flown so high in 2006. Iraqi forces captured the emir of Baghdad—Manaf al-Rawi—in the spring, and he subsequently gave up the location of Abu Omar and Abu Hamza as well as dozens of leaders around the country.[72] The evisceration of the leadership structure in 2010 pushed the organization further underground for a well-needed retooling, something requiring some tough introspection.

Expansion to the Caliphate, 2011–2014

The measure of the decline of the Islamic State at this point is usually constructed from reports of its leadership losses: just eight of forty-two leaders were at large in 2010.[73] However, while the decapitation campaign was putting tremendous pressure on the upper parts of the structure, the grassroots was reorganizing and conducting a vicious campaign against the Sunni Sahwa militias allied to the Iraqi government to win back their coveted sanctuaries in Iraq.[74] The Islamic State's loss of significant operational capability to conduct widespread guerrilla warfare forced the leadership to rely on suicide bombings as well as special operations—such as the seizure of Our Lady of Salvation Church in Baghdad, resulting in the death of dozens of Christians in the assault during mass.[75] These acts of semidesperation were claimed by the Islamic State media, and driven by the leadership's strong need to establish that the movement was still alive and capable of resisting the Iraqi government and its coalition allies. This rebuilding phase set the conditions for a movement resurgence from 2011 to 2014 that saw new initiatives by al-Furqan, which created the popular video series *Clashing of the Swords* (beginning in June 2012) and the *Windows upon the Land of Epic Battles* (2013). The combination of original battle footage with original *nasheeds* (Islamic a capella songs) as a score achieved breakout success for the Islamic State.[76]

It is hard to know what the inspiration for these changes was, but it is known that al-Adnani began to play a more influential role in the media organization after his 2010 narrations. The voice behind al-Furqan videos in 2010, by January 2011 he appeared in *The Spring of Anbar*.[77] In that video, al-Adnani is shown in the roles of preacher during a doctrinal lesson and of trainer during military drills in the Iraqi western province. Al-Adnani spoke (with face blurred) in another video released by al-Furqan in July eulogizing Osama bin Laden[78] and sang (face masked, no name indicated) in a third video by al-Furqan celebrating five years of the Islamic State shortly thereafter.[79] After these anonymous appearances, al-Furqan's first official mention of al-Adnani's name as spokesman was in a speech released in August 2011, "Indeed the Islamic State Will Remain."[80] The public acknowledgment of the Islamic State's new official spokesman, as well as an open campaign of assassination against the Sunni "traitors," is an indicator of the rising confidence of the leadership of the Islamic State in 2011. Interestingly, at this point Abu Bakr al-Baghdadi still had not made his first audio speech, which did not happen until July 2012.[81]

If the media unit was getting closer to its breakthrough in the highly influential video category, success certainly did not come easy. While the Islamic State media had produced videos since 2004, five years later the videos had improved in professional quality but not in content, consisting of tedious political broadsides against its enemies that mostly contained outtakes from Western and Arab media. New leadership of the ministry changed the format and, by August 2012, the release of *Salil as Sawarim 2* (The Clashing of the Swords)[82] demonstrated a new formula made up of brief interviews, sharp transitions between scenes, and a logical script sequence with scenes from training camp, leadership speeches, close-up battle footage, executions of the enemy, close-ups of mutilated enemy casualties, loading of captured booty, and ending with the honoring of their own martyrs. The narration is tight, with elimination of all dead time common in previous releases which, for instance, showed men cooking, doing dishes, or sitting in a room just doing nothing.

While the more recent history of the media department has been a closely guarded secret outside of the public spokesman role, there has been some reporting about the officials that have been involved in managing the department since 2013, if not before then. In addition to spokesman al-Adnani, an oversight council of three prominent figures has made decisions on policy and content: the Syrian militant Amr al-Absi, Saudi Bandar Sha'lan, and Wa'el al-Rawi, with al-Rawi serving as the media emir.[83] Neither of the first two was on the oversight council for their media expertise, which serves as an example of the Islamic State's inclusion of multinational consultation on their many oversight boards. This vision usually runs contrary to various caricatures of the movement and its leadership practices, a factor that continues to lead analysts and reporters astray.

While al-Absi was critical in the Islamic State's expansion into Syria before he was killed by a drone strike in 2016,[84] and Sha'lan is little known,[85] it was the secretive Wa'el al-Rawi who was most likely the driving force behind much of the Islamic State media's transformation since 2012. In addition to the changes in the basic design or formula for video formats, the council adopted a change in philosophy to expand its consumer base. Long relegated to posting to a narrow audience in the jihadi community, the media department embraced the popularity of social media and other methods of reaching new audiences, in contrast to their previous "top-down websites" and jihadi forums.[86] A result of this new policy was the creation of almost a dozen central media organs with diverse purposes, mediums, and target audiences.

The first, named al-I'tisam, jumped into the social media domain and began disseminating Islamic State of Iraq products on Twitter and other social media platforms in 2012, the first time that media products were released outside traditional semiclosed jihadist circuits. While not the first jihadist group to do so, their popularization and development of online cadres produced synergistic effects in recruitment, foreign fighter flow, and fund-raising, and an improved brand image. J. M. Berger notes that, unlike previous eras where new information technologies either improved the speed of communication or enhanced community sharing, the new online social media uniquely combined both functions. The use of emotionally charged and highly ideological content leveraged the speed and community aspects of the medium to achieve what Berger notes was a form of social contagion—in this case, of the millenarian type.[87]

This new push outward was also exemplified by the creation of Al-Hayat Media Center, which publishes material in languages other than Arabic—a longtime dream of jihadist theorists such as al-Suri.[88] Another recently created media center, al-Furat, focuses on the non-Arab contingents that have joined the Islamic State movement and ensures that the products are targeted to their respective populations at home.[89] Al-Ajnad produces *nasheeds* that were featured in several popular video releases and eventually became extremely popular tunes on social media outlets, as ringtones, and as the score for many homemade jihadist products. The use of *nasheeds* in the background of videos was not a new innovation for jihadi groups; al-Zarqawi's group used one as early as 2003 in a videotape of a suicide bomber saying his farewell.[90] What was new was how these original and catchy tunes went viral in the early phases of the Islamic State resurgence, thanks to the phenomenon described above.

Another evolution of standard practice was the creation of a weekly online newsletter named *al-Naba,* which served to package the multitude of reports and short stories that had been published sporadically in the past in a regularly published compilation of Islamic State military activity and other stories. The establishment of the A'maq News Agency was an attempt by the Islamic State to create an "independent" service that produces scoops by movement insiders to sway a target audience that might be hostile or skeptical of Western or regional media outlets.[91] Ironically, in practice A'maq serves as an allegedly legitimate source for these same international print and cable outlets to cite, which in turn amplifies the official message of the Islamic State. This venture into a grey zone version of the information wars could be the Islamic State's boldest experiment to date. Finally, and no less importantly, al-Bayan was created to manage radio broadcasts in the ever growing territory of the Islamic State.[92] It is the Islamic State's ground game and the use of kiosks to market propaganda to locals, which often goes unmeasured in any assessment of the efficacy of the Islamic State media.[93]

The current flood of releases of all formats from the Islamic State media outlets is a by-product of this recently expanded structure and the long professionalization of its workers and staff, combined with technology that facilitates peer-to-peer interaction and encrypted software that has fueled an expansion of outlets for viewers attracted to either the message or the spectacle. Most of this is happening at the *wilayat* level. According to researcher Thomas Joscelyn, the Islamic State's annual report released by the *al-Naba* newsletter for 1436 AH (October 2014–October 2015) summarized media output from all of its different formats.[94] (See Table 13.2.)

Further analysis of one week in April 2015 of the Islamic State media by Aaron Zelin found that the products focused primarily on Iraq and Syria despite the fact that only nineteen of the thirty-three claimed provinces are located in parts of these two countries; the majority (88 percent) were visual (mostly pictures) as opposed to text—a change from 2007 where text was dominant; and they were overwhelmingly (78 percent) locally produced at the provincial level. Another interesting finding was that out of 123 releases by official outlets that week, almost half of them (60) were not related to Islamic State violence or military operations. Instead, these messages focused on governance, religious norms, and promotion of the caliphate.[95]

Conclusion

Much like its experience in 2006–2008, the return of the Islamic State movement to prominence has resulted in active resistance, this time by an even larger coalition of Sunni militant groups, hostile local governments, and foreign interventionists. On 7 September 2016, Wa'el al-Rawi was

Table 13.2   Islamic State Media Ouput

Media Source (Type, Location)	Videos	Audios	Nasheed (religious songs)	Recitations	Magazines	Photo-reports	Images
Islamic Army of Iraq	241	6	1				
Wilayets (all, provincial media outlets)	710					1,787	14,000
Al-Furqan media (video focus, central)	7	6					
Al-Hayat Center (foreign language, central)	15		13		18		
Al-Ajnad (audio, central)			45	99			

killed in a precision strike near Raqqa, Syria.[96] This strike was most likely related to two previous strikes: one on 6 September that killed al-Rawi's media deputy for Syria and Iraq—Abu Harith al-Lami, and a strike on 30 August, which killed the public face of the Islamic State for so long—al-Adnani.[97] This dual elimination of the spokesman and media emir marks the third time since 2006 that the spokesman and the media emir were killed or captured within a short period of each other. There is not a lot yet to write about the almost unknown Wa'el al-Rawi but, based on media eulogies of their past leaders, and the archived material that is frequently released after key deaths, there will be more to write about him in the future.[98] In comparison, al-Adnani—who served as the public face of the media department and was a first-generation fighter and Camp Bucca veteran—is much better known. Al-Adnani's influence as the spokesman for the Islamic State during its return to prominence had expanded much beyond his role as media attack dog.[99] Whether it was directed at the Sunni of the Sahwa or his former boss in al-Qaeda, al-Adnani was the sharp-tongued emotional firebrand of the Islamic State behind the seemingly imperturbable Abu Bakr al-Baghdadi. Once again, the Islamic State had a leader in the media organization that transcended simple videos and messages, and performed crucial functions for the larger organization.

The effect of the killings of both leaders of the media department is hard to predict or assess, particularly since we know so little about one of the characters—and the one who had made most of the executive decisions. What we learned about the media department in its previous phases of evolution could not be pieced together until now. And even then this is a partial picture and probably mistaken in some aspects, based on the available material released by an organization that has perfected operational security in the face of an overwhelmingly technically oriented and abnormally efficient killing apparatus. Furthermore, even when its physical infrastructure and key personnel were under significant pressure, the department was able to continue its vital mission of producing products designed to create the perception of a vibrant and dynamic movement—even when it decidedly was not.

This case study reveals the growing significance of the information domain in the modern era, as recognized by many of the theorists debating the concept of hybrid war. Groups such as the Islamic State are using increased access to information sources that include popular theorists and ideologues, and lessons from past conflicts, as well as current trends that spur innovation and adaption to survive the relentless pressure from technologically superior foes. This effort, in turn, has strengthened the group's actions on the battlefield and in the cities of its enemies. Whether the looming defeat of the Islamic State is in fact imminent, other groups and possibly states will soon be examining and adopting some of its best practices and putting them to use in their multidomain conflicts with others.

Notes

This chapter is based on *Lighting the Path: The Evolution of the Islamic State Media Enterprise (2003–2016)*, by Craig Whiteside, originally published by the International Centre for Counter-Terrorism—The Hague (ICCT), 15 November 2016, doi: 10.19165/2016.1.14.

1. Aaron Zelin, "Picture or It Didn't Happen: A Snapshot of the Islamic State's Official Media Output," *Perspectives on Terrorism* 9, no. 4 (2015): 85–97; Charlie Winter, "Documenting the Virtual 'Caliphate,'" Quilliam Foundation, October 2015, p. 12, http://truevisiontv.com/uploads/websites/39/wysiwyg/doctors/jihad/FINAL -documenting-the-virtual-caliphate.pdf.

2. Thomas Rid and Marc Hecker, *War 2.0: Irregular Warfare in the Information Age* (Westport, CT: Praeger Security International, 2009), pp. 135–136.

3. Craig Whiteside, "The New Masters of Revolutionary Warfare: The Islamic State Movement (2002–2016)," *Perspectives on Terrorism* 10, no. 4 (2016): 4–18.

4. Joby Warrick, *Black Flags: The Rise of ISIS* (New York: Anchor Books, 2015), pp. 106–114.

5. Bobby Ghosh, "Twelve Years On, Remembering the Bomb that Started the Middle East's Sectarian War," *Quartz,* 28 Aug 2015, http://qz.com/476191/remembering -the-bomb-that-started-the-middle-easts-sectarian-war/.

6. Hanna Rogan, "Al Qaeda's Online Media Strategies: From abu Reuter to Irhabi 007" (Norwegian Defense Research Establishment [FFI], 2007).

7. Abdullah Azzam, "Join the Caravan," 1987, https://archive.org/stream /JoinTheCaravan/JoinTheCaravan_djvu.txt.

8. Neville Bolt, *Violent Image: Insurgent Propaganda and the New Revolutionaries* (London: Hurst, 2012); Andrew Exum, "The Spectacle of War: Insurgent Video Propaganda and Western Response, 1990–Present," *Arab Media and Society,* May 2008, pp. 3–4.

9. Rogan, "Al Qaeda's Online Media Strategies," p. 15.

10. Ibid., pp. 28–29.

11. Mustafa Hamid and Leah Farrell, *The Arabs at War in Afghanistan* (London: Hurst, 2015).

12. John Lancaster, "Brexit Blues," *London Review of Books,* 28 July 2016, www.lrb.co.uk/v38/n15/john-lanchester/brexit-blues.

13. The name, Tawhid wal Jihad (TwJ), means monotheism and struggle in Arabic.

14. Abu Musab al-Zarqawi's partner Abdul Hadi Daghlas had been killed in a US bombing of the Ansar al-Islam camp early in the war.

15. The website was alansar.com, the world's first jihadist forum, which was subsequently chased off-line.

16. Pam Benson, "CIA: Zarqawi Tape 'Probably Authentic,'" CNN.com, 7 April 2004, www.cnn.com/2004/WORLD/meast/04/07/zarqawi.tape/index.html?_s=PM:WORLD.

17. One veteran jihadist of Chechnya and Afghanistan conducted a suicide attack on the Iskandariyah Police Station resulting in fifty-five dead in February 2004. See Abu Ismail al-Muhajir, "Part VI of the Series, Biographies of Eminent Martyrs: Saif al Ummah," 11 December 2005, OSC Report No. GMP20051215371006.

18. Truls Tonnessen, "The Islamic Emirate of Fallujah," paper presented at the International Studies Association Conference, March 2011.

19. Matthew Alexander, *How to Break a Terrorist: The US Interrogators Who Used brains, Not Brutality, to Take Down the Deadliest Man in Iraq,* with John R. Bruning (New York: Free Press, 2008).

20. Abu Musab Al-Zarqawi, "Pledge of Allegiance to al-Qaeda," in *Mu'asker al-Battar,* no. 21, 17 October 2004, translated by Jeffrey Pool, Jamestown Foundation, www.jamestown.org/single/?tx_ttnews[tt_news]=27305#.Vpcp0_GlY7A.

21. Craig Whiteside, "The Smiling Scented Men" (PhD diss., Washington State University, 2014).

22. Abu Omar Al-Baghdadi, "Harvest of Prosperity," audiotape, Al Fajr Media, 17 March 2009.

23. Media Wing, Jama'at al-Tawhid wa al-Jihad, "Urgent—Clarification Statement," 20 July 2004, retrieved from Al-Anbar Network, OSC Archive Document GMP20040720000253.

24. Matt Barber, "Meet the Badris," *Syria Comment* (weblog), 13 March 2015, www.joshualandis.com/blog/meet-the-badris/.

25. Islamic State of Iraq, "Number Forty-Six of the Biographies of Eminent Martyrs: Abu-Maysarah al-Iraqi," Al-Furqan Establishment, disseminated on jihadist websites by Al-Fajr Media Center, https://azelin.files.wordpress.com/2011/08/biographies-of-the-prominent-martyrs-issue-46-e28094-abc5ab-maysarah-al-e28098irc481qc4ab.pdf (accessed 1 June 2017).

26. Arians Cha, "From a Virtual Shadow, Messages of Terror," *Washington Post,* 2 October 2004.

27. Ibid.

28. Sean Naylor, *Relentless Strike: The Secret History of Joint Special Operations Command* (New York: St. Martin's Press, 2015).

29. Scott Peterson, "Document Released by Iraq's Government Appears to Show that Al Qaeda in Iraq Feels Vulnerable," *Christian Science Monitor,* 16 June 2006.

30. Nibras Kazimi, "The Caliphate Attempted," *Current Trends in Islamist Ideology* 7 (July 2008), www.hudson.org/content/researchattachments/attachment/1137/20080701_kazimicaliphateattempted.pdf.

31. Stanley McChrystal, *My Share of the Task* (New York: Portfolio, 2013).

32. Alexander, *How to Break a Terrorist,* p. 88.

33. Jenna Jordan, "Attacking the Leader, Missing the Mark: Why Terrorist Groups Survive Decapitation Strikes," *International Security* 38, no. 4 (2014): 7–38.

34. Abu Abdallah Al-Baghdadi, read by Abu Ammar al-Dulaimi, "This Is What Allah and His Messenger Had Promised Us," Media Commission of the Mujahideen Shura Council (MSC), audio file posted to the Islamic Renewal Organization online, 1 July 2006, OSC Archive Document GMP20060703302001.

35. Islamic State, "Sheikh Abu Ali al Anbari, Accepted by God," *al-Naba,* no. 41, 16 August 2016, http://jihadology.net/2016/08/02/new-issue-of-the-islamic-states-newsletter-al-naba-41/.

36. Kazimi, "The Caliphate Attempted."

37. For an example of AQI/ISI's control and state-building efforts in Ramadi in 2006–2007, see Michael Silverman, *Awakening Victory* (Havertown, PA: Casemate, 2011).

38. Brian Fishman, "Dysfunction and Decline: Lessons Learned from Inside Al Qa'ida in Iraq" (West Point: Combating Terrorism Center at West Point, 2009), p. 4.

39. Jacob Shapiro, *The Terrorist's Dilemma*: *Managing Violent Covert Organizations* (Princeton: Princeton University Press, 2013), p. 89.

40. Benjamin Bahney, Howard J. Shatz, Carroll Ganier, Renny McPherson, and Barbara Sude, *An Economic Analysis of the Financial Records of al-Qa'ida in Iraq* (Santa Monica: RAND, 2010).

41. Islamic State of Iraq, "Number Forty-Six of the Biographies of Eminent Martyrs: Abu-Maysarah al-Iraqi," August 2011.

42. Kazimi, "The Caliphate Attempted."

43. The "stranger" code word is a common Salafi term that roughly equates to a "warrior-monk" image.

44. Truls Tønnessen, "Heirs of Zarqawi or Saddam? The Relationship Between al-Qaida in Iraq and the Islamic State," *Perspectives on Terrorism* 9, no. 4 (2015): 50; Abu Omar Al Baghdadi, "The Promise of Allah," Islamic State of Iraq, September 2008, translation available at https://kyleorton1991.wordpress.com/2017/02/11/the-islamic-state-explains-its-secret-to-success/#more-3642.

45. The first cabinet of the Islamic State was announced in April 2007 and posted on the Jidhadology website: http://jihadology.net/2007/04/19/video-message-from-the-islamic-state-of-iraqs-shaykh-mu%E1%B8%A5arib-al-jaburi-the-first-cabinet-selection-for-the-islamic-state-of-iraq/.

46. Aymenn Tamimi, "A Complete History of Jamaat Ansar al Islam," December 2015, www.aymennjawad.org/2015/12/a-complete-history-of-jamaat-ansar-al-islam.

47. Aymenn Tamimi, "An Account of Abu Bakr al Baghdadi by Abu al-Waleed al-Salafi," *Aymenn's Blog,* January 2016, www.aymennjawad.org/2016/01/an-account-of-abu-bakr-al-baghdadi-islamic-state.

48. Kevin Bergner, "Situational Update," MFNI-Iraq, 18 July 2007, www.MNF-Iraq.com.

49. B. Roggio, "US Targets Al Qaeda's Al Furqan Media Wing in Iraq," *Long War Journal,* 28 October 2007, www.longwarjournal.org/archives/2007/10/us_targets_al_qaedas.php.

50. Bill Roggio, "Hunting al Qaeda in Iraq's Propaganda Cells," *Long War Journal,* 28 November 2007, www.longwarjournal.org/archives/2007/11/hunting_al_qaeda_in.php.

51. Haroro Ingram and Craig Whiteside, "Don't Kill the Caliph: The Islamic State and the Pitfalls of Leadership Decapitation," War on the Rocks, 2 June 2016, http://warontherocks.com/2016/06/dont-kill-the-caliph-the-islamic-state-and-the-pitfalls-of-leadership-decapitation/.

52. Ali Hashem, "The Many Names of Abu Bakr," *al Monitor,* March 2015, www.al-monitor.com/pulse/en/originals/2015/03/isis-baghdadi-islamic-state-caliph-many-names-al-qaeda.html.

53. Daniel Kimmage and Kathleen Ridolfo, "Iraqi Insurgent Media: The War of Images and Idea," Radio Free Europe/Radio Liberty, 2007, p. 15.

54. Islamic State of Iraq, "Words from the Media Spokesman of Wilayat Ninewa," 1 May 2008, can be found on Aaron Zelin's Jihadology website with English subtitles at http://jihadology.net/2008/05/01/video-message-from-the-islamic-state-of-iraq-words-from-the-media-spokesman-of-wilayat-ninawa/.

55. Whiteside, "Smiling Scented Men."

56. Aymenn Tamimi captured this defector's take on the Islamic State, which included an acknowledgment that al-Mashadani had been captured by the United States: www.aymennjawad.org/2016/01/an-account-of-abu-bakr-al-baghdadi-islamic-state (accessed 1 June 2017).

57. Abu Omar Al-Baghdadi, "For the Scum Disappears Like Froth Cast Out," al-Furqan Media Production, 5 December 2007, https://scholarship.tricolib.brynmawr.edu/bitstream/handle/10066/4650/AOB20071204.pdf?sequence=3&isAllowed=y.

58. Fred Baker, "Al Qaeda in Iraq Duped into Following Foreigners, Captured Operative Says," US Department of Defense website, 18 July 2007, http://archive .defense.gov/news/newsarticle.aspx?id=46764.

59. Charts that accompanied the Department of Defense press release can be found at http://archive.defense.gov/DODCMSShare/briefingslide/309/070718-D -6570C-001.pdf (accessed 1 June 2017).

60. Malcolm Nance, *The Terrorists of Iraq*, 2nd ed. (Boca Raton: CRC Press, 2014), p. 287. See also Silverman, *Awakening Victory*.

61. Al Furqan, "Biographies of the Prominent Martyrs: Issue 45, Abu Zahra al 'Isawi,'" 18 July 2010, http://jihadology.net/2011/05/09/an%E1%B9%A3ar-al -mujahidin-english-forum-translates-issue-46-in-the-biography-of-the-prominent -martyrs-series-on-abu-zahra-al-isawi/.

62. Islamic State of Iraq, *Second Cabinet Reshuffle*, September 2009, http:// up1430.com/central-guide/pencil/elit/the_sum/the_sum_3/pages/emir/13/index.php.

63. Al Furqan, *Rising From the Dead*, video, 9 March 2010, link no longer available.

64. Abu Turki bin Mubarek al-Binali, "A Biography of IS Spokesman Abu Muhammed al Adnani as Shami," edited and translated by Pieter Vanostaeyen, 1 November 2014, justpaste.it, https://pietervanostaeyen.wordpress.com/2014/11/02 /a-biography-of-is-spokesman-abu-muhammad-al-adnani-as-shami/.

65. Ibid.

66. Abu Muhammad al-Adnani al-Shami, "And Those Who Lived in Faith Would Live upon Evidence," Jihadology.net, edited by Aaron Zelin, 21 May 2016, http://jihadology.net/2016/05/21/new-audio-message-from-the-islamic-states -shaykh-abu-muhammad-al-adnani-al-shami-and-those-who-lived-in-faith-would -live-upon-evidence/.

67. Al Furqan, "Suicide Bombing at Peshmerga Base," 11 January 2010, https:// ent.siteintelgroup.com/Multimedia/site-intel-group-1-13-10-isi-crusher-peshmerga -video.html.

68. Al Furqan, "Raid of the Prisoners," 30 March 2010, https://archive.org /details/Gazwat-Alaseer1.

69. Al Furqan, "Raid of the Prisoners II," 8 September 2010, https://archive.org /details/GhzwAssir_02.

70. Aymenn Tamimi, "The Islamic State Billboards and Murals of Tel Afar and Mosul," personal blog, www.aymennjawad.org/2015/01/the-islamic-state-billboards -and-murals-of-tel (accessed 1 June 2017).

71. Islamic State of Iraq, "Letter to Emir of Faithful from Abu Ibrahim," Captured Records Research Center, Document No. AQ-MSLF-D-001-681.

72. "Interview with Al Qa'ida's Baghdad Governor, Manaf al-Rawi," Al Arabiyah Television, 14 May 2010.

73. "US Says 80% of al Qaeda Leaders in Iraq Removed," *BBC News*, 4 June 2010, www.bbc.co.uk/news/10243585.

74. Craig Whiteside, "The Islamic State and the Return of Revolutionary Warfare," *Small Wars and Insurgencies* 27, no. 5 (2016): 743–776.

75. Brian Fishman, "Fall and Rise of Islamic State of Iraq," Policy Paper (New America Foundation, August 2011), p. 6, https://static.newamerica.org/attachments /4343-redefining-the-islamic-state/Fishman_Al_Qaeda_In_Iraq.023ac20877a644 88b2b791cd7e313955.pdf.

76. Alberto Fernandez, "Here to Stay and Growing: Combating ISIS Propaganda Networks" (Washington, DC: Brookings Institution, October 2015), p. 8.

77. Al Furqan, "The Spring of Anbar," 17 January 2011, https://ent.siteintelgroup .com/Latest-Multimedia-from-Islamic-State-of-Iraq-ISI/site-intel-group-1-17-12-isi -video-anbar-spring.html.

78. Al Furqan, "Eulogy for Osama bin Laden," 19 July 2011, https://archive.org/details/RethaAlEmamMnRboiDawlatAlIslam.

79. Al Furqan, "ISI Celebrated Five Years Since Establishment," 21 August 2011, https://ent.siteintelgroup.com/Multimedia/isi-video-celebrates-five-years-since-establishment.html.

80. Abu Muhammad Al-Adnani, "Indeed the Islamic State will Remain," Islamic State of Iraq, 7 August 2011, https://ent.siteintelgroup.com/Latest-Multimedia-from-Islamic-State-of-Iraq-ISI/isi-spokesman-stresses-continuity-of-groups-mission.html.

81. Abu Bakr Al-Baghdadi, "But Allah Will Not Allow but that His Light Should Be Perfected," al Furqan, 21 July 2012.

82. Lyrics translated by Aymenn Tamimi, "Clashing of the Swords—New ISIS Nasheed from Ajnad Media," *Aymenn's Blog,* June 2014, www.aymennjawad.org/2014/06/clashing-of-the-swords-new-isis-nasheed-from.

83. The media council of three executives is mentioned by Abu al-Waleed in Tamimi, "An Account of Abu Bakr al Baghdadi."

84. Charles Lister, *The Syrian Jihad: Al-Qaeda, the Islamic State and the Evolution of an Insurgency* (London: Hurst, 2016), p. 134.

85. Kyle Orton, "Governing the Caliphate: Profiling Islamic State Leaders" (Henry Jackson Society, 2016), p. 61.

86. Aaron Zelin, "The State of Global Jihad Online: A Qualitative, Quantitative, and Cross-Lingual Analysis" (New America Foundation, January 2013).

87. J. M. Berger, "The Metronome of Apocalyptic Time: Social Media as Carrier Wave for Millenarian Contagion," *Perspectives on Terrorism* 9, no. 4 (2015): 61–71.

88. Thomas Joscelyn, "Graphic Promotes the Islamic State's Prolific Media Machine," *Long War Journal,* 25 November 2015, www.longwarjournal.org/archives/2015/11/graphic-promotes-islamic-states-prolific-media-machine.php.

89. Charlie Winter, "Signs of a Nascent Islamic State Province in the Philippines," War on the Rocks, 25 May 2016, http://warontherocks.com/2016/05/signs-of-a-nascent-islamic-state-province-in-the-philippines/.

90. Michael Ware, *Only the Dead See the End of War,* documentary, Home Box Office, 2016, www.hbo.com/documentaries/only-the-dead-see-the-end-of-war/index.html.

91. Alex Kassirir, "The Rise of an ISIS Affiliated Media Unit: A'maq," *Flashpoint,* 25 May 2016, www.flashpoint-intel.com/the-rise-of-an-isis-affiliated-media-unit-amaq/.

92. Winter, "Documenting the Virtual 'Caliphate,'" p. 16.

93. Tyler Golson, "Islamic State's Local Propaganda Key to Understanding Appeal," *World Politics Review,* 18 May 2015, www.worldpoliticsreview.com/articles/15791/islamic-state-s-local-propaganda-key-to-understanding-appeal.

94. Joscelyn, "Graphic Promotes the Islamic State's Prolific Media Machine."

95. Zelin, "Picture or It Didn't Happen," pp. 85–95.

96. US Department of Defense, "Statement from Pentagon Press Secretary Peter Cook on Airstrike Against ISIL Senior Leader," press release no. NR-326-16, 16 September 2016.

97. Charlie Winter, "6. Context: Abu al-Harith al-Lami, Formerly in Charge of #Iraq/#Syria Media, Killed 6 Sept & Dr Wa'il, 'Information Minister,' Killed 7 Sept," Twitter, 5 October 2016, https://twitter.com/charliewinter/status/783626508963311616.

98. The Islamic State's media released a statement acknowledging the death of its information minister (abu Mohammad al Furqan, an alleged alias of Wael al-Rawi) on 10 October 2016, https://twitter.com/Raqqa_SL/status/785562692509659136.

99. Eric Schmitt, Rukmini Callimachi, and Anne Barnard, "Spokesman's Death Will Have Islamic State Turning to Its "Deep Bench," *New York Times,* 31 August 2016.

PART 4

Conclusion

14

"Hybrid" and "Information": New Labels, Old Politics

James C. Pearce

War is an extension of politics by other means, regardless of the modes and characteristics. The labels that can be attached to *war* aside, the boundaries of its definitions are often crossed and confused. No war or conflict is confined purely to one space, is fought solely by military means, or spans a period that can be defined explicitly by military actions. In the West a great deal of emphasis is placed on technology and, for this reason, technology can help us to better understand the character of war and how it is fought. Of course, as technology develops, so does the character of war, the boundaries of our understanding and, as an outcome, the definition itself. When comparing different regions, countries, states, and nonstate actors, the mold of this definition usually has particular characteristics. Yet the edges and tools that shape it remain the same.

In an attempt to understand the conflicts of the twenty-first century, analysts, practitioners, and scholars alike have struggled to package these as something entirely new. Simply referring to the ongoing standoff between Russia and the West as a "new Cold War" or "Cold War 2.0" is, on some levels, intellectually idle. The nature of this standoff bears little resemblance to the actual Cold War. This event, however, is within our recent historical memory and, therefore, its familiarity does not test the boundaries of our knowledge and understanding. Rather, it is a more fashionable way of describing the geopolitical climate. This all points to something much bigger and important. The usage of different terms to describe the evolving character of conflicts has been driven by scholars and political analysts shaping the debate surrounding the events following the beginning of the Ukrainian crisis in 2014. The ideas of a new

Cold War, hybrid warfare, information warfare, and *gibridnaya voyna* are all products of the political environment rather than a serious examination of what has been happening on the ground and, therefore, they do not necessarily reflect the reality of the current situation.

The term *hybrid warfare* has multiple implications and uses as it is. The fact that Russian understanding of the term significantly differs from its Western counterpart merely reflects its malleable nature. One area of agreement that deserves attention is the rejection of political hostilities alone as warfare. As such, the current situation with Russia and the West is hard to label. Whatever one's personal feelings, it does not seem (at the time of this writing) to be a form of tension that truly deserves to be called a "war." It is, however, the broadness of the term *hybrid warfare* that causes confusion. As this book has discussed, hybrid warfare is far from a grand strategy of either Russia or the West. Yet as Frank Hoffman and many others have noted, it is a mixture of regular and irregular forces, of methods and means. That is what makes it an interesting phenomenon and a politically powerful term in modern confrontations.

All definitions of *hybrid war* discussed by the authors throughout this book are multidimensional and integrate many different aspects of fighting into a single domain. In the case of the Russian concept of color revolutions, hybrid warfare becomes an organizational model that can offer enhanced tactics to achieve the desired goals. In this scenario, it is usually based on existing interstate struggles that can bring out a nonmilitary type of confrontation (protests, terrorism, etc.). Similar to military conflicts, revolutions go through a series of stages and have no less destabilizing power. As is often the case, however, protests can (and do) go hand in hand with military force of some kind; thus, they are hybrid by their very nature and combine military and nonmilitary activities. Military and political goals become the same and the focus turns to destabilizing (and reconstructing) the domestic security. In this context hybrid warfare, and revolution within it, is no different from conventional war, although it is worth stressing that the costs (economic and material) are different.

This also reflects the importance of information. The rapidly changing media landscape has significant implications on politics and, by extension, on national security. Messaging of the state, both at home and abroad, has become more critical than ever and is being heavily mediated through all available technologies. As such any state, be it Russia, the United States, or even Qatar, is more easily able to talk directly to foreign populations and to influence their domestic politics. This has been seen with outlets such as RT and Sputnik International in the recent past but, during the Cold War, one could easily be referring to Radio Liberty or the Voice of America. One key difference from the Cold War, however, is that the current media atmosphere has caused a considerable information overload and uncertainty, rendering official messages insecure. In many respects, the world is engulfed in a clash of interpretations, which may be settled only through a mastery of techniques of strategic communication. Important to note here is that the criteria for identifying one's international, political, and military opponents widen to include anyone who threatens said actor's command of the information space. The rising geopolitical tensions and public anxiety associated with information campaigns deployed by hostile state and nonstate actors, who seek to shape public opinion and attitudes in pursuit of their own strategic objectives, further show the complexity of the many existing dimensions. A recent example of this from the United Kingdom is the reaction of the British press Labour Party leader Jeremy Corbyn's stance on the Skripal poisoning and British air strikes that followed a chemical attack by the Syrian government.[1]

In the United States, the nature of political warfare changed as the Cold War broke out; however, it never properly armed itself for certain challenges. This trend seems to have continued. Many who have testified before Congress since 2017 (including former FBI director James Comey, former director of national intelligence James Clapper, former attorney general Eric Holder, and former deputy attorney general Sally Yates) have stated that incumbent president Donald Trump has shown little concern about the alleged Russian interference in the 2016 US presidential election.[2] Seemingly, this is a historical precedent. During the Cold War, the United States Information Agency (USIA) was constantly fighting for resources as it played a role that was often misunderstood or arguably undervalued. Surrounding this, however, are other issues peculiar to US politics that ought to be considered. First, allocating more taxpayer dollars to government-funded bodies and programs is always a hard sell to the Republican Party. The one exception is military spending and, therefore, an extended definition of *war* could prove to be a useful political tool in this regard. Second, the use of information in conflicts may need to be settled by the Supreme Court for possible breaches of the First and Fourth Amendments. The court's decisions in the coming years will be pivotal in defining the future direction of the United States on many political and social issues, including how the US government and its military uses the information domain for national security. This is especially true because of the court's current demographics. Two justices, Anthony Kennedy and Ruth Bader Ginsburg, are over the age of eighty years, are beyond the requirement of serving twenty-five years, and are considered moderate and liberal judges respectively. Trump could fill these potential vacancies with conservative justices who would tilt the court to the right. It is these kinds of political matters that plague the information space and cloud judgment on finding long-term and meaningful responses to hybrid threats and conflicts.

By contrast, hybrid warfare and information security are high-profile topics in demand in Russia today. This is both a blessing and a curse; although its response could be more rounded, there currently is no consensus over the key issues, as the authors of Chapters 3, 4, and 5 rightly point out. As such, the conceptualization of hybrid warfare and information security has limited, if any measurable, success. An interesting point to reconsider follows on from the previous paragraph. It is well agreed among scholars that particular historical, cultural, geographic, economic, and even religious and psychological mechanisms play a key role in the modernization of the armed forces. While these may not be the main obstacle in implementing effective strategies of information warfare, neither can they be dismissed. Military technologies and information and communication technology (ICT) do not differ drastically between armies, but the applications of different strategies do vary and that is why this deserves attention. As this book has discussed, Russian military doctrines have been impacted in many ways by the Soviet ideology. By contrast, the appointment of a judge in Russia is unlikely to affect Russian strategies as it would the United States.

In connection with this is the linguistic discourse. The terminology used in Russia is often borrowed from the West. *Information warfare* was strictly extraneous in USSR while *ideological struggle* was a substitute bearing a close meaning. Without a homegrown theory, some Russian authors tend to reflect foreign research, speculating on the "true" nature of Western concepts. The problem of a clear definition is getting worse due to the absence of translation standards. The consequence is a lack of real understanding in the West, which is instead replaced with confusion and hyperbole. The popular trends also coincide with media discourse, in Russia and abroad. This, in turn, creates false ideas about the relevance and significance of the Russian practice for domestic and foreign audiences. Although terminology problems will likely continue, this book has addressed these in different ways and assessed their significance.

Concerning information warfare and the rise of the Islamic State this nonstate organization uses three foundations for its information campaign: distinct warfare, victimhood, and utopia. In late 2016 to early

2017, the organization expertly used propaganda to repudiate enemy information operations and establish a strategic narrative that would ultimately enable it to emerge from its lost battles conceptually unscathed. In many ways, propaganda weathered a bad storm for the Islamic State during the Mosul campaign. It did, however, show an ability to adapt to the specific situational exigencies of the time. Even when its physical infrastructure and key personnel were under significant pressure, the Islamic State was able to continue its vital mission of producing products designed to create the perception of a vibrant and dynamic movement, which was clearly no longer the case. This propaganda was extremely effective in Russia's North Caucasus region and some European Union (EU) countries, revealing certain vulnerabilities in these societies. Many of its recruits had higher education and came from affluent backgrounds, yet they had become disillusioned with their countries of origin for many different sociopolitical reasons. Moreover, it shows that even when the Islamic State eventually falls, the reasons so many young Muslims are attracted to it remain and can be exploited by another group in the future. Of course, this is only assuming that this future group will possess the sophisticated means and organizational skills to do so. After all, the Islamic State is an artificial political construction (with an ideology of radical jihadism) that can be improved and replicated. This likely means the ways that its successor will be defeated involve tried and tested methods employed against the information warfare of the Islamic State and others of its kind.

One reason for its propaganda success could be the makeup of the leadership of the Islamic State: secret service officers from other sovereign powers in the Middle East. The organization started precariously with a few stateless individuals operating far from their homelands and grew into one of the most successful and far-reaching insurgent groups in recent history. It developed with an experienced high professional level of officer corps, management personnel, propaganda mechanisms, and experts in the sphere of internal security. The fact that it was mimicked from a former Iraqi security service also gave it a huge organizational and strategic benefit over other Islamic fundamentalist groups. The Islamic State formed its own security council and possessed a high level of military experience. The morale of its fighters was high and they developed specific (if unconventional) tactics and combat units. Indeed, it successfully intimidated its adversaries and was feared by them. The brutal nature of information warfare was justified in the name of establishing a caliphate and returning to the times of "purified Islam." In other words, the Islamic State is a systemic megaproject posing a systemic threat to global security. The fact that it is Islamic in nature does not make the goal of eliminating it any more reasonable in the near future. The nature of this conflict weakened the US position in the Greater Middle East, shaking the established balance of power between different regional actors. There is no obvious counterweight to Iran—a goal the United States has sought to achieve since the Iranian revolution. Moreover, this is the only military-political vanguard of the entire Islamic world in confrontation with the West. Its eventual defeat and demise will attract others with the same goal who may model themselves on the Islamic State.

The success of the Islamic State in attracting young followers all over the world shows the growing significance of the information domain in the modern era, as recognized by many of the theorists debating the concept of hybrid war. Groups such as the Islamic State use increased access to information sources that include popular theories and ideologues, failures from past conflicts, and current trends that spur innovation and adaption required to survive the relentless pressure from technologically superior foes. Important lessons can and should be drawn from successes of the Islamic State, if we want to defeat similar groups in the future.

What can be said is that the political and media environment of the Western world often hinders progress. The fact remains that decisions and solutions relating to warfare and conflicts require political solutions. The media has played an instrumental role in directly shifting public opinion and, indirectly, policy. For example, former British prime minister, David Cameron, failed to obtain parliamentary approval to launch air strikes in Syria 2013. Parliament was recalled for a vote during the summer recess when members of Parliament (MPs) were at home talking to their constituents. Sensing the mood, both MPs and the British press expressed skepticism over the move, and Cameron lost by just thirteen votes.[3] This has not been a stand-alone incident or one confined to the UK. Following Trump's election in 2016, a Pew poll showed that support among Republicans for bombing Syria had risen from 22 percent (2013) to 86 percent (2017). But support among registered Democrats was practically unchanged (38 percent in 2013 and 37 percent in 2017, respectively).[4] Scholars have taken note of the increased tribalism in recent years and, when this filters through into government and partisan media, foreign policy in general suffers.

Labels matter, but the contents of conflicts and warfare have been overlooked as a result. As Chapter 13 notes, little has been written about the origins and foundations of the Islamic State. Most of the attention in the public space has surrounded its nature as a terrorist organization.

The consequence is that few understand why it has been so hard to defeat. Regarding Crimea, most of the media coverage and the national governments in the West were fixated on the illegality of the peninsula's annexation. Hardly any effort went into understanding the historical context and situation within, which means that Russia could easily be depicted as a bad actor. As a former editor of the *Moscow Times* aptly wrote of the situation in eastern Ukraine: "There is excellent field reporting from Ukraine in the western media, but they make only a modest part of the general message. Public opinion is shaped largely by analytical articles and op-eds."[5] Taking this further, most newspapers in the United States and the United Kingdom have a political slant of some kind, meaning the message is filtered to begin with. The discussion needs to be wider, occurring in multiple spaces at the same time between the different actors and in a similar language. This is not to suggest that no such dialogue already occurs. However, this book demonstrates that political reasons affect the choice of a label that we put on the bottle of war more than what this bottle actually contains and, thereby, they ultimately shape not only the way we perceive the character of contemporary conflicts but also how we conduct them.

Notes

1. The "Skripal poisoning" refers to Sergei Skripal, a former KGB and double agent, who was poisoned along with his daughter by a nerve agent in Salisbury in March 2018. The UK government's response was quick in blaming Russia for directly or indirectly using a Novichok nerve agent produced in the USSR. Labour leader Jeremy Corbyn criticized the Conservative government for being too quick to blame Russia for the attack without the facts. With respect to Syria, he expressed concern over the legality of the air strikes. See Tim Sculthorpe, "Corbyn Refuses to Blame Assad for Chemical Attack in Syria and Demands All Sides Work Together on a Ceasefire," *MailOnline,* 9 April 2018, www.dailymail.co.uk/news/article-5594765/Corbyn-refuses-blame-Assad-chemical-attack-Syria.html#ixzz5DUJAfGIV.

2. These public figures have all taken part in several hearings by the congressional Judiciary and Intelligence Committees that have formed part of the "Russia investigation."

3. "Syria Crisis: Cameron Loses Commons Vote on Syria Action," *BBC News,* 30 August 2013, www.bbc.co.uk/news/uk-politics-23892783.

4. "Public Supports Syria Missile Strikes, but Few See a 'Clear Plan' for Addressing Situation," 12 April 2017, Pew Research Center, available at www.people-press.org/2017/04/12/public-supports-syria-missile-strikes-but-few-see-a-clear-plan-for-addressing-situation/1-18/.

5. Nabi Abdullaev, "Biased Journalism Robs the West of Its Moral Authority," *The Guardian,* 4 August 2014.

Selected Bibliography

Acheson, Dean. *Present at the Creation: My Years in the State Department*. New York: Norton, 1969.

Adamsky, Dima. *The Culture of Military Innovation: The Impact of the Cultural Factors on the Revolution in Military Affairs in Russia, the US, and Israel*. Stanford: Stanford University Press, 2010.

Adkin, Mark, and Mohammad Yousaf. *Afghanistan—The Bear Trap: The Defeat of a Superpower*. Havertown, PA: Casemate, 2001.

Alberts, David, John Garstka, and Frederic Stein. *Network Centric Warfare: Developing and Leveraging Information Superiority*. Washington, DC: Command and Control Research Program, 1999.

Alexander, Matthew. *How to Break a Terrorist: The US Interrogators Who Used Brains, Not Brutality, to Take Down the Deadliest Man in Iraq*. With John R. Bruning. New York: Free Press, 2008.

Aliyev, Kachivek, Zagir Arukhov, and Kaflan Khanbabayev. *Religiozno-politicheskiy ekstremizm i etnokonfessional'naya tolerantnost' na Severnom Kavkaze* [Religious-Political Extremism and Ethno-Confessional Tolerance in the North Caucasus]. Moscow: Nauka, 2007.

Arbatov, Alexey, and Natalia Bubnova, eds. *Bezopasnost i kontrol nad voruzheniyami 2015–2016: Mezhdunarodnoe vzaimodejstviye v borbe s globalnymi ugrozami* [Security and Arms Control 2015–2016: International Cooperation in Fighting Against Global Threats]. Moscow: IMEMO RAN; ROSSPE, 2016.

Armstrong, Matthew. "No, We Do Not Need to Revive the U.S. Information Agency." War on the Rocks. https://warontherocks.com/2015/11/no-we-do-not-need-to-revive-the-u-s-information-agency/ (accessed 12 May 2017).

Arquilla, John, and David Ronfeldt. *Networks and Netwars: The Future of Terror, Crime, and Militancy*. Santa Monica: RAND, 2001.

———. *Swarming and the Future of Conflict*. Santa Monica: RAND, 2000).

Aryamova, Anna. "'Tsvetnye revolutsii' kak instrument vneshney politiki stran anglo-amerikanskogo politicheskogo bloka" ["Color Revolutions" as an Instrument of Foreign Policy in the Countries of the Anglo-American Political Block]. *Vlast'*, no. 8 (2015): 206–210.

Bachmann, Sascha-Dominik, and Håkan Gunneriusson. "Terrorism and Cyber Attacks as Hybrid Threats: Defining a Comprehensive Approach for Countering

21st Century Threats to Global Peace and Security." *Journal on Terrorism and Security Analysis* 9 (Spring 2014): 26–36.

Bahney, Benjamin, Howard J. Shatz, Carroll Ganier, Renny McPherson, and Barbara Sude. *An Economic Analysis of the Financial Records of al-Qa'ida in Iraq*. Santa Monica: RAND, 2010.

Barabash, Victor. *Globalizaciya i problema vojn v sovremennom mire* [Globalization and the Problem of War in the Contemporary World]. Moscow: Peoples' Friendship University of Russia, 2011.

Bartosh, Alexander. "Gibridnaya voyna: Interpretatsii i real'nost'" [Hybrid War: Interpretations and Reality]. *Nezavisimoe Voennoe Obozrenie*, 16 September 2016. http://nvo.ng.ru/concepts/2016-09-16/1_war.html.

———. "Kompleks podryvnykh tekhnologiy 'Tsvetnaya Revolyutsiya—Gibridnaya Voyna' kak ugroza natsional'noy bezopasnosti Rossii" [The Complex of Subversive Techniques "Color Revolution—Hybrid War," as a Threat to Russia's National Security]. *Bezopasnost' Yevrazii* 1 (2015): 245–247.

Bel'kov, Oleg. "'Gibridnaya voyna': Novaya real'nost' ili novoye slovo o starykh veshchakh?" ["Hybrid War": A New Reality or a New Word About Old Things?]. *Bezopasnost' Yevrazii*, no. 1 (January–July 2015): 231–234.

———. "Ponyatie 'voyna' i yego aberratsii v otechestvennom diskurse" [Concept of "War" and Its Aberrations in Domestic Discourse]. *Vlast'*, no. 9 (2009): 6–7.

Belozerov, Vasily, and Alexey Solov'ev. "Gibridnaya Voyna v otechestvennom politicheskom i nauchnom diskurse" [Hybrid War in Domestic Political and Academic Discourse]. *Vlast'*, no. 9 (2015): 5–11.

Berger, J. M. "The Metronome of Apocalyptic Time: Social Media as Carrier Wave for Millenarian Contagion." *Perspectives on Terrorism* 9, no. 4 (2015): 61–71.

Betz, David. "Communication Breakdown: Strategic Communications and Defeat in Afghanistan." *Orbis* 55, no. 4 (2011): 613–630.

———. *Carnage and Connectivity: Landmarks in the Decline of Conventional Military Power*. London: Hurst, 2014.

Bolgov, Radomir, Natalya Vasil'eva, Svetlana Vinogradova, and Konstantin Pantzerev. *Informacionnoye obshchestvo i mezhdunarodnye otnosheniya* [Information Society and International Relations]. (Saint Petersburg: Saint Petersburg State University, 2014).

Bolt, Neville. *Violent Image: Insurgent Propaganda and the New Revolutionaries*. London: Hurst, 2012.

Bukharin, Sergey, and Vladimir Tsyganov. *Informatsionnyye voyny v biznese i politike* [Information Warfare in Business and Politics]. Moscow: Akademicheskiy proyekt, 2007.

Castells, Manuel. *Communication Power*. Oxford: Oxford University Press, 2013.

Chekinov, Sergey, and Sergey Bogdanov. "Evoliutsiia sushchnosti i soderzhaniia poniatiia 'voi'na' v XXI stoletii" [The Evolution of the Nature and the Content of the Concept of "War" in the 21st Century]. *Voennaya Mysl'*, no. 1 (2017): 30–43.

———. "O kharaktere i soderzhanii voyny novogo pokoleniya" [The Nature and the Content of a New-Generation War]. *Voennaya Mysl'*, no. 10 (2013): 13–24.

Clausewitz, Carl Von. *On War*. Edited and translated by Michael Howard and Peter Paret. Princeton: Princeton University Press, 1976.

Cull, Nicholas. *The Cold War and the United States Information Agency: American Propaganda and Public Diplomacy, 1945–1989*. Cambridge: Cambridge University Press, 2008.

Darczewska, Jolanta. "The Anatomy of Russian Information Warfare: The Crimean Operation, A Case Study." Point of View No. 42. Warsaw: Centre for Eastern Studies, 2014.

Demidov, Oleg. "Obespecheniye mezhdunarodnoy informacionnoy bezopasnosti i rossiyskie nacionalnye interesy" [Ensuring International Information Security and Russian National Interests]. *Indeks Bezopasnosti,* no. 104 (2013): 129–168.

Devji, Faisal. *The Terrorist in Search of Humanity: Militant Islam and Global Politics.* New York: Columbia University Press, 2008.

Dridze, Tamara. *Tekstovaya deyatel'nost' v strukture sotsial'noy kommunikatsii: Problemy semiosotsiopsikhologii* [Text Activity in the Structure of Social Communication: The Problems of Semio-Socio-Psychology]. Moscow: Nauka, 1984.

Druzhinina, Mariya, ed. "Politicheskaya mediametriya" [Political Media-Metrics]. Russian Institute for Strategic Studies (RISS), 30 March 2015. https://riss.ru/smi/11189.

Dugin, Aleksandr. *Setevyye voyny: Ugroza novogo pokoleniya* [Network Wars: The Threat of a New Generation]. Moscow: Yevraziyskoye dvizheniye, 2009.

Ellul, Jacques. *Propaganda: The Formation of Men's Attitudes.* Translated by Konrad Kellen and Jean Lerner. New York: Vintage Books, 1973.

Epstein, Charlotte. *The Power of Words in International Relations: Birth of an Anti-Whaling Discourse.* Cambridge, MA: MIT Press, 2008.

Farwell, James. *Persuasion and Power: The Art of Strategic Communication.* Washington, DC: Georgetown University Press, 2012.

Fedorov, Alexander, and Vitali Tsygichko, eds. *Informatsionnye vyzovy nacionalnoy i mezhdunarodnoy bezopasnosti* [Information Challenges to National and International Security]. Moscow: PIR Center, 2001.

Filimonov, Georgy, Nikita Danyk, and Maxim Yurako. *Perevorot* [Coup D'état]. Saint Petersburg: Piter, 2016.

Filimonov, Georgy, Oleg Karpovich, and Andrey Manoylo. *Tekhnologii "myagkoy" sily na vooruzhenii SShA: Otvet Rossii* [The US Techniques of "Soft" Power: Russia's Response]. Moscow: RUDN University, 2015.

Fletcher, Tom. *Naked Diplomacy: Power and Statecraft in the Digital Age.* London: William Collins, 2016.

Freedman, Lawrence. "Stop Overestimating the Threat Posed by Russia's 'New' Form of Warfare." World Economic Forum, 4 January 2017. www.weforum.org /agenda/2017/01/stop-overestimating-the-threat-posed-by-russia-s-new-form-of -warfare.

———. "Ukraine and the Art of Limited War," *Survival* 56, no. 6 (2014): 7–38.

Freyer, Nathan. "The Defense Identity Crisis: It's a Hybrid World." *Parameters* 39, no. 3 (2009): 81–94.

Fridman, Ofer. *Russian "Hybrid Warfare": Resurgence and Politicisation.* London: Hurst, 2018.

Galeotti, Mark. *Hybrid War or Gibridnaya Voina? Getting Russia's Non-Linear Military Challenge Right.* Prague: Mayak Intelligence, 2016.

Gareev, Makhmut. *Esli zavtra voyna* [If War Happens Tomorrow]. Moscow: Vladar, 1994.

———. "Voyna i voennaya Nauka na Sovremennom Etape" [War and Military Science in Their Contemporary Stage of Development]. *Voenno-Promyshlennyy Kuryer* 481, no. 13 (2013): 5.

Gerasimov, Valery. "Po opytu Sirii: Gibridnaya voyna trebuyet vysokotekhnologichnogo oruzhiya i nauchnogo obosnovaniya" [According to the Experience in Syria: Hybrid War Requires High-Tech Weaponry and Scientific Foundation]. *Voyenno-Promyshlennyy Kurier,* no. 9 (2016). http://vpk-news.ru/articles/29579.

———. "Tsennost' nauki v predvidenii: Novyye vyzovy trebuyut pereosmyslit' formy i sposoby vedeniya boyevykh deystviy" [The Value of Science Is in the Foresight: New Challenges Demand Rethinking the Forms and Methods of Carrying Out Combat Operations]. *Voyenno-Promyshlennyy Kurier,* no. 8. http://vpk-news.ru /articles/14632 (accessed 28 November 2016).

Giles, Keir. "The Next Phase of Russian Information Warfare." Riga, Latvia: NATO Strategic Communications Centre of Excellence, 2016.

———. *Handbook of Russian Information Warfare*. Rome: NATO Defense College, 2016.

Golson, Tyler. "Islamic State's Local Propaganda Key to Understanding Appeal." *World Politics Review,* 18 May 2015. www.worldpoliticsreview.com/articles /15791/islamic-state-s-local-propaganda-key-to-understanding-appeal.

Gray, Colin. *Another Bloody Century: Future Warfare*. London: Weidenfeld and Nicolson, 2006.

Grushin, Boris, and Leon Onikov, ed. *Massovaya informatsiya v sovetskom promyshlennom gorode: Opyt kompleksnogo sotsiologicheskogo issledovaniya* [Mass Information in the Soviet Industrial City: Experience of Complex Sociological Research]. Moscow: Politizdat, 1980.

Hafez, Mohammed. "Martyrdom Mythology in Iraq: How Jihadists Frame Suicide Terrorism in Videos and Biographies." *Terrorism and Political Violence* 19, no. 1 (2007): 99–103.

Hallahan, Kirk, Derina Holtzhausen, Betteke Van Ruler, Dejan Verčič, and Krishnamurthy Sriramesh. "Defining Strategic Communication." *International Journal of Strategic Communication* 1, no. 1 (2007): 3–35.

Hamid, Mustafa, and Leah Farrell. *The Arabs at War in Afghanistan*. London: Hurst, 2015.

Hammes, Thomas. *The Sling and the Stone: On War in the 21st Century*. Saint Paul: Zenith Press, 2006.

Hayden, Craig. *The Rhetoric of Soft Power: Public Diplomacy in Global Contexts*. Lanham, MD: Lexington Books, 2012.

Hoffman, Frank. *Conflict in the Twenty-First Century: The Rise of Hybrid Warfare*. Arlington, VA: Potomac Institute for Policy Studies, 2007.

———. "Gibridnyye ugrozy: Pereosmysleniye izmenyayushchegosya kharaktera sovremennykh konfliktov." *Geopolitika*, no. 21 (2013): 45–63. Translated from Hoffman, Frank. "Hybrid Threats: Reconceptualising the Evolving Character of Modern Conflict." *Strategic Forum*, no. 240 (April 2009).

———. "Hybrid Threats: Reconceptualising the Evolving Character of Modern Conflict." *Strategic Forum*, no. 240 (April 2009).

———. "Hybrid Warfare and Challenges." *Joint Force Quarterly*, no. 52 (2009): 35–36.

Huber, Thomas, ed. *Compound Warfare: That Fatal Knot*. Fort Leavenworth, KS: US Army Command and General Staff College Press, 2002.

Hundley, Richard, and Robert Anderson. *Security in Cyberspace: An Emerging Challenge for Society*. Santa Monica: RAND, 1994.

Joint Irregular Warfare Center. *Irregular Adversaries and Hybrid Threats, An Assessment–2011*. Norfolk, VA: Joint Irregular Warfare Center, 2011.

Jordan, Jenna. "Attacking the Leader, Missing the Mark: Why Terrorist Groups Survive Decapitation Strikes." *International Security* 38, no. 4 (2014): 7–38.

Kalinovsky, Oleg. "Informatsionnaya voyna—Eto voyna?' [Is Information War a War?]. *Voennaya mysl*, no. 1 (2001): 57–58.

Karsh, Efraim, and Inari Rautsi. *Saddam Hussein: A Political Biography*. New York: Grove Press, 1992.

Kazimi, Nibras. "The Caliphate Attempted." *Current Trends in Islamist Ideology* 7 (July 2008). www.hudson.org/content/researchattachments/attachment/1137/20080701 _kazimicaliphateattempted.pdf.

Komov, Sergey, ed. *Mezhdunarodnaya informacionnaya bezopasnost: Diplomatiya mira* [International Information Security: Peace Diplomacy]. Moscow: Voeninform, 2009.

Konopatov, Sergey, and Vladimir Yudin. "Traditsionnyj smysl ponyatiya 'voyna' ustarel" [The Traditional Meaning of the Concept of "War" Is Obsolete]. *Voennaya mysl,* no. 1 (2001): 53–57.

Korybko, Andrew. *Hybrid Wars: The Indirect Adaptive Approach to Regime Change.* Moscow, RUDN University, 2015.

Krasnoslobodtsev, Vladimir, Alexander Raskin, and Igor Tarasov. "Gibridnaya voyna: Ponyatiye, sushchnost', napravleniye protivodeystviya" [Hybrid War: Definition, Nature, the Direction of Counter-Measurement]. *Strategicheskaya stabil'nost'* 1, no. 74 (2016): 6–9.

Kuleshov, Yuriy, Boris Zhutdeev and Dmitrii Fedotov. "Informatsionno-psikhologicheskoye protivoborstvo v sovremennykh usloviyakh: Teoriya i praktika" [Information-Psychological Warfare in Modern Conditions: Theory and Practice]. *Vestnik Akademii voyennykh nauk,* no. 1 (2014): 104–110.

Lasconjarias, Guillaume, and Jeffrey Larsen, eds. *NATO's Response to Hybrid Threats.* Rome: NATO Defense College, 2015.

Lind, William, Keith Nightengale, John F. Schmitt, Joseph W. Sutton, and Gary I. Wilson. "The Changing Face of War: Into the Fourth Generation." *Marine Corps Gazette,* October 1989, pp. 22–26.

Lisichkin, Vladimir, and Leonid Shelepin. *Tret'ya mirovaya (informatsionno-psikhologicheskaya) voyna* [The Third World (Information-Psychological) War]. Moscow: Eksmo, Algoritm, 2003.

Lister, Charles. *The Syrian Jihad: Al-Qaeda, the Islamic State and the Evolution of an Insurgency.* London: Hurst, 2016.

Macmahon, Arthur. *Memorandum on the Postwar International Information Program of the United States.* Washington, DC: US Government Printing Office, 1945.

Manoylo, Andrey. "Tsvetnye revolutsii i tekhnologii demontazha politicheskikh rezhimov" [Color Revolutions and the Techniques to Dismantle Political Regimes]. *Mirovaya Politika,* no. 1 (2015): 1–19.

McChrystal, Stanley. *My Share of the Task.* New York: Portfolio, 2013.

McCulloh, Timothy, and Richard Johnson. *Hybrid Warfare.* Tampa: MacDill Air Force Base, Joint Special Operations University Press, 2013.

McWilliams, Sean. *Hybrid War Beyond Lebanon: Lessons from the South African Campaign 1976–1989.* Fort Leavenworth, KS: US Army Command and General Staff College, 2009.

Mearsheimer, John. "Why the Ukraine Crisis Is the West's Fault: The Liberal Delusions that Provoked Putin." *Foreign Affairs,* no. 93 (2014): 77–89.

Mee, Charles. *The Marshall Plan: The Launching of the Pax Americana.* New York: Simon and Schuster, 1984.

Messner, Evgeny. *Vsemirnaya Myatezhvoyna* [Worldwide Subversion-War]. Moscow: Zhukovskoye Pole, 2004.

Miskimmon, Alister, Ben O'Loughlin, and Laura Roselle. *Strategic Narratives: Communication Power and the New World Order.* New York: Routledge, 2014.

Monaghan, Andrew. "The 'War' in Russia's 'Hybrid Warfare.'" *Parameters* 45, no. 4 (Winter 2015–2016): 65–74.

Murray, Williamson, and Peter Mansoor, eds. *Hybrid Warfare: Fighting Complex Opponents from the Ancient World to the Present.* Cambridge: Cambridge University Press, 2012.

Nance, Malcolm. *The Terrorists of Iraq,* 2nd ed. Boca Raton: CRC Press, 2014.

NATO Strategic Communications Centre of Excellence. *Analysis of Russia's Information Campaign Against Ukraine.* Riga, Latvia: NATO Strategic Communications Centre of Excellence, 2015.

Naylor, Sean. *Relentless Strike: The Secret History of Joint Special Operations Command.* New York: St. Martin's Press, 2015.

Neklessa, Alexander. "Gibridnaya Voyna: Oblik i palitra vooruzhennykh konfliktov v XXI veke" [Hybrid Warfare: The Armed Conflicts Shape and Palette in the 21st Century]. *Ekonomicheskiye strategii,* no. 8 (2015): 78–85.

Nikolaychuk, Igor. "O suchshnosti gibridnoy voyny v kontekste sovremennoy voenno-politicheskoy situatsii" [On the Essence of the Hybrid War in the Context of the Contemporary Military-Political Situation]. *Problemy natsional'noy strategii* 36, no. 3 (2016): 85–104.

———. *Politicheskaya mediametriya: Zarubezhnyye SMI i bezopasnost' Rossii* [Political Media-Metrics: Foreign Media and Security of Russia]. Moscow: RISS, 2015.

Ninkovich, Frank. *The Diplomacy of Ideas: U.S. Foreign Policy and Cultural Relations, 1938–1950.* Cambridge: Cambridge University Press, 1981.

North Atlantic Treaty Organization. *BI-SC Input to a NEW Capstone Concept for the Military Contribution to Countering Hybrid Threats.* Brussels: NATO, 2010.

———. *Wales Summit Declaration: Issued by the Heads of State and Government Participating in the Meeting of the North Atlantic Council in Wales from 4 to 5 September 2014.* Brussels: NATO, 5 September 2014.

Nye, Joseph. *Soft Power: The Means to Success in World Politics.* New York: Public Affairs, 2004.

Nye, Joseph, and William Owens. "America's Information Age." *Foreign Affairs* 75, no. 2 (1996): 20–36.

Orlyansky, Vladimir. "Informatsionnoe oruzhiye i informatsionnaya borba: Realnost i domysly" [Information Weapons and Information Warfare: Reality and Fiction]. *Voennaya mysl,* no. 1 (2008): 62–70.

Osgood, Kenneth Alan. *Total Cold War: Eisenhower's Secret Propaganda Battle at Home and Abroad.* Lawrence: University of Kansas, 2006.

Owen, John, IV. *The Clash of Ideas in World Politics: Transnational Networks, States, and Regime Change, 1510–2010.* Princeton: Princeton University Press, 2010.

Panarin, Igor. *Gibridnaya voyna protiv Rossii, 1816–2016 gg* [Hybrid War Against Russia, 1816–2016]. Moscow: Goryachaya Liniya-Telekom, 2016.

———. *Informatsionnaya voyna i kommunikatsii* [Information Warfare and Communications]. Moscow: Goryachaya liniya—Telekom, 2016.

———. *Informatsionnaya voyna i tretiy Rim* [The Information Warfare and the Third Rome]. Moscow: NOU ShO "Bayard," 2003.

———. *SMI, propaganda i informatsionnyye voyny* [Mass Media, Propaganda and Information Warfare]. Moscow: Pokolenie, 2012.

Possony, Stefan Thomas. *A Century of Conflict; Communist Techniques of World Revolution.* Chicago: H. Regnery, 1953.

Prozorov, Stanislav, ed. *Islam na territorii byvshey Rossiyskoy imperii: Entsiklopedicheskiy slovar* [Islam on the Territory of the Former Russian Empire: Encyclopedic Dictionary]. Moscow: Lexicon, 2006.

Qiao, Liang, and Xiangsui Wang. *Unrestricted Warfare: China's Master Plan to Destroy America.* Panama City, Panama: Pan American Publishers, 2002.

Raskin, Alexander. "Setevyye Tekhnologii v gibridnoy voyne" [Network Technologies in Hybrid War]. *Informatsionnyye voyny* 1, no. 37 (2016): 2–4.

Rastorguyev, Sergey. *Formula informatsionnoy voyny* [The Information Warfare Formula]. Moscow: Radio i svyaz', 1999.

Razlogov, Kirill. *Konveyyer grez i psikhologicheskaya voyna: Kino i obshchestvenno-politicheskaya bor'ba na Zapade. 70-80-ye gody* [The Dream Conveyor and the Psychological War: Cinema and Socio-Political Struggle in the West, 1970s to 1980s]. Moscow: Politizdat, 1986.

Renz, Bettina. "Russia and 'Hybrid Warfare.'" *Contemporary Politics* 22, no. 3 (2016): 283–300.

Renz, Bettina, and Hanna Smith, eds. "Russia and Hybrid Warfare—Gong Beyond the Label." *Papers Aleksanteri,* no. 1 (2016).

Rid, Thomas, and Marc Hecker. *War 2.0: Irregular Warfare in the Information Age.* Westport, CT: Praeger Security International, 2009.

Rogan, Hanna. "Al Qaeda's Online Media Strategies: From abu Reuter to Irhabi 007." Norwegian Defense Research Establishment (FFI), 2007.

Ruiz Palmer, Diego. "Back to the Future? Russia's Hybrid Warfare, Revolutions in Military Affairs, and Cold War Comparisons." Research Paper No. 120. Rome: NATO Defense College, October 2015.

Sayapin, Vladislav. "Sovremennyye vyzovy virtual'nykh voyn" [The Contemporary Challenges of Virtual Wars]. *Istoricheskiye, filosofskiye, politicheskiye i yuridicheskiye nauki, kul'turologiya i iskusstvovedeniye: Voprosy teorii i prak-tiki* 3, no. 12/38 (2013): 180–185.

Shapiro, Jacob. *The Terrorist's Dilemma: Managing Violent Covert Organizations.* Princeton: Princeton University Press, 2013.

Shirin, Sergey. "Rossiyskie iniciativy po voprosam upravleniya Internetom" [Russian Initiatives on Internet Governance]. *Vestnik MGIMO-Universiteta,* no. 6 (2014): 73–81.

Slipchenko, Vladimir. *Voyny shestogo pokoleniya: Oruzhiye i voennoye iskusstvo budushchego* [The Wars of the Sixth Generation: Weapons and Military Art of the Future]. Moscow: Veche, 2002.

Smith, Paul. *On Political War.* Washington, DC: National Defense University Press, 1989.

Solovey, Valeriy. *Absolyutnoye oruzhiye: Osnovy psikhologicheskoy voyny i media-manipulirovaniya* [Absolute Weapon: Fundamentals of Psychological Warfare and Media Manipulation]. Moscow: Eksmo, 2015.

Stern, Jessica, and J. M. Berger. *ISIS: The State of Terror.* London: HarperCollins, 2015.

Tønnessen, Truls. "Heirs of Zarqawi or Saddam? The Relationship Between al-Qaida in Iraq and the Islamic State." *Perspectives on Terrorism* 9, no. 4 (2015): 48–60.

Tsygankov, Pavel, ed. *"Gibridnyye Voyny" v khaotiziruyushchemsya mire XXI veka* ["Hybrid Wars" in the Chaotizing World of the 21st Century]. Moscow: Moscow University Press, 2015.

US Army Training and Doctrine Command. "Islamic State of Iraq and the Levant, Threat Tactics Report." November 2014. https://info.publicintelligence.net /USArmy-TRISA_ISIL.pdf.

US House of Representatives Committee on Foreign Affairs. *The United States Information Service in Europe.* Washington, DC: US Government Printing Office, 1948.

Vladimirov, Alexander. "Gosudarstvo, voyna i natsional'naya bezopasnost' Rossii" [State, War and the National Security of Russia]. *Prostranstvo i Vremya* 3, no. 1 (2011): 26–38.

Volkogonov, Dmitry. *Psikhologicheskaya voyna: Podryvnyye deystviya imperializma v oblasti obshchestvennogo soznaniya* [Psychological War: Subversive Actions of Imperialism in the Field of Public Consciousness]. Moscow: Voinizdat, 1983.

Warrick, Joby. *Black Flags: The Rise of ISIS.* New York: Anchor Books, 2015.

Whiteside, Craig. "The Islamic State and the Return of Revolutionary Warfare." *Small Wars and Insurgencies* 27, no. 5 (2016): 743–776.

———. "The New Masters of Revolutionary Warfare: The Islamic State Movement (2002–2016)." *Perspectives on Terrorism* 10, no. 4 (2016).

Whitton, John Boardman, and Princeton University. *Propaganda and the Cold War; a Princeton University Symposium*. Washington, DC: Public Affairs Press, 1963.
Winter, Charlie. "Documenting the Virtual 'Caliphate.'" Quilliam Foundation, October 2015. http://truevisiontv.com/uploads/websites/39/wysiwyg/doctors/jihad/FINAL -documenting-the-virtual-caliphate.pdf.
———. "Signs of a Nascent Islamic State Province in the Philippines." War on the Rocks, 25 May 2016. http://warontherocks.com/2016/05/signs-of-a-nascent -islamic-state-province-in-the-philippines/.
———. "The Virtual 'Caliphate': Understanding Islamic State's Propaganda Strategy." Quilliam Foundation, July 2015. www.stratcomcoe.org/charlie-winter-virtual -caliphate-understanding-islamic-states-propaganda-strategy.
Wither, James. "Making Sense of Hybrid Warfare." *Connections* 15, no. 2 (2016): 73–87.
Yablokov, Ilya. "Conspiracy Theories as a Russian Public Diplomacy Tool: The Case of Russia Today (RT)." *Politics* 35, nos. 3–4 (2015): 301–315.
Yakh'ev, Mukhtar. "DAESh: Ideyjno-politicheskie istoki terroristicheskoy organi- zatsii" [ISIS: Ideological and Political Origins of a Terrorist Organization]. *Islamovedenie*, no. 4 (2016): 16–29.
Yarlykapov, Akhmet. "'Islamskoye gosudarstvo' i Severnyy Kavkaz v blizhnevos- tochnoy perspektive: Vyzovy i uroki dlya Rossii" ["The Islamic State" and North Caucasus from the Perspective of the Middle East: Challenges and Les- sons for Russia]. *Mezhdunarodnaya analitika* 17, no. 3 (2016): 112–121.
Zagorskiy, Andrey, and Nataliya Romashkina, eds. *Information Security Threats During Crisis and Conflicts of the XXI Century*. Moscow: IMEMO, 2016.
Zelin, Aaron. "The State of Global Jihad Online: A Qualitative, Quantitative, and Cross-Lingual Analysis." New America Foundation, January 2013.
Zhiveynov, Nikolay. *Operatsiya "PW": "Psikhologicheskaya voyna" amerikanskikh imperialistov* [Operation "PW": "Psychological War" of the US Imperialists]. Moscow: Politicheskaya literatura, 1966.
Zinovieva, Elena. "Analiz vneshnepoliticheskih iniciativ RF v oblasti mezhdunaro- dnoy informacionnoy bezopasnosti" [An Analysis of Russia's Foreign Policy Initiatives in the Field of International Information Security]. *Vestnik MGIMO-Universiteta*, no. 6 (2014): 47–52.

The Contributors

Matthew Armstrong is an author and adviser on public diplomacy, international information, and propaganda.

David Betz is professor of war in the modern world and head of the Insurgency Research Group at the Department of War Studies and deputy director in the King's Centre for Strategic Communications at King's College London.

Radomir Bolgov is associate professor in the School of International Relations at Saint Petersburg State University.

Georgy Filimonov is director of the Institute for Strategic Studies and Predictions and professor in the Department of Theory and History of International Relations at RUDN University, Moscow.

Ofer Fridman is director of operations in the King's Centre for Strategic Communications and lecturer in the Department of War Studies at King's College London.

Mervyn Frost is professor of international relations in the Department of War Studies at King's College London.

Vitaly Kabernik is senior expert in the Centre for Military-Political Research at Moscow State Institute of International Relations (MGIMO), and a fellow expert at the Carnegie Endowment for International Peace and PIR Center.

Nicholas Michelsen is senior lecturer in the Department of War Studies and director of resarch in the King's Centre for Strategic Communications at King's College London.

James C. Pearce is a PhD candidate in history at Anglia Ruskin University, Cambridge, UK.

Vladimir Sotnikov is senior research associate in the Institute for Eastern Studies at the Russian Academy of Sciences, visiting senior lecturer in the Centre for Military-Political Research at Moscow State Institute of International Relations (MGIMO), and an expert at the Russian International Affairs Council (RIAC).

Oxana Timofeyeva is lecturer in the National Research University Higher School of Economics and the Russian Presidential Academy of National Economy and Public Administration.

Craig Whiteside is associate fellow at the International Centre for Counter-Terrorism (ICCT), associate professor at the Naval War College, Monterey, and teaches at the Naval Postgraduate School. He also is senior associate in the Center on Irregular Warfare and Armed Groups at the Naval War College in Newport, Rhode Island, and lectures at the US Air Force Special Operations School.

Charlie Winter is associate fellow at the International Centre for Counter-Terrorism (ICCT).

Akhmet Yarlykapov is senior research fellow in the Centre for Caucasian Studies and Regional Security at Moscow State Institute of International Relations (MGIMO).

Index

About the Book

What is hybrid warfare? And what role does information play in today's conflicts? In the context of the technological/information revolution of the last two decades—which has greatly amplified the danger posed by nonmilitary means of political struggle—*Hybrid Conflicts and Information Warfare* addresses these questions from the perspectives of both Western and Russian experts.

Incorporating both theory and contemporary realities, including the case of the Islamic State, the authors offer a unique dialogue on the nature of conflict in the second decade of the twenty-first century.

Ofer Fridman is director of operations at the Centre for Strategic Communications, King's College London. **Vitaly Kabernik** is division head in the Department of Innovative Development at Moscow State Institute of International Relations (MGIMO University). **James C. Pearce** is conducting research at Anglia Ruskin University.